MAIN

APR 1 4 1998

2017

DISCARDED
From Nashville Public Library

Who
Tha

D1445621

The Public Library
of Nashville
and Davidson
County

KEEP DATE CARD IN BOOK

POCKET

GAYLORD

DISCARDED
From Nashville Public Library

Who Do You Say That I Am?

Christians Encounter Other Religions

Calvin E. Shenk

Herald
Press

Scottdale, Pennsylvania
Waterloo, Ontario

Library of Congress Cataloging-in-Publication Data
Shenk, Calvin E., 1936-
    Who do you say that I am? : Christians encounter other religions /
by Calvin E. Shenk.
      p. cm.
    Includes bibliographical references and index.
    ISBN 0-8361-9060-2 (alk. paper)
    1. Christianity and other religions. 2. Christianity and other
religions—Biblical teaching. 3. Religious pluralism. 4. Religious
pluralism—Biblical teaching. 5. Jesus Christ—Person and offices.
6. Witness bearing (Christianity) I. Title.
BR127.S46 1997
261.2—dc21   97-19784

The paper used in this publication is recycled and meets the minimum re-
quirements of American National Standard for Information Sciences—
Permanence of Paper for Printed Library Materials, ANSI Z39.48-1984.

All Bible quotations are used by permission, all rights reserved, and unless
otherwise indicated are from the *New Revised Standard Version Bible,* copyright
1989, by the Division of Christian Education of the National Council of the
Churches of Christ in the USA.

WHO DO YOU SAY THAT I AM?
Copyright © 1997 by Herald Press, Scottdale, Pa. 15683
    Published simultaneously in Canada by Herald Press,
    Waterloo, Ont. N2L 6H7. All rights reserved
Library of Congress Catalog Number: 97-19784
International Standard Book Number: 0-8361-9060-2
Printed in the United States of America
Book and cover design by Jim Butti

07 06 05 04 03 02 01 00 99 98 97 10 9 8 7 6 5 4 3 2 1

To our children, born in Ethiopia, and their spouses—
Douglas and Elaine,
Duane and Tanya,
Donna and Ryan—
all of whom have spent a semester of study
in the Middle East,
where they encountered the issues described here.

Contents

Foreword

While traveling in India in 1968, I bought a copy of *Recovery of Faith*, by Sarvepalli Radhakrishnan, the well-known Hindu philosopher who served as president of India in 1962-1967. Two things impressed me about Radhakrishnan. One was the urgency he felt to counter the effects of secularism and restore faith. The second was his characterization of Christianity. He asserted that the essence of Christian faith is its missionary vocation. Of course, Radhakrishnan disagreed with this mission, but it was clear to him that, for the church to retain its integrity, mission must remain at its heart. About the same time I came across a statement by Martin Buber, influential twentieth-century Jewish theologian and philosopher, who made the same point: mission "is the life-breath" of the Christian community.

These bracing encounters have indelibly imprinted my understanding of religious faiths. Each faith tradition has its own integrity. Remove or dilute this defining feature, and the tradition has been stripped of its reason for being. To argue against or play down the missionary essence of the Christian faith is fatally to weaken it. That is not to deny that at times, in the name of mission, Christians have brought reproach to the name of Christ and discredit to the church. But the remedy is not to attack and redefine the nature of the Christian mandate. Rather, the antidote is to bring the manner of Christian witness in line with its God-given goal.

Christians seem especially vulnerable to that imperialism of modern thought that seeks to homogenize differences among the religions in the name of an underlying universal rationality. Christians are intimidated by cultural and religious pluralism. In one generation, the West has gone from a situation in which the vast majority of people

13

could be identified as one variety or another of "Christian," and a small minority was Jewish. In recent decades adherents of religions from all parts of the world have migrated westward. In addition, the West has been a seedbed for indigenous new religious movements.

It is not easy to get one's bearings in such a restless and complex world where religious differences intertwine with ethnic particularities to create a powerful source of constant discord in many parts of planet earth. Consequently, many Christians are in retreat. They are confused and unsure about their own faith commitment. This is reflected in eroding loyalty and participation in church, especially missionary witness. Many Christians are embarrassed to be identified with a "missionary" religion.

Who Do You Say That I Am? straightforwardly addresses issues of faith and witness in today's world. Calvin Shenk is conversant with the burgeoning literature that deals with interreligious relations and understanding. Various scholarly schools of thought have developed around certain interpretive keys. Terms like exclusivist, inclusivist, and pluralist are used to describe how the Christian should understand, interpret, and relate to people of other faith persuasions. Each label is reductionist and needs to be tested against a higher authority, the Scriptures.

Out of long involvement with adherents of many religions, Shenk dares to assert that one can be profoundly respectful of people of other faith traditions and still retain the integrity of one's own faith. His many reports of personal encounters enliven his presentation.

Much of what has been written about relations between Christians and people of other faiths has paid little attention to Scripture. When the great Roman Catholic theologian Karl Rahner developed the highly influential notion of "the anonymous Christian," he did so entirely on philosophical grounds. By contrast, Shenk's aim is to clarify and present an attitude that is broadly biblical and Christlike. By selecting this text or that, it is possible to make the Bible support a wide range of positions. That is not the method used here.

The Bible is not a book about religious pluralism or the saving value of one religious system or another. It assumes religious diversity to be a part of the human condition. The human being is inveterately religious. The Bible pointedly warns us about false religion in its many guises and makes clear that religion per se cannot save. Every human construct and effort at self-help will fall short. We humans continually misjudge the reality and power of sin. God alone has the power to intervene in the human situation and provide the means to be reconciled. God the Creator is also God the Redeemer.

This book is moderate in tone and wise in perspective. It warns against pitting Christianity against other religions or arguing for the superiority of one religion over another. We have no responsibility for judging other peoples' religious understanding. Instead, Shenk makes the case for Christians to be faithful and winsome witnesses to Jesus Christ—witnessing in the spirit and compassion of the crucified and resurrected God.

—*Wilbert R. Shenk*
  Fuller Theological Seminary
  Pasadena, California

Preface

This book has grown from my fascination with religious aspects of culture. My interest developed during fourteen years in Ethiopia as I studied and wrote about Ethiopian and African religions. The interest grew as I taught religion at the Bible Academy, Mekane Yesus (Lutheran) Seminary, and Haile Selassie I University. Among other subjects, I taught Ethiopian religions, African traditional religions, world religions, sociology of religion, and comparative religious philosophy. My students included Christians and adherents of other religions.

After fourteen years we returned to the United States, where I have been a college (and sometimes seminary) teacher at Eastern Mennonite University. I have taught sociology of religion, world religions, children of Abraham (Judaism, Christianity, Islam), Christian faith and other religions, and missiology. With students I have visited religious centers in Washington, D.C.—Hare Krishna Temple, Zen Buddhist Center, Therevada Buddhist Center, Muslim Mosque, Mormon Visitor's Center, Unification Church, and Jewish synagogues. Adherents of other religions—Jews, Jehovah's Witnesses, Bahais—have addressed my religion classes.

On four occasions Marie and I led college students on semester-length Middle East study programs. During these semesters and through leading other study tours to the Middle East, I have been exposed to the practices of Judaism, Christianity, and Islam in Syria, Jordan, Israel/Palestine, Egypt, Greece, and Rome.

To be immersed in the popular expressions of religions, I have undertaken religious study tours to India, Sri Lanka, Nepal, Thailand, Korea, Hong Kong, Taiwan, Japan, and Turkey. I spent a sabbatical semester in Jerusalem studying Middle Eastern religions and another sabbatical semester teaching at Union Biblical Seminary in India and probing issues related to Hinduism.

Recently I have been dividing my time each year between teaching at Eastern Mennonite University and exploring Middle Eastern religions in Jerusalem as a research scholar at Tantur Ecumenical Institute. Situated between Israel and the West Bank, Tantur is ideally located to feel the pulse of Judaism, Christianity, and Islam. This schedule regularly includes a side trip to Ethiopia for leadership training.

My interest in religions is not merely academic. I bring a missiological perspective to other religions. Aiding in pursuit of these two interests was my service on the Overseas Committee of the Mennonite Board of Missions for more than twelve years and my ongoing membership and participation in the American Society of Missiology, Association of Professors of Mission, and International Association of Mission Studies.

I believe it is important to understand the worldview and practices of other religions but also necessary to understand how the gospel sounds in specific religious contexts. I have an increasing appreciation for Christian faith by seeing its uniqueness in contrast to other options.

Several years ago Harvey Cox noted that two of the most crucial issues in theology were liberation theology and theology of religions. This book reflects my search for a theology of religions appropriate to Christian witness. It is written with a bias—that Christ is normative for all. Since the centrality of Christ is assumed, the book does not deal specifically with how one can be sure Christ is truth for all. The emphasis is on Christ, not Christianity as a religion.

This book emphasizes the need to use the Bible as one's interpretive framework and to think theologically, not just emotively, about the religions. Assuming that Christ is the foundation for witness, the book explores methodological and attitudinal aspects of witness.

Because I am writing for the general reader rather than the specialist, some theological issues are not addressed, or at least not in depth. Likewise, notes are kept to a minimum. Though ideas cited in the footnotes have informed this writing, there are other ideas or phrases which have become part of my perspective through years of teaching whose sources are not specifically documented.

In addition, careful readers will note that though they do so in varying forms, some themes recur frequently in different chapters. This is a deliberate effort to cover key issues from a variety of interrelated perspectives.

I wish to thank Eastern Mennonite University for providing me with a sabbatical semester during which this writing was begun and subsequently granting three semester hours of released time, when I tested the manuscript with students. Lee Snyder, former dean of Eastern Mennonite University, deserves special thanks for encouraging me to pursue this project as one goal I had set for myself.

I am grateful to my students in Ethiopia, India, the Middle East, and the United States for the inspiration they brought to the classroom, their faith commitment, their questions, their critique, and their affirmation. Particularly helpful were world religion students at EMU who read and critiqued each chapter of the initial draft.

To friends and colleagues who have read and critiqued the manuscript—Myron Augsburger, Jim and Ann Hershberger, Barb Fast, Tom Finger, Norman Kraus—I express deep appreciation.

Alas, I am one of those people who still thinks best in longhand, not having mastered computer skills to the degree of being able to write a book on computer! Fortunately Lila Collins, who among other tasks served the Bible and Religion department at EMU, was able to decipher my handwriting and patiently typed and revised multiple drafts of the manuscript. She did so not only with speed and accuracy but with graciousness. Words are inadequate to express my thanks.

Michael A. King, book editor for Herald Press, deserves special thanks for his encouragement, critique, concern for ideas, and carefulness for detail. It was a delight to work with one so competent.

I am profoundly grateful to Marie, with whom I have shared and processed many of the experiences and ideas reflected here. She not only typed preliminary drafts of some chapters but read the entire manuscript and made editorial suggestions. Her wisdom, sensitivity to detail, and editing skills were invaluable. I am most appreciative of her constant encouragement and emotional support.

—*Calvin E. Shenk*
Harrisonburg, Virginia, and Jerusalem

Who Do You Say That I Am?

1

Introduction to Religious Plurality

In 1961 my wife, Marie, and I sailed from New York to serve as missionaries in Ethiopia. Our ship went by way of Libya, Egypt, Lebanon, Sudan, and Djibouti (formerly French Somaliland). In each country we saw a religion unfamiliar to us—Islam. In Ethiopia this exposure increased. I was a teacher; among my students were Muslims, most of whom were nicer than I expected. The conduct of some was an implicit rebuke to nominal Christianity. They observed our lives and heard our Christian confession. Some believed; most did not. A few who believed in Christ later became church leaders. Some suffered hostility from their families; others were imprisoned for their confession.

Several things happened to me in Ethiopia. I developed an increasing respect for religious variety and was fascinated by the relationship of religion to history and culture. I pondered the religious search of human beings. But at the same time, my confidence in the uniqueness of Jesus Christ in the context of other religious options was strengthened.

Since our return from Ethiopia in 1975, I've discovered Christians are asking a different set of questions than we were asking in Ethiopia. Many questions reflect equivocation about the meaning of Christian faith in relation to other faiths. Is Jesus the only way to salvation? What about sincere seekers in other religions? How can we be so certain about our faith? Is there room for other religious beliefs? Often asked by students, these are not merely academic questions. They are asked also by Christians in congregations.

Religious Plurality

Such questions are sparked by our increased exposure to religious plurality. Though Christians in all periods of history have faced religious plurality in one form or another and have learned to adapt to such contexts, several factors make this a crucial issue for our time.

In the past, knowledge of other religions was often limited to a few people. Today plurality is a global phenomenon to which we've been increasingly exposed through the news media, travel, cross-cultural study programs, mission/service assignments, international relations, and economic relationships. We know more about other religions than our parents did because of the explosion of knowledge about other religions and through personal acquaintances. Misunderstanding and stereotypes are being replaced by a more sympathetic understanding of the nobility and riches of other religions.

A consequence of globalization is that differing cultures and religions previously separated from each other now live in close proximity. Living in a global village precludes isolation. Religions coexist and interact, no longer confined within particular boundaries. Hare Krishna devotees celebrate in St. Peter's Square. I've been present for Friday prayers at the mosque on Massachusetts Avenue in Washington, D.C. Some North Americans, enamored with Indian and Asian spirituality, have fled the "materialistic" West in search of the "spiritual" East. I've seen scores of Westerners gathered around Hindu gurus (teachers) or ashrams (communities) in India, revering Sai Baba (one who claims to be a manifestation of God) or Raj Neesh (a guru who promoted diverse sexual practices).

Religious plurality is no longer a distant phenomenon; North American and European societies are becoming increasingly pluralistic. When we are forced to deal with the presence of rival religions in our midst, the plurality of religion can't be ignored. When Eastern gurus come to North America, some North Americans are converted to Buddhism or Hinduism. However, many more are impacted by Eastern ideas—monism, reincarnation, meditation—through syncretistic movements such as the New Age, even if they don't become Buddhists or Hindus. Something of Eastern thought, particularly of India, has become part of the unconscious furniture of our minds.

Many of the new religions in North America—Islam, Hare Krishna, Zen—are no longer only passively present. Buddhism, Hinduism, and Islam have launched active missionary movements. Hindus are increasingly prominent in North America. Several million

Buddhists live in the United States. Buddhist monasteries are found in most Western countries. Many mosques are being constructed in the United States and Canada. It is estimated that there will soon be more Muslims than Jews in the United States. There are already more Muslims than Methodists in Britain. Since Islam is the second largest religion in France after Roman Catholicism, Muslims outnumber Protestants. Adherents of other religions are now our neighbors, and their children are in school with our children. They come as immigrants or to study in our universities.

The increasing religious plurality has come as a surprise. At the end of the nineteenth century, many in the Western world believed that world religions could not survive the collision with modern Western civilization. They predicted people would leave their traditional religions (Hinduism, Buddhism, Islam) and become Christians. Westernization and secularization were seen as allies to Christian witness. Secularization and modernity had an important impact upon religion. But instead of collapsing, the world's religions have experienced revival and resurgence. Some religions actively resist further conversion from their ranks or reclaim those converted to Christian faith. Indeed, there has been a call to return to the fundamentals of these religions.

A return to the fundamentals has sometimes led to negative fundamentalism, often in chauvinistic, nationalistic, absolutist, or fanatical forms. I was in Jerusalem at the time of the Hebron massacre, when a fundamentalist Jew shot many Muslims as they prayed in the Mosque of Abraham, and during the time Islamic suicide bombers killed many Israelis in retaliation. In the United States a Christian fundamentalist killed a doctor who performed abortions. In India, Hindu and Islamic fundamentalists assault each other. When people feel threatened, they retreat and build barriers of authoritarianism, rejecting secularism and religious pluralism. They are afraid of losing their religious commitment in a pluralist society.

Clearly, there is worldwide religious ferment. Several years ago I heard Harvey Cox from Harvard Divinity School lecture on the renewed interest in religion. He maintained that God is not dead but that we are today witnessing a "rebirth of the gods." He cited the importance of Shinto ritual at the funeral for the Japanese emperor and the religious outrage against the publication of *The Satanic Verses*. Cox noted that Buddhist monks in Tibet continue to resist China. He highlighted the impact of the Roman Catholic Church on Solidarity in Poland, and the reassertion of Russian Orthodoxy with the demise of the Soviet Union.[1]

I found Cox's comments diverging from what he wrote in 1965. Returning from Ethiopia for a year's leave in graduate school, I read *The Secular City*, in which he theologized about secularization's impact upon religion.[2] His later book, *Religion in the Secular City*, describes the resurgence of religion.[3]

Peter Berger, a sociologist, also wrote about secularization in his book, *The Sacred Canopy*.[4] Subsequently he penned, *A Rumor of Angels*, in which he calls attention to "signals of transcendence." He contends that our society, rather than being only secular, has phenomena that point beyond secular reality to the transcendent. Humans cannot dismiss the question of meaning. He criticizes secular thought which tries to invalidate religious reality.[5]

Secularization has been a powerful movement. Those enamored by it have had difficulty with the supernatural, which they have imagined as absent or remote, and to be dismantled. Secularization has emptied many churches. People have believed our world could be explained without the hypothesis of God. Dogmas were reduced to myths, and myths became fiction. Thinking that life has no meaning or purpose, people have filled their lives with sensation. But some have discovered that one "does not live by bread alone." They have tried autonomy but have not found freedom. They have wanted individualism but not the consequences. They have been left without hope.

There has been a backlash against the scientific, rational, and logical consciousness of secularization. When former religions have eroded, new religions have taken their place. Religions have survived not necessarily because true but because of the universal human need for transcendence. Secular meaning systems have not been able to replace religion. The more the secularists have proclaimed the absence of God, the more there has been recovery of a sense of need for God.

The resurgence of multiple religious forms in the West adds to religious plurality. Today there is not only religious skepticism but religious enthusiasm. People are turning again to religion. Secularization and modernity have failed us. Now the children of the people who despised religion are becoming religious.

Religious Subjectivism

Western culture did not simply return to its former religion. The collapse of Christian orthodoxy led to a proliferation of many new religious movements to fill the spiritual vacuum. As religious plurality increased in the West, syncretistic streams of religious thought and devotion emerged which undermined the historical Christian faith.

Some religions moved away from creed and authority to experience, emphasizing the development of the ego and going within for salvation rather than looking outside for help. Some people experiment with altered states of consciousness through Transcendental Meditation, yoga, chanting, channeling, or forms of asceticism.

Often religious consciousness, religious feeling, or religious sensitivity are ends in themselves. When experience is desired, there is no end to experimentation. People become devotees of anything. When I was in India, I pondered the difference between a devotee and a disciple. In India, a devotee of one god is usually tolerant of other objects of devotion because of the Hindu belief in the multiplicity of divine manifestations. In contrast, a disciple is devoted to one; a disciple is more exclusive in devotion.

North American culture is obsessed with immediacy of experience. This is particularly true in religion. Any religion is thought to be better than no religion. Many have a functional view of religion—for birth, marriage, holidays, illness, death—rather than a religion concerned for ultimate truth. They are consumers of religion, any kind of religion. What the consumer wants, the consumer gets. We hear, "Everyone should have a religion of one's own." Religious preference emphasizes subjectivity, with focus on emotion and intuition as the norm. This focus causes tension between subjective knowledge and objective knowledge.

Some want an all-inclusive religion, religion for religion's sake. In the name of tolerance and pluralism, many treat religion like a taste or a style of life. Worldview, belief, values, and lifestyle are chosen on the basis of what one prefers. The "church of your choice" has become the "religion of your choice." Religion is chosen as one purchases a car. Consumerism makes God into what the consumer wants. The experiential dimension is an important component to any valid religion, but the immediacy of religious experience is not sufficient if the content of faith is neglected.

Self-Criticism

Renewed expressions of religious plurality in the world and in North America have led to Christian reflection and soul searching. Christians are becoming self-critical when they see the sins of Western culture—crusades, colonialism, the Holocaust—or the faults of the church which give rise to new religious movements. The West is no longer sure its culture is universally valid. More attention is now given to the cultures of the East and the South. Christians feel guilt about the too-close association of Christian faith with Western culture. They acknowledge the fallibility of faith expression both historically and culturally.

Embarrassment about some aspects of the missionary movement causes excruciating pain, particularly its association with racism and imperialism (political, economic, cultural). Many are disillusioned with the institutional church because of its bigotry and aggression in associating the superiority of the gospel with supposed Western superiority. In the minds of many, conversion was associated with force, bribery, proselytizing, and deculturalization. Militant language—fighting, warring, winning—was used to witness to the Prince of Peace.

In our disillusionment with Christianity, we sometimes over-idealize other religions and raise doubts about the Christian faith. We resolve to listen to other religions and learn from their insights. We seek to be fair and positive toward them. Through our exposure to other religions, we discover that many of their adherents are good people. We determine to divest ourselves of all arrogance, triumphalism, and superiority, and to wonder about our understandings of exclusivity. Christians are no longer as confident and certain as before, differing about the tenets and truth claims of Christian faith. They are more open to other religions and other ways of looking at the world.

Quest for Unity

Given so much social fragmentation and unrest in the world, we are asked to explore new forms of unity which can promote a more stable world. All desire unity, but on what basis is unity achieved? The function of religion in this quest is explored precisely because religion has been used to divide humankind. Christians in particular are blamed for narrowness and intolerance by seeking to convert others. The contemporary Christian, it is said, should live harmoniously by helping Hindus to be better Hindus and Buddhists to be better Buddhists. Religious pluralism is said to provide a new basis for human unity as religions collaborate for a more just world.

Some suggest that as the ecumenical movement has brought churches together to form one fellowship in spite of doctrinal differences, so the world's religions can bring unity of purpose. In light of problems such as the threat of nuclear war or the global ecological crisis, an aggressive claim on the part of one religion to have the truth for everyone is regarded as treason against the human family. It is assumed that one particular religion cannot provide the basis for unity.

The interreligious issue is compounded by the intercultural issue, assuming that if we are not religious pluralists we are somehow against other cultural groups. We are never to call our neighbors wrong but to love them, for only love can unite. Truth, it is suggested, cannot unite because it judges, polarizes, and divides.

Yet the search for something universal, some new form of unity, frequently results in a soft religious pluralism. In seeking peaceful coexistence and reconciliation, a worthy goal, some call for a larger ecumenicity and replace Jesus with a commitment combining the spiritual resources each religion has to offer. They may suggest that one should choose whatever religion meets one's needs.

Truth and Relativism

Differing answers are given in response to the truth claims of the religions. Some have turned their back on religion, considering all religions untrue. Doubt, or at least resolve to remain uncommitted, seems more respected than faith. Others believe that all religions contain part of the truth and point in the same direction, toward unseen transcendent reality. Truth is said to be larger, richer, and more complex than can be contained in any religion. According to them, it is wrong to absolutize one perspective of looking at the world. One is encouraged to be a humble seeker after the truth, with an open mind to all that comes in a variety of religious experiences. Another view claims that one religion is true, and all other religions are false or untrue. Christians have traditionally considered Christ as the final revelation and the norm for all truth and have insisted on connecting truth and salvation.

Meanwhile, academic interest in "comparative" religion, sociology of religion, and anthropology of religion has tended to homogenize religions by minimizing differences rather than dealing with underlying presuppositions and questions of truth in each religion. Greater personal exposure to and study of the world's religions have made us aware of the historical conditioning of all religions, raising questions concerning aspects of Christian faith. We ask whether imperialism is a result of "dogmatic" Christianity. If we relativize our culture, should we relativize truth claims? If we divest ourselves of racial or national superiority, should we downplay the finality of Christ? Is Christ indeed the way, the truth, and the life? Are we arrogant if we use such absolute language? Our culture is suspicious of anyone who claims to know the truth or holds to the superiority of a particular religion;

there is growing distrust of exclusivism of any kind.

Pluriform religion persists, but who is asking the truth questions? If we are committed to religion in general, what are the criteria for truth? Religious plurality and postmodernity easily give birth to relativism and subjectivism. Truth is defined by each individual or community. Truth is said to be one, but humans call it by different names. Some insist that "my karma is as good as your dogma." Differences between religions are not considered to be truth or falsehood but different perceptions of the truth. But with such understandings of religious plurality, the authority of all religions tends to be undermined, leaving no certainty, fixed points, or final truths. On what basis does one choose a worldview, beliefs, and values?

Relativism is expressed in differing understandings of truth and morality. Frequently one hears that morality is a matter of history, culture, and context. The Bible and Jesus are said to be important for Christians, just as the eightfold path is valuable for Buddhists. But if God's truth is reflected to some extent in all religions, how can one make any claim for normative truth? Can truth be defined in conflicting ways and still be correct?

Allan Bloom, in *The Closing of the American Mind*, is critical of subjectivism. According to Bloom, we talk about values, commitments, and lifestyles, but not about right and wrong, truth and error. He suggests that when values take the place of virtue, when commitment replaces morals, truth is undermined. Bloom says the danger we have been taught to fear is not error but intolerance. We have been taught that relativism is essential for openness. Openness and relativism become moral virtues. Few wrestle with what is good, what is right, or what is true. Humans want to choose their own beliefs, worldviews, and values. The self has replaced the soul. Openness and autonomy have usurped authority.[6]

Many Westerners think there is no such thing as normative truth. One can believe anything, they say, so long as one doesn't claim it is normative truth. They believe that people of different religions all worship the same God, that people can define truth in conflicting ways and still be correct.

Since relativism is in vogue, those who object to it are said to be insensitive or divisive. Relativism is considered more optimistic, whereas Christian faith is regarded as narrow and negative. Christian faith is questioned, repudiated, or ignored; certitude is lost. Relativism says one choice is not better than another. Relativism erodes authority, dissolves absolutes, and washes away the foundation of faith. In the name of plurality and relativism, religion is treated like a preference for a particular lifestyle. It is considered wrong to condemn the lifestyle of another.

Is there truth, or only your truth, my truth, the truth for this time and place? Many are not asking, "Is it true?" but "Are you sincere?" They prefer "it seems to me" or "I feel." They don't speak of right belief or right behavior but of the need to be authentic on the basis of one's choice of values. From those who don't wish to impose their values upon others, we may hear, "Who am I to judge?"

Yet is there no place for discernment? Can categories of true and false, right and wrong, be omitted from religious discussion? Is it enough to listen to what the heart says while ignoring what Scripture says? Pluralism, relativism, and openness have led to confusion about belief, the meaning of truth, and acceptable morality. Pluralism, relativism, and openness have become the new trinity in Western culture!

Religious Plurality and Religious Pluralism

It is common for the witness of the church to take place in the context of religious plurality. But in recent years our society has moved beyond the *fact* of plurality (descriptive pluralism), "plurality of religions," to an understanding of pluralism that assumes the dimension of an *ideology* (prescriptive pluralism). Religious plurality is not being discussed for the first time, but the diversity is being reinterpreted. Religious pluralism is not then simply a statement of fact but a theological or philosophical assessment of other religions which celebrates plurality. Religious pluralism is considered less bigoted and more loving.

Emphasis on the *fact* of religious plurality acknowledges the differences in religious traditions and the need from a social point of view to live together harmoniously. People of differing cultures, creeds, and religions must live together in the same communities. Plurality is part of our social existence. Until recently most people lived together in societies where one religion was dominant and the others were marginal. It is no longer possible to insist that everyone be subject to the dominant culture. Different cultures and different religions must get along together. New sociocultural understandings of other religious communities are important. Religious freedom, peace, justice, and human rights belong to all.

However, religious pluralism as an *ideology* frequently establishes theological conditions for living together harmoniously. These conditions require one to downplay the question of truth and falsehood in religion or to accept divergences as different understandings of the same truth. Each religion is then partial and only one of the ways. Or religious pluralism goes beyond universal toleration to acceptance of all religions as true. Such religious pluralism undermines the authority of all religions. Belief is weakened and fragmented by reductionism. It is considered a mistake to suggest that anyone's culturally conditioned religious insights could have universal validity.

Religious pluralism as an ideology relativizes all claims that any religion makes about the truth of its doctrine or practices. Choices are said to be good, no matter what is chosen. To speak of the truth or falsity of one religious stance in comparison to another is considered bad manners at best or imperialism at worst. Such claims are regarded as condescending or paternalistic.

As long as other religions were in distant lands, it was easy to believe in the uniqueness of Christ. But now these people are our neighbors. How do we understand the gospel and the mission of the church within this new plurality of cultures and religions? When the fact of plurality is reinforced by ideological pluralism, convictions about religious truth are easily weakened. It is problematic when Christian faith is placed in the same theological category as other religions.

Ideological religious pluralism seeks for unity beyond diversity. All gods are considered a manifestation of one divine reality. The soul of religion is one but encased in a multitude of forms. Each person searches for the unspoken center we all share. All search for the same noble ideal, the ultimate, the source. It is frequently said that all rivers flow from the same reservoir or all rivers flow to the same ocean. Sometimes religions are described as differing spokes in a wheel, differing colors in a rainbow, differing branches of one tree, or differing fingers on one hand. It is suggested that one can get to the second floor of a building by a rope, a pole, stairs, an elevator, or a ladder, just as one can take different paths to the top of the same mountain.

Each religion is said to be a culturally conditioned way, pointing to the same destination. Though all religions are fragmented and partial, and are interim in character, all contain truth. These understandings move beyond plurality as a *fact* to a *justification* of religious pluralism. Religious pluralism becomes the new dogma. Do all religions indeed point in the same direction or have the same goal?

Religious Pluralism and Cultural Pluralism

Religious pluralism is often confused with *cultural pluralism* because culture and religion are interwoven. Yet the two must not be confused. Cultural pluralism is an attitude that welcomes different cultures and lifestyles within a society as enrichment to human life. No culture is by definition considered superior to another or inferior to another. From a biblical perspective, all cultures are relative. None are absolute. The God revealed in Jesus Christ is for all cultures and all people. Cultural pluralism is not the enemy of faith. Christian faith enhances variety in cultures.

Many of us have learned to appreciate the variety, creativity, and beauty of other cultures. Opportunities in mission and cross-cultural educational experiences have shaped us. Some of us are internationalists. We have learned new dimensions of cultural pluralism—that one culture is not necessarily more right than another. I consider myself a cultural pluralist.

However, a potential danger of cultural pluralism is an undiscerning cultural relativism which assumes that every aspect of culture is relative. Though cultures are relative, total cultural relativism is problematic because not all aspects of culture are morally neutral (e.g., sexual promiscuity or abortion on demand). In our concern for global solidarity and global sensitivity and in our reaction against cultural imperialism, we can too easily become normless cultural relativists.

Cultural pluralism is sometimes used to relativize faith commitments by raising doubts about universal norms. Blind celebration of cultural or religious diversity separated from norms is never desirable. The discussions about religious plurality and cultural pluralism force us to wrestle with how to name Jesus amidst competition with other norms.

Christ as Center

Religious plurality forces us to rethink the uniqueness of Jesus Christ. When we listen to our culture, we hear that Christian faith may be true for me but Islam or Buddhism may be true for others. God is said to have had a hand in the formation of the *Quran* and the Buddhist *Sutras*. We are told that a common thread runs through all religions so that in the end all religions say the same thing and hold to a common moral code.

Sometimes Christians who have developed a global vision ask, "In the context of religious plurality, how can I say that Christ is the definitive self-revelation of God? If Christ is so crucial, why have not more followers of the world's religions been attracted to him? If only one-third of the world's population professes faith in Christ, what is Christ's relationship to the other two-thirds? Will the majority be excluded from salvation?"

How do we live as disciples of Jesus Christ in the midst of a highly pluralistic and relativistic society? Many questions compete with each other in our minds. Is Jesus Christ merely *a* savior, one among many, or is he the *unique Savior* of humankind? How do we understand Jesus in a pluralistic world where others are as convinced as we that what they believe is right? If God is love, can we believe that God will provide saviors in other cultures? Is Christian faith simply one religion among others, the one we happened to be born into?

These questions concerning Christ and religious plurality are raised around the world and in our homes and churches. Responses vary widely. Some want to affirm all religions as paths to salvation. Others insist that to regard all faiths as equally valid leads to apathy, and that tolerance of religious plurality has its limits. They seek to make claims about Christian faith without downgrading other religions, to express their loyalty to Jesus Christ without arrogance and contemptuousness.

In much of the discussion on religious plurality, Christians are asked to choose between mutually exclusive options. They are expected either to accept religious pluralism and thereby cast doubt on the uniqueness of Christian faith, or to reject religious pluralism to remain faithful to the Christian tradition. Are these the only options? To what degree is Christian commitment compatible with cultural and religious plurality?

Religious plurality poses a problem for Christian churches and Christian theology. This is not a new question, but in recent years it has acquired new significance and urgency. In the last decade religious plurality has emerged as the most debated religious question. No other issue presents more challenge than the issue of Christian faith and other faiths. This is a theological and missiological issue. What is the relationship between God's redemptive activity in Jesus Christ and people of other faiths? Our understanding of the theological significance of other religious traditions determines our approach and attitude to people of other faiths.

The issue of Christian faith and other religions cannot be dismissed. If it is not dealt with, other people will define our theology for us. Response to religious pluralism must be on the basis of biblical norms, norms that must be rethought and expanded, not abandoned. Without norms, we are swept along with the current. Christology is at the center of the debate on Christian attitudes toward other religions. Christians cannot deny Christ as Lord and Savior, but Christian theology will need to be formulated in the presence of other religions, as it was in the Jewish and Greco-Roman context of earlier centuries. Our challenge is to remain faithful to Christ as we seek to understand the faith of others.

As Christians we know that we need to witness to Christ in an increasingly pluralistic world. But in the face of religious plurality and relativism, and with guilt for past mistakes, we sometimes equivocate in our conviction for the truth of Christian faith and the missionary character of the church. Are we prepared to deal with religious plurality missiologically? This calls for creative thinking about a theology of religions for witness.

This book deals with several models Christians have used in evaluating Christian faith and other religions. It examines Old Testament and New Testament perspectives on God's covenantal revelation and God's relationship with other religions. Later chapters identify theological issues that emerge when Christians reflect on other religions, and seek to assess other religions from the perspective of biblical revelation. This is followed by a discussion of Christology, the meaning of witness to Christ, and appropriate forms of witness. Consideration is then given to the difficult issue of those who have not heard of Christ. The book concludes by recommending appropriate styles of witness.

2

Response to Religious Plurality—Exclusivism and Inclusivism

In the history of Christian theology, three major positions were developed in response to religious plurality—*exclusivism, inclusivism,* and *pluralism*. The three approaches tend to be too sharply defined since we are dealing with people and not just systems. Within each of these categories, there is a significant amount of variation; some persons hold positions that bridge the categories. In this chapter exclusivism and inclusivism are defined, described, and evaluated.

Exclusivism

Definition

Exclusivists insist that Christ is unique, final, decisive, and normative as the self-revelation of God, for the salvation of the world. In Christ, by grace alone and through faith alone, people are saved. The Christian faith is unique because the cross is reconciliation at God's initiative. Christian faith, so long as it is centered in Christ, is the single particular religious tradition which embodies the uniquely authentic response to divine reality. Exclusivism as presented here is used in a theological sense, not in a personal, attitudinal, or social sense.

Exclusivists hold that God is made known through Hebrew Scripture and through Jesus Christ. From an Old Testament perspective, Yahweh and Baal were different; Yahweh was never just an extension of another god. All gods were forbidden except Yahweh. The

New Testament acknowledges that "salvation is from the Jews" (John 4:22) and witnesses to full salvation through Christ.

Specific texts used by exclusivists include these: "There is no other name under heaven given among mortals by which we must be saved" (Acts 4:12). "I am the way, and the truth, and the life. No one comes to the Father except through me" (John 14:6). "No one can lay any foundation other than the one that has been laid; that foundation is Jesus Christ" (1 Cor. 3:11). "There is one God; there is also one mediator between God and humankind, Christ Jesus, himself human, who gave himself a ransom for all" (1 Tim. 2:5-6).

Exclusivists believe that Jesus Christ is the sole criterion by which all religions, including Christianity, should be understood and evaluated. Christian faith is not just an extension of the work of God that is equally apparent in other religions. The incarnation, death, and resurrection of Christ are profoundly significant; they form the center of history. Christ did not come just to make a contribution to the religious storehouse of knowledge. The revelation which he brought is the ultimate standard. Since in Christ alone is salvation and truth, many religious paths do not adequately reflect the way of God and do not lead to truth and life. Jesus is not, therefore, just the greatest lord among other lords. There can be no other lord besides him. This exclusive claim is not a footnote to the gospel. It *is* the gospel.

Description

The exclusivist position had been the dominant stance of the church as a whole through most of its history until it was challenged by the Enlightenment. Modern representatives of this position included Karl Barth, Emil Brunner, and Hendrick Kraemer. Barth, though not totally exclusivist, made a radical separation between divine revelation and religion, asserting that the gospel comes by revelation, while other faiths are the product of religion. He emphasized the sovereignty of God's grace and de-emphasized human response. He understood biblical faith to be a struggle against other religions. All religions, including Christianity as a religion, come under the judgment of God.

Brunner believed Jesus Christ both fulfills and judges other religions; he is the truth for which other religions sought in vain. Other religions have some breath of the Holy but none of them is the Holy; none is without truth, but none is the truth.

Kraemer affirmed the uniqueness of Christ but recognized God's presence and activity outside the revelation of Christ. The religious and moral life of human beings is evidence that God is wrestling with the world. But God's presence must be tested by the gospel because humans distort their religion by efforts of self-deliverance.

Exclusivists agree that if Jesus is unique and the only way to salvation, other faiths are excluded from being true in the same way or from being alternate ways of salvation. A true glimpse of Jesus and the cross shows the incompleteness of other religions. Other religions have virtues, but these are considered irrelevant for salvation. One can appreciate what is good, true, and beautiful but not confuse virtue with redemption. Religions, including Christianity, are often flawed responses to God; they are either misleading or inadequate. Exclusivism holds that there is radical discontinuity between Christian faith and other religions in the understanding of God and of salvation. Religions can even be a stumbling block to knowing God and are under God's judgment. The primary emphasis of exclusivists is not on sincerity and dedication to one's religion but on repentance and acceptance of the free gift of salvation in Jesus Christ.

For most exclusivists, conscious confession of Christ during one's lifetime is necessary for salvation; through explicit faith one appropriates the grace of God. Exclusivists make a strong argument for evangelism and conversion. Christians should go into all the world to witness to the gospel because it is important that the gospel be heard and believed.

Exclusivists have a major challenge in discerning how to balance the universal goal of salvation with God's particular revelation in Jesus Christ. They acknowledge that the scandal of particularity and exclusive statements about the person and work of Christ were no more acceptable in the first century than they are today. Exclusivists argue that the New Testament world was religiously plural—many lords, many gods—but Christians said Jesus alone was Lord. The gospel was foolishness to Greeks and scandal to Jews. Holding to the uniqueness of Christ made early Christians countercultural.

Carl Braaten contends that Christians cannot surrender the finality of the person and work of Christ, for if we compromise this claim to accommodate religious pluralism, we have a different gospel. The apostolic church, called into existence from religious pluralism, encountered pluralism when it witnessed to Jews, Greeks, Romans, and the syncretisms of Hellenized culture. But the church's relationship to the world was shaped by its particular identity in the gospel: the world's salvation had arrived in Jesus. Braaten writes, "The Christian faith has a particular content. It makes a particular claim to the truth."[1]

If we equivocate about the ultimacy of this truth or place alongside it other events of equal validity, we "fall into idolatry and apostasy."[2] If we place Jesus into the pantheon of spiritual heroes, we resemble the Gnostics of the second century.

Response and Evaluation

Exclusivism as a term is unfortunate. For many it suggests narrow-mindedness, arrogance, insensitivity, self-righteousness, or bigotry. Exclusivists are accused of not respecting other religions. But Christian exclusivism does not suggest that all claims of other religions are false; some claims of other religions are true. It does not suggest that other religions are without value or that one cannot learn important principles from people of other faiths.[3] Exclusivism rather gives strong expression to the particularity and distinctiveness of Christian faith. Exclusivism relates to one's understanding of salvation, not to God's activity in the world. God is clearly active beyond the boundaries of Israel and the church. It is unfortunate if the distinctiveness of Christian faith leads to neglect of or easy dismissal of the universal action of God in history. Later we will deal with the crucial theological issue of how one relates this activity to God's specific activity in Christ.

We observe that Christian exclusivism is not the only kind of exclusivism. Other religions also claim that their affirmations are true and reject counterclaims. Many religions are exclusivist in some sense. Monotheistic religions tend to be more exclusivist than others. For example, Islam is not prepared to give up its claim that Muhammad is the final prophet or that the Quran is the most complete revelation. Though Judaism, by suggesting that the righteous of all nations have a part in the world to come, expresses tolerance of other religions, Christians learned some of their exclusivism from the Jewish rejection of idolatry.

The strength of exclusivism is its conviction that salvation is alone through Christ and its attempt to be faithful to the gospel. If one believes that the central claims of Christian faith are true, conflicting claims of other religions are in some sense false. For example, if one believes Jesus is the Messiah, then denial of Jesus as Messiah is a false understanding. If Jesus Christ is the incarnation of God and the only Lord and Savior, the idea that salvation might be found in the structures of other religions is unacceptable and is seen as a violation of the Christian message.

Exclusivism is clear in understanding the nature of sin and salvation. Exclusivists do not equivocate in their allegiance to Christ and the church. They do not feel obliged to surrender that which they consider true—the superiority and finality of Christ. Believing that salvation is only in Christ, they are keen to witness to those who have not heard of Christ.

Today exclusivism is not only criticized by other religions but from within the Christian community. If salvation is found in Christ alone, many people question the moral character of a God who allows people to be born where they have no access to the way of salvation. Is God loving, gracious, good, just, and righteous if through no fault of their own most of the world's people have not heard the gospel? If God wills all to be saved, what is the means to such fulfillment? These questions have led some people to inclusivist or pluralist understandings.

Those who criticize the exclusivist position believe it takes the Bible and Christ seriously but doesn't take other religions seriously enough. Parallels between Christian faith and other faiths are downplayed. They think there is too much emphasis on the transcendence of God and object to the great distinction made between revelation and religion. Some suggest that exclusivism compromises the sovereign freedom of God. Others believe that exclusivism in the Bible developed as a particular theological position because of specific historical-cultural circumstances. They admit that the interpretation of Jesus as the unique incarnation of God may have been appropriate for the early church but suggest it is not necessarily binding in the modern world.

Some insist that exclusivism is immoral and violates Christian values. Wilfred Cantwell Smith argues, "Exclusivism strikes more and more Christians as immoral. If the head proves it true, while the heart sees it as wicked, . . . then should Christians not follow their heart? Maybe this is the crux of our dilemma."[4] Smith insists that Christian values are concerned with reconciliation, dignity of the neighbor, peace, and respect.

Others argue that counting Jesus as the only way for salvation (John 14:6) sounds arrogant in a pluralist culture. They suggest that such an exclusive claim should be challenged or discounted. Indeed, they wish that Jesus had said, "I tell you about a way of life" (like the Buddha), instead of claiming to *be* the way. They deny that Jesus made such a claim or that John recorded it accurately, suggesting that someone wrote the statement to bolster the faith of a minority community or fabricated it to promote a particular theology. But this is problematic for those who believe one must not discount biblical affirmations because they conflict with other religious or philosophical systems. Peter Cotterell asserts, "It is not that Jesus *knows* the way, or that he *shows* the way, but that he *is* the way."[5]

A few have sought to deal with Acts 4:12 ("there is no other name") as confessional language rather than propositional language. Krister Stendahl, referring to Acts 4:12, believes that confessional language or love language is given to exaggeration. He compares it to a husband who says to his wife that she is the most beautiful woman and is the only one for him. Such a statement is true for him but not universally true. He has difficulty accepting the negative side of that confession and asks, "How can I sing my song to Jesus without telling dirty stories about others?" He believes the Christian apologetic is often used to bear false witness against one's neighbor. It is like putting on a black tie to make one's dirty white shirt look whiter. Stendahl believes insistence on the uniqueness of Christ satisfies a Christian need for certainty.[6]

Wesley Ariarajah says that when his daughter tells him he is the best daddy in the world, she is speaking the truth, for this comes out of her experience of him as her father. But in the next house, another little girl also thinks her father is the best in the world. She also is speaking the truth. Ariarajah suggests these expressions are true but not absolute truth because they are the language of love. Similarly, he considers the language of Acts 4:12 to be the language of love and faith, which should not be made into absolute truth.[7]

The declaration of Acts 4:12 is reinterpreted to be an affirmation for Jesus without ruling out the possibility of other saviors. Exclusive statements are said to reflect the manner in which people spoke. But exclusivists insist that Acts 4:12 is consistent with the larger thrust of the New Testament. It is unwise to judge exclusivist passages of the New Testament on the basis of our cultural presuppositions, which tend to relativize the uniqueness of Christ.

How does one understand the narrowness of exclusivist texts? Some suggest that the exclusive claim of the gospel be attributed to the outdated cultural situation in which the New Testament originated. Others argue that one can no longer justify exclusivism simply by referring to texts such as John 14:6 and Acts 4:12 because we don't know whether Jesus really spoke those words or what Peter really meant. Christian faith is blamed for making Christ final, definitive, and normative.

Some hold that the name of Jesus symbolizes the grace and love which Jesus represents but which can be found under the names of other religions also. For example, Donald Dawe reinterprets the name of Jesus by emphasizing the translatability of the name of Jesus. The name of Jesus symbolizes human goodness and new being. When one sees human life being renewed and virtue expressed in other religions, there the work of God is actualized, but the criterion for this actualization is in Jesus Christ. Jesus models new being, self-negation rather than self-assertion (Phil. 2:5-8). The name of Jesus is the encoding of the motif of death and resurrection as the key to new being. But this motif is brought to expression in vastly different ways in various religions as they become vehicles for human renewal and fulfillment.[8]

In response to Dawe, exclusivist Christians agree that humanization and new being can be affirmed where the name of Jesus is not specifically known and confessed. But is humanization and new being always to be equated with the name of Jesus? To separate the name of Jesus from the specific history of Jesus is problematic. Dawe seems to supply his own definition for the name of Jesus. Christian faith is deprived of its essence if one minimizes the particularity of Jesus or takes away the names which symbolize his unique meaning. If Jesus is not what he claimed to be and what his disciples claimed him to be, who is he? Can Jesus be reduced to what our age prefers for him to be?

With the unprecedented exposure of people in the West to neighbors, friends, or colleagues who adhere to other faiths, some Christians challenge what right one has to tell followers of other religions that "my religion is right and yours is false." Christians sometimes ask, "If Hinduism is false, how could Gandhi live such a moral life? How could Buddha be so compassionate? How does one account for the moral sensitivity of Confucius?"

However, exclusivists explain that when Jesus said he is the truth, he did not mean he was teaching a number of good and true ideas. He meant that in him the total structure of the universe was for the first time and forever disclosed. This truth is not merely set forth in propositions to which we give intellectual assent, but in personal forms which demand surrender. We see Jesus as the truth, and we seek to do the truth.

Many Christians believe God acting in Christ is different from anything found in other religions and from the way humans have imagined God in their fantasies. This is not to say that other religions will not rebuke, instruct, or inspire us (e.g., Islamic prayer and fasting, Buddhist self-discipline). The crisis we face results from the mistakes we have made in history and from the fact that Christianity as a religion is mixed with much error. But the basis of our confidence and conviction in the unique self-revelation of God is in Jesus' incarnation, teaching, death, and resurrection. Is it reasonable to suppose that if God could have adequately been revealed in any other way, God would have taken the incredible road of incarnation and death?

Even some critics agree that exclusiveness has strong biblical support and is consistent with Christian orthodoxy through the centuries. Early Christians believed salvation was available to all—Jews and Gentiles—because of the unique person and work of Jesus Christ. The early church was critical of the religious practices and beliefs of Hellenistic paganism. Historically, the Western church, following Augustine, has tended toward exclusivism and particularism.

Must one abandon exclusiveness to be more accepting of other religious traditions? Critics accuse exclusivists of understanding the missionary task as conquest, triumphalism, manipulation, and aggressiveness born of a superiority complex. One cannot deny the particular claims of Christ and the gospel, but how one speaks of Christ is quite important, and the tone in which one argues is crucial. Exclusiveness must not make one dogmatic, ethnocentric, or imperialistic. Temptations to dominance, absolutism, condescension, or contempt lurk close by. Belief in the triumph of Christ should not make us triumphalistic in manner. We must be invitational in tone when we speak of the finality of Christ, or of Christ as the foundation for one's faith.

Theological exclusivism must not be used by Christians to oppress people of other faiths. By devaluing other religions, one can sometimes inadvertently devalue the other's humanity. It must not be confused with cultural prejudice or political superiority. If we are theologically exclusive, we should not let that position lead us to socially excluding people or denying their rights. Without Christian love, exclusivism can too easily express hostility or be patronizing.

Exclusivism is considered by critics as minority language and therefore survival language, born of ignorance and parochialism. Though such criticism is harsh, exclusivists need to be more aware of how they sound to others. Are exclusivists too possessive of God and Christ? I sometimes wince when I hear "my God," "my Jesus," or "our God," "our Jesus." We do not possess God; God possesses us. A definition of "us" must leave space for the other. There is great danger in negative attitudes toward the rest of the world. We must resist a self-enclosed faith. We don't want to give the impression that salvation is confined to Christianity as a religion. Paul rebuked the arrogant attitude of God's covenant people.

Any emphasis on exclusivism must be related to Christ, not Christianity as an institutionalized religion. Christ is exclusive in relation to other gods, but he is universal and available to all. Exclusivism has not dealt adequately with the fate of those who have not had meaningful exposure to salvation in Christ. Are exclusivists too pessimistic about salvation for the adherents of other religions?

Since exclusiveness sounds so restrictive, is *particularity* a better term? The gospel concerns the particularity of Christ's incarnation, death, and resurrection. Indeed, that particularity was a scandal. But the uniqueness of that particularity should not translate into separateness or abrasive exclusivism. That particularity calls for Christian modesty and graciousness.

Christian exclusivists (or particularists) should not diminish the all-inclusive intent of God. Does one's belief in Jesus open doors or shut doors, remove barriers between people or erect higher barriers? Christ is the one who opens doors and breaks down the walls of partition. One's exclusivism must consider the inclusiveness of Christ. Jesus was inclusive in his relationships, but he was not inclusive of all religious ideas or practices (e.g., Samaritan woman, John 4).

Exclusivism is said to absolutize particular doctrinal understandings, institutions, or fallible Christian expressions. This can serve as a reminder that exclusivists should rather speak of an absolute God, since "absolute" is an attribute of God alone. The revelation of God in Christ is an absolute norm, and Christ makes an absolute claim on believers.

Christ's exclusive claims must be held in tension with his inclusive hope for all humankind because he is the *only* Son for *all* who believe. The church as a community of believers must be clear: God wishes all to be saved, and the invitation is to all. Yet holding to the finality of Christ does not release one from exploring the relationship between Christian faith and other religions.

There are differences of opinion among those who espouse exclusivism. All agree that salvation is in Christ alone, but views differ concerning the need to have actual knowledge of Christ and conscious faith in him. They are seriously troubled about those who have never heard. In this respect exclusivism resembles inclusivism.

If we surrender Christ as norm, we surrender the essence of Christian faith. That is why the issue of religious plurality is so crucial in Christian theology. As Braaten says, "The question whether there is the promise of salvation in the name of Jesus, and in no other name, is fast becoming a life-and-death issue facing contemporary Christianity. In the churches this issue will become the test of fidelity to the gospel. . . ."[9]

Inclusivism

Definition

Inclusivism is a mediating position between exclusivism and pluralism. Inclusivists in the Christian theology of religions both accept and reject other faiths. They accept the divine presence in other religions but consider them insufficient for salvation apart from Christ. Inclusivists believe God offers all humans the light of faith and grace, but this is always because of Christ and in relationship to Christ. Inclusivists seek to avoid confrontation with other religions. Two binding convictions are held in tension: the operation of the grace of God in all the religions of the world working for salvation, and the uniqueness of the manifestation of the grace of God in Christ, who is the final way of salvation. Inclusivists disagree with exclusivists on how the particular grace of God in Christ is made manifest.

Inclusivists want to avoid monopolizing the gospel of redemption. They acknowledge the possibility of salvation outside of Christian faith or outside the walls of the visible church, but the agent of such salvation is Christ, and the revelation in Jesus is definitive and normative for assessing that salvation. Jesus Christ is believed to be the center, and other ways are evaluated by how they relate to him. Other religions are not just a preparation for Christ, but Christ is actually present in them. Some elements in other religions are even willed by Christ.

Inclusivism assumes that God's saving presence in Christ impacts the wider world and other religions. Since all truth is God's truth, Christ must include all that is true in other faiths. If all truth and goodness is from Christ, then all religions belong in some way to Christ. Inclusivism emphasizes continuity between other faiths and Christian faith; that which is hidden in other religions has been fulfilled by Christian faith. Inclusivism attempts creatively to integrate non-Christian faiths with Christian theological reflection.

Inclusivists believe that non-Christian religions have a positive saving potential similar to Judaism in the Old Testament; they can serve as preparation, bringing people to Christ. They can be the means by which God's salvation reaches those who have not yet heard the gospel. Alternate religious traditions may even mediate divine grace found in the particular Christian tradition. Those who believe can relate savingly to God either apart from their religious practices or through specific elements of their religious tradition.

Inclusivism, like exclusivism, emphasizes that people are not saved apart from Christ on the cross, but inclusivism would not place so much emphasis on explicit faith. Grace is explicit in Christian faith but is more implicit in other religions, offered freely even without making a personal decision about Christ. Inclusivists ask how much one must know to be saved; if God knows the person's heart, is knowledge really necessary to be a believer? Is saving faith *knowledge about God* or *trusting in God* for salvation? Those who are saved, however, are not saved because of their religion but in spite of their religion. John Sanders wrote, "Inclusivists hold that while the source of salvific water is the same for all people, it comes to various people through different channels."[10]

Inclusivists insist that God works decisively in the singular and particular event of Jesus (one person and place, not several persons and places), who is the source of redemption and forgiveness. If Christ saves Buddhists, Hindus, or Muslims, they are drawn to him as a magnet and are saved through him. God's grace can flow through other religious instruments but only because of Christ. Christ's grace and power magnetize the good in all religions and people. Truth and salvation are present because Christ's saving grace is there even though people may be unaware of it.[11]

Description

In recent years Roman Catholics have led the way in inclusivist understandings. Vatican II (early 1960s) changed the Catholic view that "there is no salvation outside the church," but it did not explicitly state that other religions are a means of salvation, though sometimes that is implied. Yet Vatican II was a watershed in the Christian attitude toward other religions. Vatican II took the position that Christ's atoning work is broader than was earlier thought.

Since Vatican II, the Roman Catholic Church is more explicit that other religions reflect rays of truth, seeds of truth, or spiritual and moral truths that enlighten all humans. But this understanding is balanced with the uniqueness of Christ as Savior. Catholics have a high regard for other religions and for the grace of God through creation. Those who do not know of Christ but who, moved by grace, seek God with a sincere heart according to their conscience, may receive eternal salvation apart from explicit faith in the gospel. But Christ must be proclaimed because he is the fullness of life. Witness is necessary because the good in other religions is not yet fully Christian.

In the early 1960s, Karl Rahner, a Roman Catholic, coined the phrase "anonymous Christians." Rahner accepted God's revelation in Christ but did not limit salvation to those who responded to the revelation in Christ. He believed God's grace, was mediated to adherents of other religions and insisted that other religions could be a positive means of gaining a right relationship with God and receiving salvation. Religions are not only natural knowledge of God; they contain supernatural elements of grace given by Christ and can function as vehicles for salvation. According to Rahner, grace comes to each of us through God's offer. Rahner narrowed the gap between nature and grace. When persons accept this grace, they are accepting Christ though not consciously naming him. They are "anonymous Christians." Because God can work anonymously within religion for salvation, Christ becomes the final fulfillment of the "revelation of grace." Those who respond to the revelation of grace which they have experienced implicitly, though never having heard the good news of Christ, are justified through Christ. Christ alone is Savior; salvation is always Christian salvation.

Rahner insisted that only one religion is true, yet followers of other faiths who sincerely practice their religion can be saved because they are covert followers of the one true faith. Even if their faith is not overt, they live in the state of Christ's grace. Rahner's ideas were revolutionary. Other religions were not totally rejected. God's saving work was not only in the church but could be encountered in other religions. Rahner sought to preserve the morality of God by insisting that the unwillingly blind are not condemned for their blindness but are judged by the extent of their desire to see.[12] Rahner is optimistic concerning salvation. He believes God wills all to be saved. He moved from a church-centric to a Christo-centric theology of religions. In other religions Rahner recognized supernatural elements of grace, not just values, which he believed were given to human beings through Christ, in whom the highest and final truth is found.

On a study visit to India in early 1981, I read *The Unknown Christ of Hinduism* (1964), by Raimundo Panikkar, who expresses another Roman Catholic view of inclusivism. The author quotes Hebrews 1:1-2, "Long ago God spoke to our ancestors in many and various ways by the prophets, but in these last days he has spoken to us by a Son, whom he appointed heir of all things, through whom he also created the worlds." Panikkar argued that Christ not only inspired the prophets of the Bible but also those of Hinduism and other religious traditions. For Panikkar, Christ has inspired the truth and goodness in Hinduism and is present in the Hindu spiritual and moral principles. He suggested that Hinduism and Christian faith meet in Christ; good Hindus are saved by Christ, not by Hinduism. The mystery of Christ works in hidden ways within religious rituals and institutions.

In relating Christ to Hindu prayers, Panikkar sees a possible equation between Christ and Isvara (personalized form of the Hindu god Brahman, the Ultimate or Absolute). He asks whether Christ might be the fulfillment of the Hindu longing to know Brahman, comparing the "Unknown God" in Hinduism to the "unknown god" of the Greeks in Athens (Acts 17:23).[13]

In a later revision of his book (1981), Panikkar rejected his earlier inclusivist stance for a more pluralist position and emphasized Christ as the universal symbol more than the historical Jesus. Christ as universal symbol, he believes, is recognized in some way as people worship the Hindu gods Rama, Krishna or Purusha. Though hidden and unknown, Christ is actively involved in each authentic religion.

Hans Küng, a Roman Catholic theologian, suggests that if some who are ignorant of the gospel of Christ do sincerely search for God with the help of divine grace and seek to do God's will as known to them through conscience, they can attain eternal salvation. Salvation is made available through the religion of their historical situation. As humans seek the hidden God within their religion, they are confronted with the revelation of Jesus Christ.[14] This he calls the *ordinary way* of salvation. Those directly confronted by Christ through the Christian tradition are saved by the *extraordinary way*. (Some suggest the *ordinary way* is through the Christian tradition, and the *extraordinary* way is through other religions, thereby reversing Küng's concepts.)

Küng's inclusivism was not intended to ignore the newness of the gospel. He believes in an inclusivism which does not impose Christian faith on the adherents of other faiths but listens to and respects the insights and theological truths expressed in other religions. He wants to create a synthesis in which the isolated, scattered, and distorted ideas can be brought to full realization in Christian faith, which is the final arbiter of truth.

Heinz Schlette based his inclusivism on the unfolding of the revelation of God at particular times and stages in the history of the world. He made a distinction between *general* and *special* sacred history. He believes *general sacred history* points to the covenant made between God and all humanity through Noah. *Special sacred history* points to the covenant made between God and Israel and reaching fulfillment in Christ and the church. The covenant with Noah authenticates the response of non-Christians to God, but all religions are not equal ways to salvation. Special sacred history is related to general sacred history not as truth to falsehood, but as complete to incomplete, perfect to imperfect, plant to seed.

Though Catholic approaches to religious plurality vary, some generalizations are possible. If people sincerely search for God under the influence of grace and seek to do the will of God through the guidance of conscience, they may obtain salvation. The goodness and truth of other religions are seen as preparation for the gospel, given by the One who enlightens everyone (John 1:9). The good in people, cultures, and religions can be made whole through Christ. Nothing that is true and holy in other religions is rejected. But Christ is the full embodiment of truth, and fullness of life is found in him.[15]

Roman Catholics teach that if human sin is universal, Christ's salvation is all the more universal. Since everyone born into the world stands in solidarity with the disobedience of Adam, all are part of the new humanity whose new head (Christ) has overcome sin and death.[16] Every person without exception has been redeemed by Christ and united with Christ even when the person is unaware of it. The Spirit working in the depth of conscience moves persons toward the truth. This means that those who, through no fault of their own, have not known of the gospel or the church, can be moved by God's grace to receive salvation and do the will of God.

Protestant inclusivism is similar in some ways to Roman Catholic perspectives. At the World Council of Churches Assembly in 1961, Joseph Sittler, a Lutheran, drawing from the Greek Patristic tradition rather than Augustine, emphasized the "Cosmic Christ." He argued in favor of an all-embracing cosmic Christology, the uniting of humans and religions under one new head, the cosmic Christ (based upon Colossians 1:15-20 and Ephesians 1:10).[17] Paul Tillich described those who follow Christ but who are not fully aware of Christ as part of the "latent church."

Inclusivists, while holding firmly that God is supremely manifest in Jesus, also affirm the universal presence of God's Spirit through the whole of creation. They argue that God's saving power and presence is defined by the life, death, and resurrection of Jesus, but that salvation is not confined to Jesus of Nazareth. Through the *Logos* (Word) and the Spirit, God acts to bring salvation to other people and cultures who may not have heard of Jesus.[18]

More recently some evangelicals, concerned about those who haven't heard, have suggested a universally accessible salvation apart from evangelization, based upon a faith response to the revelation that one has. Persons are then saved or lost on the basis of their commitment, or lack thereof, to the God who saves through Jesus Christ. Saving grace is mediated through general revelation and God's providence. The particularity and finality of salvation in Jesus Christ is affirmed, but knowledge of his work may not be necessary.

Such evangelicals insist that no one can be saved apart from Jesus Christ, but one need not be aware of his work to benefit from it. People can receive the gift of salvation without knowing the giver or totally understanding the nature of the gift. Faith, not explicit knowledge, is necessary for salvation. If redemption is for all, and if God wishes all to be saved, it must be possible for people in each history, culture, or geographic region to receive salvation. People are not saved by their righteousness or merit. But those who walk in the light they have, are accepted by Christ because they yield themselves to the light.[19]

To summarize, inclusivism, like exclusivism, claims that the central teachings of Christian faith are true. However, inclusivism is more positive toward other religions than is exclusivism. Inclusivists hold to the finality of Jesus for salvation but are more willing to believe that God's salvation is accessible through non-Christian religions. Jesus is still normative, unique, authoritative, and definitive. However, those who through no fault of their own do not know the gospel, yet who are moved by grace and sincerely seek God, may receive eternal salvation. Some suggest that the goodness and truth in other religions was placed there by Christ (John 1:17) as preparation for the gospel and should not be rejected. This more positive view of religion sees Christ in some sense as the origin, center, and destiny of the various religions.

Inclusivists have different understandings of mission. Some insist that it is very important for those who have implicit faith to come to a fuller understanding of salvation by trusting Jesus of Nazareth so that the one they know only vaguely they can know explicitly. As they discover Jesus Christ, a movement toward Christian faith often takes place.

Yet for many inclusivists, the task of mission is not to displace another religion but to engage in conversation with other religions. Such a mission will inform people that they are already potentially saved by Christ. If Christ is present in the *Logos*, though not explicitly known and confessed, the task is not to bring Christ to religion but to help people discover and unveil Christ who is already there. Some inclusivists say that Christ is the unknown child hidden in the womb of other religions, and that the church functions as midwife in bringing Christ to birth. Or they claim that Christ is sleeping in the night of religion and must be awakened. Witness to the historical Jesus Christ, not just the anonymous Christ principle, calls forth the elements of the hidden Christ in other faiths. Some would argue that it is much more important for a religion (e.g., Hinduism) to become more Christian than to convert a few followers of another religion (e.g., Hindus).

Response and Evaluation

Inclusivism seeks to preserve the uniqueness and centrality of Christ but conditions our understanding of the exclusive Christ. It preserves the heart of the faith but is also open to people of other faiths. Inclusivism seeks to make sense of God at work in other religions, openly acknowledging that people in other faiths have genuine glimpses of the majesty and greatness of God, yet holding to Jesus Christ as the norm for discerning God's activity. Since humans, though fallen, are still in God's image, there is truth and grace in other religions.

Inclusivism is so attractive because of its teaching that God does not condemn those who have no opportunity to hear the gospel. Those who respond to the light they have, will be saved even if they do not identify the light with Jesus Christ. Inclusivism is optimistic concerning salvation, refusing to limit the grace of God to the confines of the church. Inclusivism is based on the premise that all people have a chance to be saved. No human being is excluded from the possibility of benefiting from God's grace. An all-loving God would not consign the majority of humankind to perdition, because if God desires to save all, God will act to accomplish it. One is asked to open one's arms to those who are loved by God. Inclusivists understand God's salvation as wider than often assumed by exclusivists. Exclusivists tend to leave the other's salvation up to God's mysterious workings.

The strength of inclusivism is that Christ is brought back to the center. Jesus is the normative and decisive criterion. By affirming the reality of Christ's grace and presence, one is free to be more open in looking for Christ's presence and the Holy Spirit at work in religions. One is conditioned to look for continuities between Christian faith and other religions. By playing down negative judgment, inclusivism is more tolerant and benevolent than exclusivism.

Inclusivism tries to combine two convictions—the universal will of God to save, and the unique particularity of Christ. But the boundary between Christian faith and other religions is easily blurred. Sometimes more attention is given to the universal than to the particular. Discussed below are numerous objections to the inclusivist view.

Chris Wright expresses caution about inclusivism: "It obviously wants to steer between the rocks of callously dogmatic exclusivism and the whirlpool of relativism and pluralism. I find myself both attracted to it because of the problem it is trying to avoid, and yet wary of it because of the result it seems to lead to."[20] Inclusivism which is too open-ended soon becomes relativistic and universalistic, downplaying the objective action of God in historical revelation and salvation. When inclusivism is vague, it moves toward pluralism. Inclusivism can easily minimize the importance of making Christ known as Lord and Savior.

Some inclusivisms seem to minimize the uniqueness of the incarnation by placing too little emphasis on the historical Jesus. Some theologies of *Logos* and cosmic Christ which acknowledge that Christ is active outside of the incarnation have extended their theologies beyond what Scripture would seem to warrant. They have a cosmic amorphous Jesus or separate the Spirit from Jesus. Such theologies lessen the necessity for conversion or else modify it in significant ways. Does the presence of God's grace in the lives of non-Christians result in salvation? If one has so much openness to the grace of God in other religions, is one not diminishing the uniqueness of Christ or minimizing the newness of the gospel?

Inclusivism raises the issue of how one understands religions. Do religions mediate grace? Does God use religion to reach people and confront them directly with grace? Is Christ *within religion, above religion,* or *against religion*? Often religions are not seeking God but leading away from God. Error and depravity in religion is not denied but seems to be de-emphasized. It is important to find the way between God's amazing grace and the appalling sins of the world. Does God confront and work through religion? Does God confront people who are within religion in spite of their religion?

How does one understand the term "anonymous Christian"? Being an anonymous or "honorary" Christian or even experiencing a self-awakening is hardly the same as conversion. Do people want to be called "anonymous Christians"? If the uniqueness of Christ is non-negotiable, will other religions not object to inclusivism as much as to exclusivism? It is coercive to make people anonymous Christians when they have not asked for Christian faith or even resist it. Adher-

locus of religious truth. Rather, since knowledge of God is partial in all faiths, including the Christian faith, religions must acknowledge each other if the full truth about God is to be available to humankind.

Pluralism implies that a "whole" religious vision requires a variety of approaches even if those approaches appear to be contradictory. Since no religion is perfect and each grasps only part of the Real, there needs to be mutual enrichment, interaction, interdependence, and reciprocal challenge of one's limited, defective, or misleading understandings. Each religion stimulates the other to growth. One religion does not provide everything needed.

Such pluralists say that God does not just allow a plurality of religions; God *wills* them. The rites and doctrines of religions are impulses of God's grace. If the knowledge of God is equally available in different religions, one should place all religions on an equal footing, not just for the sake of religious freedom, but for the sake of theology.

Social Conditioning

According to pluralists, God has provided various mediators for different geographical and cultural contexts. Perceptions of God differ because of differing historical and cultural conditions. Each religion is a historical-cultural variation of a common authentic conviction. Christian faith works best in some settings; other faiths are preferable in other settings.

In whatever religious environment one was born, there one should remain: primal religions for Africans, monotheism for Arabians, Christian faith for Western culture, Hinduism for India. Sufi Muslims teach that one can dig a Jesus well, a Buddha well, or a Krishna well; but if one only digs a little in each well, it is difficult to find water.[3] The implication is that one needs to dig deeper in one well and not change wells. Christians should continue to believe in Jesus Christ but should not impose their path on those who follow other ways.

Specialization of Religion

Some pluralists understand each faith as a specialization with different strengths and weaknesses, just as each person is different. Or each faith is considered a different building material which contributes to the construction of one house of God. Instead of emphasizing the core of faith, they point to the convergence of faiths. They welcome a global theology in which each faith is corrected by the strengths of the other: Jews and Muslims emphasize the oneness of God; Hindus emphasize the variety of God. The linear, historical, and prophetic character of the Near Eastern religions will be enriched by the circular, eternal, and mystical strengths of the Southeast Asian religions. According to this view, God is present in each faith, though only partially present. Salvation is available in each faith, but religions are not homogenized.[4]

Other pluralists come close to inclusivists when they acknowledge the distinctiveness of each faith but give special attention to Christ. Truth is dispensed among all religions, but though God is known in other faiths and people seek and find God in other faiths, God is most fully known in Christ. Christ embodies not just partial truth but fullness of truth. Sufficient knowledge for salvation is found in other faiths, yet to a lesser degree. One sees most clearly in Christ what God is doing outside of Christ. Christ is considered the highest peak of the mountain among mountain ranges. He is without peers, yet not alone.[5]

Twentieth-Century Pluralism

Earlier in this century religious pluralism was advocated by Arnold Toynbee, William Ernest Hocking, and Ernst Troeltsch. Toynbee believed all the "higher" religions come from God, and each presents some facet of God's truth. Toynbee assumed that God's revelation was given in different forms and different degrees according to individual and cultural differences. He wanted to preserve the spiritual dimensions of one world in order to eradicate favoritism, self-centeredness, or arrogance.

Hocking based his theological understanding on the premise that all religions contain an inalienable core of truth expressed in diverse ways. He believed that Christian faith anticipated the essence of religion but represents only one cultural response to the divine initiative. Christianity cannot claim a monopoly of religious truth. Troeltsch wanted to evaluate all religions by the historical method and judge them by objective facts. Initially he thought Christian faith was the highest example of personal spiritual faith, but he later disclaimed Christian faith as the supreme expression of religious life. For Troeltsch, Christian faith became one manifestation of God in one culture, one faith among others. All religions come from the same source and tend toward the same goal, with God as the final arbiter in matters of truth.

More recently Wilfred Cantwell Smith, John Hick, and Paul Knitter have become leading proponents of religious pluralism. Knitter argues for a "unitive pluralism," a new understanding of religious unity but not "one world religion." He rejects syncretism, indifference, or lazy tolerance, but accepts all religions as equally valid and believes other revealers and saviors may be as important as Jesus Christ.[6] He believes the religions of the world are more complementary than contradictory.

In a recent book, *The Myth of Christian Uniqueness*, edited by Hick and Knitter, the authors propose a pluralist theology and claim to be "crossing the theological Rubicon" (like Caesar precipitating civil war by crossing the Rubicon River in 49 B.C.). Christians should abandon claims about the uniqueness of Christ and the possibility of definitive revelation, accepting a plurality of revelations and a parity of religions in which Christian faith is one among many options.[7]

Theocentrism

John Hick advocated a "Copernican revolution" in theology, a shift from Christ or Christian faith as the center of the religious universe to the realization that God is at the center. All religions revolve around God instead of Christ.[8] He replaced Christ-centeredness *(Christocentricism)* with God-centeredness *(theocentrism)*. As fuller knowledge recognized the sun rather than the earth at the center of the planetary universe, so God ought to replace Christ at the center of the religious universe. God is the sun whom all religions reflect in their different ways. Religions should not be rivals, just as planets are not rivals. Hick does not believe in one revelation received in one theological form. Differences in belief and practice reflect the cultural forms which embody individual experience. Hick believes that the major faiths make unique sounds that contribute to a symphonic whole. Religions are complementary, not mutually exclusive.

Theocentrists argue that Jesus was theocentric because he proclaimed the kingdom of God, never claiming to be God or the Son of God. Nor did he place himself or the church at the center but put God at the center. The "I am" sayings of Jesus are not considered the words of the historical Jesus. It is said that Christ placed himself below God by proclaiming, "The Father is greater than I" (John 14:28). Paul declares Christ to be ultimately subject to God by asserting, "When all things are subjected to him, then the Son himself will also be subjected to the one who put all things in subjection under him, so that God may be all in all" (1 Cor. 15:28).

Some say that Jesus preached the kingdom, but the church preached Jesus; it was the New Testament writers who made Christian faith Christocentric. They note statements like these: "No one comes to the Father except through me" (John 14:6), or "The Father and I are one" (John 10:30). They claim such sayings are additions of the early church community rather than the words of Jesus. The New Testament pictures of the exclusive and normative character of Jesus (Acts 4:12; John 1:14; 14:6; 1 Cor. 15:21-22; Heb. 9:12) are attributed to the medium of the New Testament rather than to its message.

In theocentrism, Christ and Christian faith are placed on a par with other religions in their orbit around God. Inclusivism moved from church-centeredness to Christ-centeredness, but pluralism has moved from Christ-centeredness to God-centeredness. Theocentrism provides a common denominator for all religions, so there is no privileged position for any one. Theocentrism accommodates complementary views of God.

Hick and Knitter believe that God-centeredness is less divisive than Christ-centeredness. According to them, God unites, Christ divides. God is to some extent defined by Jesus but not confined to Jesus. Since Jesus cannot be regarded as the one measure of what God is like, one needs a fuller vision and richer understanding of God. Christ is only one among many who have borne witness to Ultimate Reality. Other traditions correct our partial glimpses of God. In the theocentric pluralist perspective, the data of world religions become the norm; Christ is not the norm.

Salvation-Centeredness

A few pluralists have moved beyond God-centeredness to salvation-centeredness (soteriocentrism) because religions which are ambivalent about belief in God (e.g., forms of Buddhism and Chinese religions) share a common quest for some form of salvation. Soteriocentrism seeks to include all religions, but in the process "salvation" is frequently redefined. Salvation/enlightenment/liberation is assumed to be a reality common to all major religious traditions.

Enlightenment is a particular concern of Eastern religions. Liberation resonates with Western religious interests in liberation theologies, which interpret salvation in terms of social liberation. Emphasis is placed on what religions *do* more than what they *say*. Consideration is given to the spiritual and moral fruit of faith. All are saved in their own way; all religions are salvific.

Pluralism assumes that everyone will be saved by whatever means available. If we believe that only those born within a particular thread of history will be saved, we are parochial and make God into a tribal deity. Since belief in the normativeness of Christ leads to repression rather than liberation, it is morally and theologically wrong. Salvation/enlightenment/liberation is a more inclusive set of terms than God and leads to greater religious cooperation, in this view.

Religious Experience

Often religious pluralists deny that God can be identified with any specific name, form, image, or story. They are ambivalent about the very existence of God. When there is no objective reality (God) to provide the center, the only center remaining is religious experience. Religious differences are then reduced to private opinions and experiences. Revelation is said to come to the person in some sort of individualistic spirituality or imaginative creativity. People search for core mystical experiences which are larger, richer, and more complex than can be contained in any one religious tradition. With an open mind, they listen to the religious experiences of others.

Instead of starting with propositional formulations about God and Christ, pluralists unite by engaging in a collective search for the meaning of the sacred and by emphasizing similarities, parallels, overlappings, and commonalities of religion. Since the object and content of religious experience is infinite, no one religion has the final word. To bring differing religions together, each contributes to the pool of religious values such as justice, compassion, truth, and righteousness.

Experience is preferable to doctrine because doctrine divides. Each religion represents a common core experience of the Ultimate; common experiences central to all religions are also sought. Pluralists from Christian traditions are quick to suggest that the way other people describe their experience of the Transcendent is remarkably close to the experience of Christians, with Christian faith differing only in degree. At the experiential level, humans are said to be in contact with the same Ultimate Reality.

Wilfred Cantwell Smith distinguishes between "cumulative tradition" and "personal faith." He places priority on personal faith.[9] Personal faith is the individual's relationship with the divine, but cumulative tradition represents the cultural framework in which people have been nurtured. Like Hick, Smith ignores christological dimensions of the issue and puts God at the center instead of Christ. Christians are blamed for equating their religion with God by making their religion final and absolute, a form of idolatry. They are asked to repent of their idolatry by giving up exclusivism or inclusivism for pluralism. Raimundo Panikkar and Stanley Samartha understand all religions to participate in and reflect the mystery which no one can own.[10]

Reinterpreting Christ

Pluralism reduces the significance of Jesus Christ by rejecting the idea that God has been revealed in any normative or unique way in Jesus Christ. Rather, God is revealed in all religions; Jesus is merely one of the great religious leaders who is used by God to provide salvation. Since Jesus Christ is not the completeness of God's self-revelation, pluralism denies that Jesus is the one by whom all religions are evaluated. Andrew Kirk's observation of pluralism is appropriate: "Rather than confessing that Jesus Christ is the one Lord over all, this view asserts that the one Lord who has manifested himself in other names is also known in Jesus."[11]

Hick says, "God is *truly* to be encountered in Jesus but not *only* in Jesus."[12] He asserts that Christ is "wholly God" but not the "whole of God."[13] Knitter doesn't believe one can say there is "no other name" or "no other gospel" because there are many revelations and many saviors. He advocates a "non-normative theocentric Christology," believing it does not contradict the New Testament.[14]

Some pluralists make a distinction between the *Jesus event* and the *Christ principle*. Panikkar suggests that Jesus is the name for Christians, but Christ may have other names in other faiths and cultures. Christ is not less than Jesus of Nazareth, but Christ is not bound by Jesus of Nazareth, and Christians can't say Christ is only Jesus. Every authentic name enriches and qualifies the mystery of Christ. Jesus is Lord for Christians, but Christ is the name above all names.[15] According to this view, "Jesus is the Christ" is not identical with "the Christ is Jesus."

Pluralism wants to free Christ from the rigid categories of the New Testament. Jesus is then reinterpreted in nonexclusive terms because, it is said, he never thought of himself as God in human flesh but as a special agent in the inauguration of God's kingdom. From this perspective, the early church and the New Testament made Jesus divine and exclusive. Jesus' theocentric view was changed by the church into Christocentrism.[16]

Pluralism accepts Jesus Christ as the way, the truth, and the life (John 14:6) for Christians, but not the only way. Christians might say, "Christ is my Lord and Savior," but this does not necessarily mean that he is Lord of all people since there are other saviors. Exclusive statements such as Acts 4:12, "There is salvation in no one else, for there is no other name under heaven given among mortals by which we must be saved," must be understood as poetic language, the language of love. Christians express "love language" toward Christ. Christ as "the one and only" could mean "I am fully committed to you" rather than "no one else is worthy of my commitment." It is an enthusiastic confession of Christ's reliability but should not be taken to mean that Christ is the only reliable one.[17] Christians are asked to respect the love language of other religions.

John Hick believes New Testament statements about Christ are mythic-symbolic, stories that are not literally true. For Hick, truth does not reside in literal interpretation but with the historical personal meaning of Scripture. Therefore, all mythic language of the New Testament must be reinterpreted. Hick considers the incarnation of Christ a myth; God is incarnate in all people insofar as they are Spirit-filled or Christlike. Incarnation is merely a way of saying that Jesus had contact with God. Hick reinterprets all religions in order to put them into the same framework.[18]

Incarnation is then a symbol (metaphor, poetry) of what God wants to accomplish. It is not a one-time event but an ideal. Logos has been interpreted to minimize incarnation because there are other incarnations, and what happened in Jesus can happen elsewhere. Jesus is not divine. He is not the second person of the Trinity. Jesus was open to God's presence. He had intense God-consciousness and tremendous spiritual authority. Son of God and Trinity are creations of the church. Similarly, resurrection is seen as a subjective experience rather than an objective event. Resurrection took place within Jesus' followers; Jesus arose in their faith. Resurrection did not cause faith; faith caused the resurrection. There may be similar resurrection events in other believers and other religions.

Thus, the uniqueness of Christ has been redefined. Uniqueness no longer means the one and only, but the only one of its kind. This belief implies that all religions are unique. The uniqueness of Christ is in degree rather than in kind. Christian faith is unique in the same way that everything else is unique. All great teachers and prophets are unique. Jesus is Lord, but so were Krishna and Buddha. Gandhi, a pluralist, was fascinated with the uniqueness of Jesus but conditioned uniqueness by his claim that "Jesus is Lord, but not a solitary Lord." For pluralists to accept Jesus as unique means that there is no one like him in any other tradition. He is unique because he is the source of truth for Christians and represents a particular view of God, but he is not qualitatively different.[19]

Religious pluralism does not entirely remove Christ from the equation but wants to redefine him to fit into the category of other great religious teachers. Within the church, Christians confess Jesus Christ as Lord and Savior, but that does not entitle them to make the same claim outside the church. We are told that Christian faith may be true for us, but not necessarily for everyone. We may claim one way, one mediator, one foundation, but that is only true for those who sub- scribe to Christian faith. Jesus may be Lord and Savior, but others who are equally sincere look to other names.

In this view, it is arrogant and condescending to insist that there is no other name given under heaven by which we must be saved (Acts 4:12). Christians are asked to be dialogical and confessional, to give up judgmentalism and claims to the finality of Christ. Jesus is no longer the final revelation or norm but is decisive and normative for Christians only. For those outside of the Christian tradition, his reve- lation is relative. Christ then becomes the pioneer who is moved from the center to the "leading edge" of the religious quest. All claims about the finality of Christ are culturally limited. To absolutize Jesus is to make an idol of him. Testimonies about Christ are not universal fact but simply expressions of individual religious experience.

Relative Truth

Pluralism leads to a relative understanding of truth—nothing is absolutely true. Alister E. McGrath notes that "the first casualty of the pluralist agenda is truth."[20] All religious knowledge is believed to be historically and culturally limited, making it impossible to evaluate the truth claims of another religion on the basis of one's own religion. It is assumed that there is no place outside of culture or history from which one can derive norms of right and wrong for making a judg- ment. There is no absolute or universal truth but only relative and subjective truth.[21] All belief systems are equally plausible, and all claims to truth are equally valid. No story is the only story. Truth is that which is true for *me*.

Christian faith is true because some consider it true, not because it *is* true. Truth is what one feels good about. Truth is not either/or but both/and. Normative claims of truth are divisive, even imperialistic. Those who dogmatically appeal to revelatory authority, special insight to truth, or absolute commitments are severely criticized. They con- sider it a kind of idolatry to believe that truth and salvation are given decisively in Christ.

Stanley Samartha once declared, "There is no reason to claim that the religion developed in the desert around Mt. Sinai is superior to the religion developed on the banks of the river Ganga."[22] According to this view, all religions contain truth; one truth is as good as another. There is truth for each setting: Hinduism is good for India, Buddhism is good for Thailand. Gandhi believed all religions were equally true in their own right. He was consistent with the Indian-Hindu understanding, in which no religion is universally normative or authoritative. For India, the best path to God is the religion into which one is born. Hinduism welcomes the gospel if Christ is merely one of the great sages and "no other name" is abandoned.

When truth is relativized, the Bible is relativized. Christ and the Bible are true for those who accept them. The Bible is only one revelation among many; it is useful within Christian faith but has no binding authority for other religions. All inspired books of religion are true for those who believe them, according to this understanding.

Response and Evaluation

Vagueness of God in Religion

Our knowledge of God may indeed be culturally conditioned, but not all such knowledge is culturally conditioned. Pluralists are also culturally conditioned by modern Western culture.

The pluralist says that all religions, despite their contradictions, point to the same divine reality. But that is difficult to believe because the basic claims of the world's religions seem incompatible. Competing traditions are not all authentic unless we say that the criterion of true faith is that it embraces everything. If all religions are in contact with one divine reality, why are there diverse understandings of divine reality? It has been suggested that God is not only expressed differently in each religion, but that there are differences within Godhead itself.[23] But do not differences within Godhead cause pluralism to come dangerously close to polytheism? Are monotheism and polytheism both true?

Pluralists say that our apprehension of the divine is distorted. But even that does not account for all the differences. How can religions that are agnostic, theistic, or naturalistic all be about the same ultimate mystery? Timothy Westergren notes,

> Though different religions all encourage openness to some higher reality, the conceptions and descriptions of the divine that they promote are mutually exclusive and contradictory. What kind of God is God if he is conceived both theistically and nontheistically, personally and impersonally?[24]

Does a religion lead to God if it denies the existence of God?

If the same reality is behind the variety of religions, how can we really understand that reality? Is there a common God in all religions? Is there a common quest for God? The theory of common essence seems to be a product of the imagination. Interreligious dialogue is not enhanced by minimizing differences, compromising religious distinctives, or reinterpreting religions to eliminate problematic elements.

Pluralist theories strip religion down to its barest minimum. Theories which deal with common essence fail to take adequate account of the very different apprehensions of God in the different religions. It is difficult to believe that all religions derive from the same source and tend toward the same goal when they characterize their essence and meaning so differently. Pluralism does not deal adequately with differences in doctrine and theological statements which occur at many levels. Theological tolerance often leads to indifference toward something that is at the heart of a particular faith. As David Bosch said, "When everything is equally valid, nothing really matters anymore."[25]

Pluralism does not take religious diversity seriously enough. We cannot believe the idea that the end of all religion is identical despite the diversity of paths. Do various paths lead to the top of the same mountain, or to different mountains? If all paths lead to God, it is possible that all could lead away from God. There is no way all religions can be fused together into a coherent whole, because the mystical core is not the same. Christian faith should not be rewritten in order to have harmony between religions.

Pluralist conversations about God are vague and impersonal. God at the center is very abstract—Real, Ultimate, Transcendent Being. Hick wants us to move away from a church-centered or Christ-centered faith to a God-centered or Absolute-centered faith. But how is the Absolute understood? God loses decisive meaning when the incarnation and resurrection are reduced to a myth or God is required to be the center of all religions, including those without any belief in God.[26] Lesslie Newbigin asks why the impersonal, undefinable abstraction is more worthy to be at the center of the universe than the One revealed in recorded history. He believes this shift to the theocentric view means that the theologian's *conception* of God becomes the reality which defines the essence of religion.[27]

Criteria for Understanding God

Where do theocentric pluralists get their criteria for understanding God? What are the characteristic attributes of the Real or God? How can one understand God as love apart from the revelation of

God in Israel and in Jesus Christ? Buddhism, Islam, and Hinduism are not nearly so clear about the love of God. Or how are we to distinguish between what is and what is not a valid response to God? Are no judgments made? Is nothing excluded?

Pluralism does not deal adequately with the problem of criteria for evaluating the different images of the divine. How does one decide between God represented by a stone phallus in a Shiva temple, and God revealed in the cross of Christ? Can Yahweh be the same as Brahman? Shouldn't the God we worship have some definite characteristics?

We may suggest that there are a number of spheres of saving contact between God and humans, and that each is partial, incomplete, or unique. If so, we lack a foundation for distinguishing good from bad, the spiritually wholesome and profound from the spiritually destitute. On what basis can we critique Jim Jones or the Branch Davidians? Why was it wrong to torture witches or slaughter Jews?

Biblical particularity is an essential criterion in the face of pluralism, which is universal, general, or abstract. Pluralists seem to be close to Gnostics of the second century, who objected to the specificity of biblical particularity. They claimed to have discovered an esoteric knowledge about ultimate reality, a knowledge or experience superior to that given to the apostles in their interpretation of Jesus Christ. For them, truth couldn't be revealed in the particular. Gnostics thought many mediators were needed to understand ultimate reality. Similarly, contemporary pluralists suggest that the many experiences and the many mediators are equally valid. But how do we know that the same divine and transcendent reality lies behind different manifestations of religious devotion unless we understand the nature of that reality? There is a profound difference between Brahman and Allah.[28]

Christ the Criterion

Christians do not claim to fully and finally comprehend God, but we have partial comprehension. We don't pretend to exhaust the divine nature, but we seek to understand the divine through God's self-disclosure in Christ and in Scripture. If we suggest that Christian faith is only one of several contributions to the religious life of humankind, we depart from New Testament foundations. Scripture emphasizes the need to worship God, not gods in general (the Canaanite option) but the God who has been made known through Christ. We cannot choose between God and Jesus Christ because God is the Father of our Lord Jesus Christ (1 Pet. 1:3).

Pluralism seeks to accommodate Christian faith to other religions by discarding distinctive doctrines of Christian faith that give it identity. But if Christian faith is simply homogeneous with other religions, its understandings of God, Christ, and salvation are drastically reinterpreted. Christian faith cannot be separated from the uniqueness of Christ.

Pluralism challenges the foundation of Christian faith—that Jesus Christ is the complete definitive self-revelation of God and that there is salvation in no other. One might declare, as does Hick (and others), that "Christ is wholly God" but not the "whole of God." Yet such a declaration must be held in tension with the Scripture which says, "For in him the whole fullness of deity dwells bodily" (Col. 2:9).

Pluralism minimizes the doctrine of the incarnation by suggesting that Christ represents one focus of the saving God or one vehicle of God's disclosure. The reinterpretation of Christ's incarnation as myth does not adequately explain why Christ came; it subverts the distinctiveness of Christ. The incarnation of Christ in history validates Christ's life, teaching, and atonement. Myth introduces an alien framework for the incarnation; our understanding of God loses meaning if the incarnation is no more than myth. Though Jesus Christ is a stumbling block for many, we are not justified in removing him from the center. Christian faith cannot disown its self-confessed identity.

Theocentrism that is not Christocentric is not a Christian theocentrism. Christ is the center but does not displace God, for God is the goal. Christ is the mediator who leads to God. Jesus is the center because he has been placed there by God. Therefore, we do not have to choose between Christocentrism and theocentrism. Jesus Christ is God turned toward humankind in self-revelation; he is not God's replacement. Christocentrism and theocentrism must embrace each other; they are inseparable. The presence of God in Jesus is not based on Christian experience or on deification of Jesus by later Christian interpreters but on Jesus' claim of relationship to the Father. Jacques Dupuis says, "There is no Christian theocentrism without christocentrism; but neither can there be a genuine christocentrism that will not at the same time be theocentric."[29]

Clark Pinnock says, "Focusing on Christ is not different from being God-centered—it is a way of being God-centered."[30] Mark Heim believes faith in Christ centers on God; it is not a substitute for God-centeredness.[31] Christology helps us to understand God's saving love. The God who loves humanity and forgives sins is God the Father of Jesus Christ, not a generic God. If the normativeness of Christ is removed, we have no basis for knowing God as personal, loving, and forgiving.

Christ is at the center of the New Testament. Though Jesus announced the kingdom of God, the New Testament focuses on Jesus. One cannot speak of the kingdom without Christ, for the reign of God is manifest in history through Christ. Jews had no objection to a theocentric view. They opposed Jesus as Messiah and Son of God. Chris Wright says, "The New Testament writings are a constant reflection of the struggle by which the God-centered faith of the Hebrew Scriptures was seen to be Christ-centered in reality."[32] Christ was the center of the theocentric universe because he was Emmanuel—God with us.

To relativize Jesus is to strip him of his distinctiveness and to deny him. Jesus is too radical to be relativized. One might say that he is central for Christians but is not absolutely unique or final. But that is hardly consistent with the New Testament declaration that God has given Christ "the name that is above every name," that "every knee should bend" at the name of Jesus, and that "every tongue should confess that Jesus Christ is Lord, to the glory of God the Father" (Phil. 2:9-11). Knitter, Panikkar, and Samartha believe that Jesus is normative for Christians but that we should not insist on him for others. But Norman Kraus understandably asks, "How can I reject the universal normativeness of God's revelation in Christ and still accept it with ultimate seriousness as final authority for myself?"[33]

Some, on the basis of mythic understanding, argue that Jesus was elevated to divine status by the church. But this is unfair to the history of the New Testament; New Testament affirmations were often made in contrast to myth (1 John, Colossians). Second Peter 1:16 declares, "For we did not follow cleverly devised myths when we made known to you the power and coming of our Lord Jesus Christ, but we had been eyewitnesses of his majesty." Chris Wright sharpens the implications by noting, "Either Jesus was God and still is, or he is not God and never has been. . . . If Jesus was not more than a man, then the whole Christian faith and all the generations of Christian worship have been one monstrous deluded idolatry."[34]

Salvation

Pluralists, though often espousing the relativity of religions, are not complete relativists when they establish criteria for assessing religions. Pluralists make a judgment that all religions are true, as others make a judgment that some religions are false. Pluralists don't want to judge other religions by Christian faith, but they judge other religions by their particular cultural traditions, which reflect a Western point of view. To what extent is pluralism a new form of Western imperialism?

Some believe that the criterion for evaluating religions is the salvation they offer. But how is salvation understood and measured? Liberation is commendable. Yet no particular event constitutes salvation. Are all religions valid ways of salvation? How does a nontheistic, nonpersonal "God" bring salvation? Vagueness about God results in a vague salvation. Is the love of a personal God the same as the love of an impersonal God? Many different models of salvation are offered, such as *moksha* (Hindu release) or *nirvana* (Buddhist release). Most offers of salvation do not acknowledge sin or respond to it, but Christian faith understands redemption to be provided through forgiveness offered by Jesus Christ. Through forgiveness, one is reconciled with God. This is vastly different from human transformation as taught by many religions.

Christians insist that salvation cannot be separated from the universal love of God manifested in Jesus. We should not separate the universal salvific will of God from God's will to save through the grace of Jesus Christ.

Truth Is Relativized

Pluralism challenges the foundation and nature of truth by attempting to free us from the authority of Scripture and denying that Jesus Christ is the unique way to God. But when we relativize Jesus, we are left with no place to stand to evaluate the truth.

In our culture much attention is given to revelation through people, their actions, and their immediate noncognitive experience. But what is the relationship between experience and truth? Can one validate truth-claims by experience? Experience of God is often separated from an understanding of God. Experience alone is not sufficient as a theological foundation; the whole variety of human experience is not equally valid. Experience must be interpreted within a framework, the framework of Scripture. Experience does not evaluate Scripture, but Scripture evaluates experience. Core religious experiences vary widely. Buddhists and Christians do not have the same experience.

Truth is frequently understood in relational and subjective terms. Truth, it is said, is that which helps us to accept and relate to others. Certainly our relationships with others are crucial, but relationships are not the sole criteria for discerning truth. Character must not be confused with truth.

How are we to answer the problem of conflicting truth claims between religions? Are differing notions of truth identical or complementary? Truth is not always complementary. There are incompatibilities and contradictions, such as God in contrast to no God. It is dishonest to ignore conflicting claims, to dissolve or discount such contradictions. The question of truth and how to test it is thereby diminished. If all faiths are equally true, can all be equally false? The existence of a religion does not guarantee its truth. Beliefs held with sincerity are not necessarily true. If everything sincerely believed and practiced is true, intellectual and moral discernment is ignored. Christians believe that some things are eternally true, that truth can be known, and that there are normative standards, ultimate truths.

Values are important, but values are not equivalent to truth. We cannot dismiss truth or abandon the search for truth but must ask truth questions and respond to them with biblical, moral, and intellectual vigor. If one accepts relativistic pluralism, how can there be a prophetic voice? How is wrong defined? There is a true and false understanding of God, a true and false understanding of devotion, a true and false understanding of behavior. Female infanticide and the burning of widows in India was wrong. Killing Muslims in the name of the cross was wrong. We believe these were wrong because of the truth revealed in Christ. There are erroneous assumptions about the nature of truth. Total pluralism leads to disorientation and confusion.

We must be culturally sensitive, but Christian tolerance should not obligate us to revise the normative declaration that Jesus Christ is Lord of all. It is not adequate to say that religions are relative to the cultures from which they emerge. Modernity and postmodernity condition us to think that one religion is not better than another—Shinto for Japan, Islam for Iran, Christian faith for the West. If we say that because birth determines one's religion, all religions are true, then truth is merely a function of birth.

It is equally inadequate to suggest that religions are in essence one. Though such a confident claim is technically opposite of relativism, many aspects of religion are nevertheless relativized. As Clark Pinnock says, "To wave a wand over religions and declare that they are saying the same thing is nonsense. This is sloppy pluralism, false tolerance, and indifference to truth."[35] Religious relativism asks people to modify the implications of their most precious beliefs—Muslims need to downplay their belief that Muhammad is the final prophet, and Christians need to reinterpret their belief in Jesus as the incarnation of God. Pluralist theology diminishes the unique significance of each religion and fails to do justice to the great diversity among the religions. It can lead to indifferentism, which fails to recognize the vision that is particular to the religion.

Truth claims of each religion must be listened to more seriously, and Christians must respect religions other than our own. But if we hold that Christ is the final revelation, we are not obliged to consider them as equal manifestations of God's will. Christians base their understanding of truth on the particularity of Christ, not on relativism.

When religious pluralism is accepted ideologically, truth is always an open question, little is considered false, no claim to truth can be considered final, and people abandon hope of finding the truth. Our culture resembles the pantheon in Rome, where there was room for all religions if only they renounced exclusive access to ultimate deity and final truth.

However, does it matter which path we follow? Is it biblical or reasonable to suggest that there are no norms by which everything else is measured? In the face of the radically new religious pluralism, must we deny the essence of the gospel or yield the possibility of making normative statements?

All religions are not walking hand in hand to the same goal. They are going in different directions. Religious pluralism has become a dogma that needs critical assessment. Pluralism is identified with relativism, but relativism itself is self-contradictory. If one says that there is no absolute truth, one makes an absolute statement. We must recover the biblical witness to God's revelation and sharpen our understanding of the nature of biblical authority in understanding truth.

Tolerance and Dogmatism

Christians need to be loving and tolerant, but each of these requires definition because love, courtesy, and tolerance are not the only religious values. Tolerance does not demand an open-minded acceptance of all ideas as true. Love need not succumb to a pluralist stance; love can object to ideological religious pluralism. While we need to model tolerance in our attitudes, tolerance does not excuse us from discerning the truth. Often the quest for tolerance is used to condemn those who cannot with good conscience be religious pluralists. Pluralists avoid judging other religions, but they readily judge exclusivists and inclusivists. By denying the validity of other points of view, they are not really pluralists. The tolerant religious pluralist becomes intolerant of nonrelativist thinking. In the name of tolerance, some become intolerant.

Pluralism easily becomes triumphalistic and exclusivist for the pluralist position. When pluralism labels some things intolerable, it can become as coercive and absolutist as what it criticizes. If pluralism insists on excluding or reinterpreting certain beliefs, is it really pluralism? The historical development of religious pluralism has led to dogmatism concerning religious pluralism. Some who criticize the dogmatism of the exclusivist or inclusivist become dogmatic in the way they hold their "nondogmatic" views. Those who do not agree with pluralism are considered intolerant, narrow-minded, and possessive of their own God. If exclusivism is extreme, so also is pluralism. Andrew Kirk aptly observed,

> In declaring, on the grounds of the present cultural consensus, what people ought and ought not to believe, the pluralist position has rightly been seen as imperialist and intolerant, the very characteristics which it denounces in the exclusivist claim of some religious traditions.[36]

Likewise, relativism can be condescending and dogmatic. Pinnock asks, "How is it that one can be relativistic about everything and not about relativism itself?"[37] We all want to live in harmony and unity with people of other religions, but what is the basis for that unity? Commitment to Christ or commitment to pluralist-relativism are both faith positions that need to be tested. Is religious pluralism the norm, or is Christ the norm? Will pluralism be a world faith replacing Christ?

Religious pluralism is not unique to the modern world. The Mediterranean setting into which Christian faith was born was much like our world. The collapse of the classical gods of Greece and Rome left a vacuum which produced popular philosophies and cults. In a fearful and capricious world, the gospel promised salvation. In contrast to cults of secrecy, the gospel was openly proclaimed. Where no truth was compelling enough to demand one's whole life, Christians were willing to sacrifice everything.[38] Early Christians knew what it meant to live under the power and authority of other lords. They were converted from a large variety of religious beliefs. They experienced conversion as liberation from oppression.

Understanding of Mission

Pluralism undermines a traditional understanding of mission. If one recognizes parallel paths to the truth, there is no need to evangelize. Why expect people to convert from other religions in which

God's grace is already at work? Conversion is considered imperialistic and socially devastating. Christian faith is only a universal message for those whose heart is touched by it. Other religious ideas will speak to other hearts. Christian mission is restricted to participation with other religions in humanitarian concerns or to sharing insights in dialogue with other religions, for change can only come from within the tradition. Another pluralist view suggests that the church's mission is to redeem and liberate that which is already Christian within the religion.

The early church proclaimed the gospel to people who followed a variety of religions—Jewish, Greek, Roman, and Oriental. They encountered rivals and alternatives to Christian faith expressed in philosophy, literature, and religion. They engaged Artemis (Diana), mystery religions, Gnosticism, Stoicism, Epicurianism, Cynicism, and the cult of the Roman emperor. The gospel transcended cultural barriers but did not accept religious pluralism and syncretism. The early Christians were confident about Jesus Christ, but they were not imperialist. They were not dominant in the culture; they came from the periphery. If the early Christians would have adopted pluralism, the gospel would not have moved beyond the Middle East.

Today's church should follow the example of the early church rather than become wedded to a pluralist ideology. Pluralists ask us to "cross the theological Rubicon," but the editors of the *International Bulletin of Missionary Research* insist,

> We need to affirm again the unique 'Rubicon-crossing' event of twenty centuries ago: the redemptive entering of the Creator into human history in the person of Jesus Christ (Heb. 1:1-3). Without the uniqueness of that person and that event, there is no gospel and no mission.[39]

Summary Perspectives on Exclusivism, Inclusivism, and Pluralism

The discussion of exclusivism, inclusivism, and pluralism in chapters 2 and 3 (above) is designed to present perspectives on Christian faith and other religions, not to suggest that these are totally adequate categories. Clearly the most serious divide is between exclusivism and inclusivism on the one hand, and pluralism on the other hand. Typologies are helpful for analyzing issues, but persons and religious systems resist too-rigid codification. Indeed, exclusivism, inclusivism, and pluralism can sometimes create unnecessary polarities. Given the many variations within them, the neatness of the categories may need to give way to a continuum, depending on the theological issues involved.

Nevertheless, each of us brings strong convictions to the issue of Christian faith and other religions because of our concern for truth claims and salvation claims. Rather than becoming obsessed with each detail of the categories, we should rather witness to our Christian faith as centered in Christ and attested to by Scripture. Thus we will allow people to consider him whom we have found to be trustworthy, Jesus Christ.

4

A Biblical Perspective on the
Religions—Old Testament

I have participated in discussions on Christian faith and other religions in which persons have argued that we can't use the Bible as our primary witness because it is biased toward Christian faith and doesn't provide a fair assessment of other religions. In this chapter on the Old Testament as well as chapter 5 on the New Testament, I assume that the Bible's perspective on other religions is a reliable foundation from which to begin our exploration of a theology of religions.

Thinking Biblically

Those who are concerned with Christian faith and other religions must take seriously the source of their faith as explicated in Scripture. How we read and interpret the Bible is crucial. Is it authoritative and normative for faith and life? Or is it one witness among many stories, one of the multiple sources? We need a systematic study of the biblical data as they relate to the questions of Christian faith and other religions, a study which includes an examination of specific texts but also considers the main thrust of the Old and New Testaments. We need to immerse ourselves in Scripture so that we think in a biblically comprehensive way.

The Bible does not present a systematic "theology of religions" or a detailed description of the religions of people surrounding Israel and the early church. But the Bible does record interaction between biblical faith and other faiths. It is a record of God's revelation and involvement in the world, which includes God's encounter with the religions. Our challenge is to discern what was meant in the Bible and what it means for today. Biblical tradition and human experience need to engage each other, but biblical material will check our opinions, hunches, and intuitions.

It is important to distinguish between God's revelation and the sometimes faulty human response to it. Often Israel's religion and Christian religion have been misused. Evaluation of other religions is not on the basis of the historical expression of Christianity but on the basis of the authority of God's word. Christians must always submit their convictions and behavior to scriptural critique. Human reasoning and action should not be placed above the biblical text.

In the Old Testament, God's revelation is most complete through Israel: and in the New Testament, God's fullest revelation comes to the world through Jesus of Nazareth, the son of Israel. God's purpose is to restore relationships broken by sin, to overcome the alienation between God and humans, between humans and humans, and between humans and the created order. The story of God's revelation in Israel and in the life of Jesus is set in the context of humanity-wide concern. Israel is to be a blessing and light to the nations, and Jesus is the light of the world.

We are concerned here with how the Bible portrays religions. From a biblical perspective, religions are multidimensional. They reflect God's activity in the world, the human search for God, and the human attempt to flee from God. They seek to reverence the God or gods they know, and they try to manipulate God or gods. They are cries for help and efforts at self-justification.

When one studies Israel, Jesus, and the early church, it is clear that biblical faith is not just a religious philosophy, a code of social ethics, or one of the possible roads up the mountain toward God at the top. Biblical faith invites humans into a covenant relationship. The covenant takes a particular form, but its intent is universal.

Covenant of Creation and Covenant with Noah: Genesis 1–11

Genesis 1–11 describes God as the Creator and sustainer of the whole universe and all the nations. Creation implies God's continuing jurisdiction over all the world. Genesis assumes that all people are created in God's image and are aware of God. They are created to respond to God and live in community with God; their lives are God-oriented. Disobedience and sin marred the image of God in humankind, but that image was not removed. People still have God-awareness; they act religiously (Gen. 4:1, 3, 26). Every human being has some relationship with the Creator, whom they understand as protector, bestower of blessing, or judge. They respond to God with offerings, pleas, or declarations.

Although God-awareness continues, sin has caused distortion, shame, and distance from God. Humans are rebellious and in hiding; they seek God and flee from God. They are alienated from God ("Where are you?" Gen. 3:9) and from each other ("Where is your brother?" Gen. 4:9). Genesis 3 helps us understand the nature of sin and the need for redemption. God's response to sin is not withdrawal from the world. God continues to show concern both in judgment and love: judgment against sin (Adam, Eve, Cain, destruction by flood, scattering at the Tower of Babel), and opportunities for new beginnings (Seth, Enoch, Noah, Shem, Abraham).

God is related to humankind through the *covenant of creation* and the *covenant with Noah*. The *covenant of creation* unites the human family because all have a common origin. Humans are one, though separate nations and peoples; God belongs to all nations and peoples, and God's witness is in all cultures. This is foundational for understanding God's action in the history of other nations in the Old Testament. The nations are blessed but not in the same way as Abraham is blessed. They are within a creation covenant, but the covenant is not as complete as that offered in Abraham. Though the nations are not elected as Abraham, they cannot be separated from the Abraham people.

H. D. Beeby says, "The nations are present theologically in every sense of the unfolding drama of redemption."[1] Creation and redemption are the two modes of God's activity in the world. The setting of redemption is against the background of creation. Beeby writes, "Blessing, therefore, comes in two distinct ways: in association with creation, and in association with a chosen people whose presence and work is to represent God's redemption."[2]

God's interest in the future of the nations, implied already in the creation covenant, is seen also in the *covenant with Noah* (Gen. 6:18; 9:8-17) and in the Table of Nations (Gen. 10). After the judgment by flood, God began anew by entering into a covenant of preservation with Noah. This was a cosmic, universal covenant, Noah representing all people. The covenant with Noah is related to God's providence, a covenant promising "common grace" that sustains the world after the Fall. Yet that covenant was not totally adequate; something more was needed. Goldingay and Wright note that "human beings in the covenant relationship initiated with Noah are still prohibited from enter-

ing fullness of life in the presence of God and tend to resist the fulfillment of their human destiny."[3]

The covenant with Noah was impersonal, unconditional, and in-
discriminate. Little response was required. But the covenant with
Abraham was specific, personal, and required a response of obedience. The covenant with Noah was not revoked by the Abrahamic
covenant; it prepared the way for the more complete revelation and
specific blessing of the nations through Abraham.

What follows the covenant with Noah is disappointing and shows
the need for a covenant of restoration through Abraham. The brokenness of community was amplified at the Tower of Babel, where there
was an attempt to form a community without God or even against
God. They sought a "name for themselves" (Gen. 11:4). They were
concerned for security, power, and fame. Attempts to build community by self-assertion, cleverness, and technique ended in failure. Judgment resulted in confusion and scattering.

Though Babel marks the end of the first chapter of humankind,
God did not abandon the nations to their fate. The call of Abraham
(Gen. 12) was against the background of creation and the world of
peoples in Genesis 1–11. Though God called Abraham, the other peoples are the continuous subjects of God's concern. It is this universal
concern that forms the backdrop for "in you all the families of the
earth shall be blessed" (12:3).

Genesis 1–11 helps us understand variety in religion. Because
people are in the image of God and share the same background
through creation, there will be parallel insights between biblical faith
and other religious traditions. Further, God's work in the wider world
through the covenant with Noah will have an impact on religious consciousness. Clearly God worked in the lives of Abel, Enoch, and Noah
(Hebrews 11 commends them). They were "people of faith" before
the existence of the "people of Israel."

However, the picture is not only positive. The Serpent deluded
humans in their desire to be as God and continues to inject evil into
religious quests. People try to dissolve the distinction between themselves and the Creator and establish their own norms for behavior.
Because of the Fall, religion is not always a fitting response to God;
sometimes it expresses rebellion against God. Religion always has this
duality or ambiguity. It seeks after God and flees from God. It manifests both goodness and alienation. When other religions share common ground with biblical faith or have a positive function, they should
be affirmed and seen as starting points, not as the finishing point.[4]

Election and Covenant Through Abraham: Witness to the Nations

After the Babel tragedy, Abraham was called to leave his country (the religio-cultural environment of Ur and Haran), his kindred, and his father's house. He was to follow God into the unknown, with nothing but promises. He will dwell in another land, he will become many people, he will be blessed, his name "will be made great" (in contrast to Babel which tried to make a name for itself). He will be a blessing to the nations.

This call was a radical breakthrough, the beginning of the restoration of the lost unity of humankind and of broken fellowship with God. What Babel lost, God promised to restore and guarantee in Abraham's election. The new community was God's answer to the fractured community of Babel. It was not a community of kinship but of covenant. Bavinck notes that covenant community is in contrast to the surrounding nations, where deities tended to be incarnate in the nation.[5] God was not just a tribal deity for Abraham people. God's actions in fulfilling the promises to Abraham have an important function for the lives of all peoples. They represent the continuation of God's dealings with the nations.

The language of election is covenantal language. To be elected is a privilege, but not without responsibility. The Abraham community was chosen for the sake of the world. Even if weak and smaller than neighboring nations, it was to carry the promise and mediate the blessing. Witness to the nations arises from covenant community (Gen. 12:3; 18:18; 22:18; 26:4; 28:14). Election was for another's blessing, not a basis for another's rejection. Other nations are invited, not ignored, forgotten, or despised.

The particularism of election is offensive to some, but when particularism is held alongside God's universal concern, it is understood as God's instrument for universal ends. If God is the God of Abraham because of the covenant made with Abraham, it is conceivable that other nations can also be included in the covenant. The people of Abraham have no peculiar claim upon God; their position is based solely on God's electing grace. Bernhard Anderson notes, "Israel's greatness would lie not in herself, but in the God who was active in her history to overcome the confusion, disharmony and sin sketched in such lurid colors in primeval history."[6] J. Verkuyl proposes that God "deals so intensely with Israel precisely because he is maintaining his personal claim to the whole world."[7]

There are two kinds of particularism. At the Tower of Babel particularism expressed itself in autonomous self-seeking, with resulting fragmentation and scattering. In contrast, Abraham's people, though particularized, were to be led and blessed by God so they could be a sign of hope for others. This particular call was not fragmentation of community but God's answer to fragmentation through an alternate community. Abraham walked the path that all humanity would be invited to follow; the covenant made with him was not the "amen" but the beginning of new possibilities. Chris Wright points out that "the tension between the universal goal and the particular means is found throughout the Bible."[8]

Abraham's call separated him from the world, giving him a unique identity for service and blessing. Separation from the nations opened the possibility of interaction with the nations. He was placed in the context of universal history, an indication that God is interested in world history, not just the narrow thread of salvation history isolated from the larger world. As John Sanders says, "The covenant with Abraham did not abrogate the older covenants; rather, it developed and articulated God's universal plans more fully."[9]

Implication of Abrahamic Faith: God and the Gods

In Israel, God worked with a covenant of redemption, initiated and sustained by grace. The covenant with Israel for blessing to the nations implies that other nations were in need of fuller revelation. They were invited to receive blessing through the Abrahamic covenant.

Yet Israel's religious understandings were not entirely original or totally separate from the surrounding culture. The Old Testament did not hesitate to use *El*, a high God worshiped in that cultural context, as a name for God. Genesis 12–50 presupposes that this God is the one whom, in a later period, Israel will worship as *Yahweh*. God is called *El Elyon* (Most High, 14:18-22); *El-roi* (He sees me, 16:13); *El Shaddai* (Almighty, 17:1; 28:3; 35:11; 43:14; 48:3); *El Olam* (Eternal, 21:33).

El was the Canaanite name for the high God. However, the use of El was not always identical with Yahweh. There were similarities between Yahweh and El (as the Canaanites knew him), but these correspondences did not constitute total identity. We cannot conclude that Canaanite and Israelite faith were equally valid alternatives depending upon the geographical, historical, or cultural location. Canaanite religion had some valid insight, but what God began in Abraham was new. Goldingay and Wright contend that "the biblical view is that the living God, later disclosed as Yahweh, accommodated his dealings with the ancestors of Israel to the names and forms of deity then known in their cultural setting."[10] But this does not endorse all Canaanite El worship. Yahweh was to be known more fully and worshiped exclusively by those who imperfectly knew him as El.

Chris Wright notes, "What we have here . . . is a situation where the living God is known, worshiped, believed, and obeyed, but under divine titles which were common to the rest of contemporary Semitic culture."[11] God's self-revelation accommodated itself to the Canaanite's existing religious framework but transcended their former understanding with new and fuller promises.

This does not suggest that all religions are equally valid ways to God. The relationship between God and Abraham was based on God's initiative and grace, not on the name of a deity Abraham already knew. God's purpose was not to validate the religion of El and his pantheon, but to lead the Abraham people beyond it into a personal relationship with God. God used what knowledge they had to prepare them for a fuller knowledge of God's name and character.[12]

This suggests that God relates to people in terms of their existing concept of deity (*El* in the Old Testament or *Theos* in the New Testament), but such initiative prepares for fuller revelation and redemption. It would be wrong to conclude that the worship of other gods is always an unconscious worship of the true God. El, understood as the creator God, was acceptable, but lesser deities and idols were not. While there was some continuity between ancient Semitic religions, the Old Testament rejected idolatry, immorality, and occult practices. Though there was selective accommodation and assimilation, syncretism was opposed. Even if other religions believed in a creator God and had elements of truth, sin often led to the distortion of truth. Followers of other religions were invited to learn from Yahweh. The salvation disclosed in Israel was for all nations.

Exodus, Sinai, Canaan: No Other Gods

When God chose Moses to lead Israel out of Egypt, God said, "I am the God of your father, the God of Abraham, the God of Isaac, and the God of Jacob" (Exod. 3:6). Later as Moses struggled with the call and asked how to identify the God who was calling him, God replied, "I Am Who I Am" (Exod. 3:14), *Yahweh*. The Most High, Eternal, Almighty Creator God was now to be known as Yahweh. Yahweh is the God who would take Israel out of Egypt, make covenant with them, and lead them to Canaan. This new experience gave new content to their understanding of God.[13] From then on, they knew that Yahweh is radically different from other gods.

The Bible suggests that the worship of Yahweh exposes the inadequacy of earlier religious understandings. Yahweh was more than God among the gods; Yahweh was often against the gods. Yahweh's self-revelation to Israel critiques other gods and religions because truth and salvation are understood to come from Yahweh above.[14] Only Yahweh can save; they could not save themselves, nor could the idols of the surrounding nations save them.

Yahweh was in conflict with the gods of Egypt. Pharaoh repeatedly refused to acknowledge the God of Israel. The plagues were acts of God's judgment on Pharaoh and Egypt in the context of their unrepentant oppression of Israel. The plagues desacralized the gods of Egypt and help us understand that God is over all the earth, not just a national deity. The plagues were attacks on the gods of Egypt, who were expected to protect Egypt from such disasters. God said, "On all the gods of Egypt I will execute judgment: I am the Lord" (Exod. 12:12). Jethro, father-in-law of Moses, blessed the God of Israel: "Now I know that the Lord is greater than all gods, because he delivered the people from the Egyptians" (Exod. 18:11).

Numbers describes the conflict between Israel and Egypt: "The Lord executed judgments even against their gods" (Num. 33:4). Israel celebrated its deliverance from Egypt by declaring, "Who is like you, O Lord, among the gods? Who is like you, majestic in holiness, awesome in splendor, doing wonders?" (Exod. 15:11).

When the Israelites arrived at Sinai and prepared to make covenant with Yahweh, Yahweh told them, "If you obey my voice and keep my covenant, you shall be my treasured possession out of all the peoples. Indeed, the whole earth is mine, but you shall be for me a priestly kingdom and a holy nation" (Exod. 19:5-6). Israel was to serve in a mediating (priestly) role and was to model holiness in the context of God's wider world. Israel was called to witness to the world through her worship and her new way of living together as a holy nation guided by *Torah* (law, instruction).

The first three of the Ten Commandments (Ten Words) pertain to Israel's understanding of God. God said,

You shall have no other gods before me. You shall not make for
yourself an idol, whether in the form of anything that is in heaven
above, or that is on the earth beneath, or that is in the water under
the earth. You shall not bow down to them or worship them; for I
the Lord your God am a jealous God. . . . You shall not make
wrongful use of the name of the Lord your God, for the Lord will
not acquit anyone who misuses his name. (Exod. 20:3-7)

Because idolatry, images, and misuse of God's name (name magic) are
ways in which God is easily misunderstood, such practices are strictly
forbidden.

The first commandment suggests that Yahweh is not a generic deity. The Lord is different from other gods in the ancient Near East.
God is not to be confused with the gods of Egypt and Canaan. The
name *Yahweh* distinguishes God from other gods. Uniqueness and finality belong to God. According to Clark Pinnock, "The major claim of
uniqueness in the Bible is the claim made on behalf of Israel's God,
and only afterward on behalf of Israel's Messiah."[15]

The uniqueness of Jesus is related to the uniqueness of Israel's
God. Israel had received a fuller knowledge of God. The Israelites
were to reject all the gods but the God known through acts of revelation and redemption. Faith in Yahweh was exclusive, but there was a
universal purpose to the particularism and exclusiveness of Israel's
faith. The Israelites had no reason to be proud of their privilege. Their
religion was not "developed" at Mt. Sinai but "received" at Mt. Sinai.
This is not a question of superiority but a question of truth. If the Israelites accept other religions as equally valid and acceptable alternatives to their own faith, that would be betrayal, not kindness.[16]

When Israel settled in Canaan, the people were tempted to follow
the fertility religion of Baal (male deity) and Asherah (female deity).
Yahweh led them through the Sinai desert, but could Yahweh guarantee agricultural success in Canaan? Israel was warned against accepting the religious worldview of the Canaanite people with its moral
degradation (Deut. 7:16, 25; 13:1-18). The worship of Baal and the
other gods and goddesses had a different status than the worship of El
because they were gods without moral character. Baal shrines were to
be destroyed, not adapted (Deut. 7:5; 12:2-4); Baalistic influence
would lead to perversion. Baalism was associated with horrendous
evil: idolatry, sexual immorality, ritual prostitution, child sacrifice, divination, spiritism, necromancy, soothsaying, and sorcery (Lev. 18:21-
25; Deut. 12:29-31; 18:9-13). The worship of El was acknowledged,

but the worship of Baal was repudiated because it implied the worship of other gods.

After Israel settled in Canaan, Joshua called for covenant renewal, asking Israel to put away the gods of Mesopotamia, Egypt, and Canaan (Josh. 24:14-28). Joshua implies that whatever polytheistic worship may have been part of Israel's ancestry, polytheism was no longer appropriate in light of Yahweh's acts of redemption in the exodus from Egypt and settlement in Canaan. Israel had not needed to choose between Yahweh and El but was obliged to choose between Yahweh and the gods of their neighbors.

There is no basis for concluding that other nations in the Old Testament were in reality worshiping Yahweh under a variety of names and should be left to worship their own gods. Instead, Israel's relationship with Yahweh was to be a witness to others; other people were invited to join in the worship of Yahweh. A "mixed company" joined Israel in the Exodus (Exod. 12:38). Others such as Rahab (Josh. 2:8-11) and Ruth (1:16) joined Yahweh's people.

Kingship, Prophets, Exile, Restoration: Protest Against Idolatry and Syncretism

Though Israel was chosen by God and warned against unholiness and idolatry, the history of kingship records repeated apostasy. Chosenness did not prevent Israel's religious response to God from degenerating. Israel received God's revelation and salvation but sinned grievously. When Israel regarded Yahweh's calling as a special privilege instead of a call for the sake of the nations, the prophets protested such religious pride. When Israel tried to fuse the worship of Yahweh and Baal into a comfortable syncretism, the prophets spoke of infidelity and called Israel to be a faithful covenant partner. Elijah challenged the people to choose between Yahweh and Baal (1 Kings 18:21). Both could not mediate salvation. They were not equal; they represented competing truth claims.

The prophets criticized Israel's unfaithfulness to the Sinai revelation; prophets distinguished between serving God for God's sake and using the name of God for one's own sake. When worship was separated from obedience, the prophets raised their voices. Many in Israel thought God's judgment was for the nations and God's salvation was for Israel, but the prophets destroyed their false sense of security.

The prophets criticized the infiltration of idolatry that deified the created order: fertility, power, rulers, sun, moon, stars. The prophets were intolerant of all other deities, especially of fertility gods and goddesses. Kings and queens of ancient Israel often tolerated other gods because they believed Yahweh ruled over the state but other deities had important designated functions. Sometimes other gods were acknowledged because of marriage or political alliances (e.g., Solomon, Ahab, and Jezebel). People sought family and local deities to help them with their work and life. They believed Baal and Asherah could produce rain, crops, family fertility, and health. Prophets like Elijah, Hosea, Amos, and Jeremiah insisted on the exclusive worship of one covenant God, Yahweh. Yahweh could not be the head of a pantheon of other gods and goddesses.

Some of the worst idolatry occurred during the reigns of Ahaz (2 Kings 16:1-20; 2 Chron. 28:1-27) and Manasseh (2 Kings 21:1-16; 2 Chron. 33:1-17). Ahaz burned his son to Moloch (a Syrian custom) as an offering, burned incense to other gods (on high places, hills, and under every green tree in the Hinnom Valley), sacrificed to the gods of Damascus, had an Assyrian altar duplicated and placed before the temple in Jerusalem, made images of Baal, placed foreign altars in Jerusalem, and closed the temple.

Manasseh built high places and pagan shrines in communities outside Jerusalem. He tried to combine the worship of Yahweh with Baal nature religion. Representations of Asherah (female deity) were made, and sacred prostitution was practiced. The astral cult of Mesopotamia was introduced with the worship of sun, moon, and star deities. Manasseh burned his own son as a sacrifice and practiced soothsaying, divination, and sorcery. He employed mediums and wizards.

The psalmist contrasts God's power with the impotence of other gods. He depicts idols as the work of human hands, having mouths that do not speak, eyes that do not see, ears that do not hear, noses that do not smell, feet that do not walk, hands that do not feel, throats that can't make a sound. Those who make idols are like them (Ps. 115:4-8). Jeremiah uses satire to demonstrate the foolishness of idolatry, describing idols as scarecrows who can't speak and need to be carried, as stupid, foolish, false, worthless, and a delusion (Jer. 10:1-16). Hosea (8:6), Jonah (2:8), and Habakkuk (2:18-19) protest the vanity of idols.

Isaiah 40–55, set during the exile, includes severe criticism of other religions. The Babylonian gods Bel and Nebo are criticized and judged. Unlike El, Bel was not accepted as the name under which the one true God could be worshiped. Yahweh alone is the Creator and Ruler of events. Written in the context of religious pluralism, Isaiah 40–55 did not affirm the surrounding multiple religions. Instead, the prophet witnessed to the mighty saving acts of Yahweh in Israel's history.

The Isaiah text conveys some of the most severe criticism of idolatry. Idols are formed of wood, gold, iron, and silver by human artisans. The same tree is used as wood for the fire and for carving an image; though people bow down to gods they have made and carry them around, they are not gods but images. They ask the idol to save, but the image is powerless (Isa. 40:12-26; 41:1-7, 21-29; 42:5-9; 44:2-4, 9–20; 45:14, 24; 46:5-7). Idolatry is illusion; idolaters are blind, deluded, misled. Often idolatry and social injustice are linked.

Much of the Old Testament describes Yahweh in conflict with the forces which seek to thwart God's plans for the world. Yahweh is too dynamic to be represented by an image. Yahweh saves; the gods of the nations are impotent. Yahweh is jealous and will not share praise with idols. Yahweh battles against false gods which human beings have fashioned from the created world, idolized, and used for their own purposes. The goal of this spiritual struggle was not that only Israel should be saved, but that every nation would acknowledge Yahweh as the only true and living God.[17]

Isaiah 40-55 might be seen as the most "exclusivist" and nationalist section of the Hebrew Bible because of its emphasis on Yahweh alone. Yet its broader emphasis is on Yahweh's relationship with Israel being significant for the whole world. That makes it at the same time "universalist." Isaiah 56-66 also combines the universalist and exclusivist perspectives.[18] Isaiah 40-66 has a strong emphasis on Yahweh as universal Creator.

During the Babylonian exile, Israel was stripped of her power but learned new dimensions of her calling as a suffering servant. Her sufferings opened the eyes of many to God's salvation (Isa. 52:13—53:12). Israel discovered that God's love for the world is not expressed in power and glory but in suffering servanthood. God's love is universal; God does not have favorites or reject the rest of the world.

In contrast to the severe critique of other gods in Isaiah 40-55, Ezra, Nehemiah, and Daniel identify Yahweh as the "God of heaven," a local title used in the Persian empire. Daniel identified Yahweh as the Lord of Heaven, the Syrian high God. Similarly, Ezra and Nehemiah express their theology using the terms of the surrounding culture (Ezra 1:2; 5:11-12; 6:9-10; 7:12, 21, 23; Neh. 1:4-5; 2:4, 20; Dan. 2:18-19, 37, 44; 5:3).[19]

God's Dialogue with the Nations

God intends to bless all the world, but not in any way that people happen to choose. Yet non-Israelites were not beyond God's activity and saving presence. Furthermore covenant blessings for Israel were not automatic; not all Israel was true Israel. Sometimes Israel acted like pagans and pagans acted righteously.

Though God's self-revelation was most fully made known to Israel (in that time before Christ), Yahweh is the universal God over all people and nations. Since God made all humans, God is involved in the lives of all and controls the destiny of all nations (Isa. 19:23-24; Amos 1:3—2:8; 9:7). God is in dialogue with all peoples of the earth (Ps. 87:4; 47:1, 8-9). But how was God concerned for and active in the nations that surrounded Israel? If God has a saving purpose for all nations (Ps. 102:15-22), to what extent do persons outside of Israel know God? Israel lived with tension—the fear of compromising with the nations, yet knowing that God was related through creation with all nations.

Clearly God acted in Israel for revelation in a special and historically particular way, but God's salvation was not limited to those who shared that tradition. God was working for the salvation of humankind outside the confines of particular revelation through Israel. Though the Old Testament establishes a normative and particular approach, there are notable exceptions.

As seen earlier, before God's covenant with Abraham, persons such as Abel, Enoch, and Noah responded positively to God. Their faith is attested to in Genesis and commended in Hebrews 11:1-7.

That some persons outside of Israel came to faith raises important theological questions. The relationship of Melchizedek to Abraham (Gen. 14:17-24) sharpens the theological issue. Melchizedek functioned as a Canaanite priest for a God he knew as El Elyon. When he and Abraham met, they showed respect for each other and worshiped God by the same name. Yet Melchizedek made his faith response within the context of another religion. How did he obtain his knowledge? Was he led to God through conscience or nature, or was it by special intervention from God? Abimelech, King of Gerar (Gen. 20:1-18), another "outsider" who met Abraham, seems to be a person of faith who had a right relationship with God. Jethro, a priest of Midian and father-in-law of Moses, may have worshiped God through the Kenite religion outside of the covenant with Israel before he met Moses. But he then joined in the worship of Yahweh, declaring that Yahweh was greater than all gods (Exod. 18:1-11).

Balaam, a Mesopotamian diviner, was employed by the Moabite king Balak to curse Israel, but Balaam could only pronounce a blessing (Num. 22–24). How are we to understand that a foreign priest-diviner, though not a member of the covenant community, was obedient to the Lord's will and could not thwart the fulfillment of the divine purpose for Israel? How is God's purpose revealed to a non-Israelite?

Rahab, a prostitute from Jericho who assisted Joshua as he sought to enter Canaan, confessed faith in Israel's God (Josh. 2:1, 11) and joined the people of Israel. In the New Testament, she is commended for her faith (Heb. 11:31). Ruth, from Moab, joined Israel and was in the lineage of Christ (Matt. 1:5). Naaman, a Syrian commander, came to Elisha requesting healing for leprosy and confessed faith in the God of Israel (2 Kings 5:1-19), though perhaps not exclusively. Job, the Edomite, was considered blameless and upright (Job 1:1) and developed a deeper relationship with God through his experience of suffering. The Queen of Sheba was attracted to what God was doing in Israel through Solomon (2 Chron. 9:1-12) and received the commendation of Jesus (Matt. 12:42).

Solomon, at the dedication of the temple, prayed for foreigners who would come to the temple:

> Likewise when a foreigner, who is not of your people Israel, comes from a distant land because of your name—for they shall hear of your great name, your mighty hand, and your outstretched arm—when a foreigner comes and prays toward this house, then hear in heaven your dwelling place, and do according to all that the foreigner calls to you, so that all the peoples of the earth may know your name and fear you. . . . (1 Kings 8:41-43)

The Old Testament proclaims that God rules all nations (Ps. 8:1; 22:27-28; 46:10; 47:1; 49:1; 50:1; 66:1, 8; 67:3; 82:8; 96:3, 7, 10; 97:9; 100:1). The Psalms indicate that God is known through nature (Ps. 19:1-6), the law (Ps. 7-13), a majestic name (Ps. 8:1, 9), righteousness (Ps. 50:6; 97:6), faithfulness (Ps. 89:5), wisdom (Ps. 104:24), and power (Ps. 29:4; 89:8).

God acted providentially through the nations to correct and to redeem Israel. The people of God were punished by Assyria, called the "rod of God's anger" (Isa. 10:5), and by Nebuchadnezzar of Babylon, whom the Lord called "my servant" (Jer. 25:9; 27:6). Cyrus the Persian, called "my anointed" (Isa. 45:1), was used by God to enable the Jews to return from exile. These nations carried out their roles under the direction of Yahweh, not through the power of their gods.

Biblical wisdom literature (Proverbs, Ecclesiastes, Job) functioned as a bridge between Israel and the nations. Awareness of wisdom in surrounding cultures served as a point of contact for witness to the nations because there were close links in wisdom's spirit, content, form, and method. While wisdom literature incorporates insights from other cultures by recognizing values, it purges wisdom of that which is not consistent with the biblical tradition. Wisdom in Israel, one of God's self-manifestations, is a divine gift to the nations. "By me [wisdom] kings reign, and rulers decree what is just; by me [wisdom] rulers rule, and nobles, all who govern rightly" (Prov. 8:15-16). The wisdom tradition is valuable for understanding other religions and for interreligious dialogue.

The examples cited above seem to point to the possibility of those in other religions coming to know God. There are hints of inclusivism here. At the same time, inclusion is held in tension with the particular Yahweh whose sovereignty extends above all.

Because of the revelatory character of creation and God's providential activity in the world, we should not be surprised to find God-awareness and uprightness in other nations. We can expect to discover common religious elements or parallel ideas between Hebrew faith and the surrounding cultures (priesthood, kingship, sacrifices).

Further, if Yahweh desires the salvation of all people, it should not shock us if people outside of Israel are drawn to the faith most fully made known to Israel. Though Israel had a unique identity in mediating redemption, Yahweh remained sovereign and was involved with all people.

How did individual God-fearers acknowledge the transcendent God and come to faith outside of the witness of Israel? Were these people seeking for the true God apart from their religion? Certainly Yahweh is active in the world independent of the particular covenant. However, the evidence suggests that the God-fearing are not entire nations but individuals within nations. And it is important to note that Israel plays a role in helping such seekers know Yahweh.

The faith of Israel is similar to other religions, but it is also unique: the moral nature of God, holiness, ethics, expiation, reconciliation, loving-kindness. When other religions serve as a preparation for understanding faith in Yahweh's nature and lordship, they have a positive function. But if religions distort the uniqueness of God's self-revelation to Israel and ignore Yahweh's expectations, they are vigorously critiqued.

Mission in Israel

God's dialogue with the world is expressed in creation and providence, but God encountered the Old Testament world uniquely through Israel. The missionary dimension of Abraham's call to be a blessing to the nations became more explicit in the prophets. The book of Jonah shows God's concern even for the enemy, Assyria. Micah proclaimed that the mountain of the Lord's house would be established as the highest of the mountains, and that people would come from many nations to the mountain of the Lord and to the house of the God of Jacob to hear the word of the Lord as it went forth from Jerusalem (Mic. 4:1-5). Jeremiah said nations would gather to Jerusalem to enjoy God's presence (Jer. 3:17). In prayer to the Lord, the prophet declared, "To you shall the nations come from the ends of the earth and say: our ancestors have inherited nothing but lies, worthless things in which there is no profit. Can mortals make for themselves gods? Such are no gods!" (Jer. 16:19). Jeremiah further indicates that Jerusalem would symbolize joy, praise, and glory before the nations (Jer. 33:9). The hope that all would come and learn from Yahweh in Jerusalem was echoed by Isaiah (Isa. 2:2-4).

Israel became most missionary during the exile. The exile was a vehicle whereby Israel's mission could be fulfilled. Israel represented Yahweh, who was in stark contrast to the gods of the nations. Thus Israel was the means whereby nations would recognize their folly and turn to Yahweh. Israel was God's *servant* to bring *justice* to the nations. Isaiah said Israel was to be a *covenant* to the people and a *light* to the nations (Isa. 42:1, 6). "Nations shall come to your light, and kings to the brightness of your dawn" (Isa. 60:3).

After the exile Zechariah declared that nations would join Israel because God's blessing was upon Israel (Zech 2:11). Israel no longer symbolized curse but blessing (Zech. 8:13). Many people and nations would seek the favor of the Lord of hosts in Jerusalem and would be attracted to Judaism through hearing that God was with the Jews (Zech. 8:20-23). They would come to Jerusalem to worship the King, the Lord of hosts (Zech. 14:16-19).

The mission impulse of Israel was a movement more *centripetal* (nations drawn to Israel like a magnet) than *centrifugal* (Israel going to the nations). Nations would come to Israel and Jerusalem as they saw what God was doing in Israel. Malachi looked forward to the day when many would acknowledge Yahweh. He prophesied, "From the rising of the sun to its setting my name is great among the nations, and in every place incense is offered to my name, and a pure offering; for my name is great among the nations says the Lord of hosts" (Mal. 1:11).

This does not automatically endorse other religious worship, but it does celebrate the fact that others will acknowledge Yahweh. The hope that all nations will ultimately acknowledge Yahweh does not suggest that all religions have the same understanding of one divine being. Some suggest that Israel's mission was to witness to light without expecting that people in other religions would have faith in the God of Israel. However, many texts from the Psalms and Prophets indicate that nations would come to Israel/Jerusalem to hear of and to follow Yahweh (e.g., Isa. 44:5).[20]

The Old Testament message is clear. Nations were invited to come to Jerusalem and become full participants with Israel in the worship and service of Yahweh. There is no hint that Israel's God is simply one among many from which the nations may equally choose. The witness of Israel is normative and has a universal content: "all nations," "all people," "all flesh." Through Israel the nations would come to know Yahweh and recognize the futility of their religions.[21]

Israel had a strong sense of being a unique community because of the uniqueness of Yahweh. Israel was chosen to witness to the uniqueness of God. The universal concern of Yahweh reflects the fact that Yahweh created all nations and peoples and rules over all. There is no need for other gods because they have no real existence. Israel's role in mission assumes that other religions need to hear of Yahweh's character and work.

Israel's story is a history among the nations: Egypt, Canaan, Syria, Assyria, Babylon, Persia, Greece. Israel's relationships to the nations are multidimensional.

1. Israel existed for the nations as a nation of priests, holy people, light to the nations, servant to the nations.

2. Israel's life was to be in contrast to the nations, against idolatry and immorality.

3. Israel lived as debtor to the nations, through selective cultural borrowing.

4. Israel was called to be in mission to the nations.[22]

Israel was truly Israel when grappling with the nations. When Israel retreated into a ghetto or became absorbed into the nations, Israel lost its soul.

New Testament Interpreting the Old Testament

New Testament interpretation intimates that the Old Testament faithful, living prior to the incarnation of Christ, were in some way connected to Christ and were saved by faith in the Messiah to come. Jesus said, "Your ancestor Abraham rejoiced that he would see my day; he saw it and was glad" (John 8:56). "Before Abraham was, I am" (John 8:58). On another occasion Jesus said, "If you believed Moses, you would believe me, for he wrote about me" (John 5:46). The writer to the Hebrews refers to Moses suffering abuse for the sake of Christ (Heb. 11:26). Paul, in describing the experience of Israel in the exodus, wrote, "For they drank from the spiritual rock that followed them, and the rock was Christ" (1 Cor. 10:4). Peter suggests that the prophets predicted the sufferings of Christ on the basis of the Spirit of Christ within them (1 Pet. 1:11).

The witness of the New Testament stands on the shoulders of the Old Testament. The covenant with Israel prepares the way for Jesus Christ, the new covenant. The uniqueness of God's self-revelation in Israel in the context of the religions of the nations provides the foundation for the uniqueness of God's revelation in Christ and for the church's response to this event in the context of the religions of the Greco-Roman era.

5

A Biblical Perspective on the Religions—New Testament

The New Testament provides multiple perspectives on religion. While the uniqueness and finality of Jesus Christ predominate, the New Testament also acknowledges that each human being has some correct God-awareness. Yet the New Testament severely critiques negative aspects of religion. This chapter examines these themes to provide a framework for looking at Christian faith and other religions.

Uniqueness and Lordship of Jesus Christ

The New Testament is both a record and interpretation of God's self-disclosure in Jesus Christ, son of Israel. The New Testament affirms the radical monotheism of the Old Testament by presenting Jesus Christ in a historically particular and normative way. God's revelation is not primarily in a set of beliefs but in the incarnation of Jesus. Jesus came to share our human existence and to make known the compassion of God for all humankind. That saving love culminated in the cross and resurrection.

Good News Replacing Lostness

The gospel is good news because Jesus has come to save us from sin, brokenness, lostness, and death. The angel announced to Joseph that Mary would bear a son whose name would be Jesus, "for he will save his people from their sins." He would be named Emmanuel, "God with us" (Matt. 1:21, 23). Jesus' work in history is a consequence and fulfillment of the purpose of God in creation. Jesus Christ functions as the Second Adam (1 Cor. 15:22, 45), making possible a reversal of the evil consequences of the first Adam.

The consequences of sin, alienation and lostness (Eph. 2:12; 4:18-19) permeate the whole of human existence. The New Testament, like the Old, presents a radical and comprehensive view of sin. Jesus described lostness by the parables of the lost sheep, the lost coin, and the lost sons (Luke 15:3-32). Humans are lost and need to be found; they are alienated and need to be reconciled.

Paul explained the interconnectedness of sin, death, judgment, and condemnation but announced God's response in Jesus Christ, offering the free gift of grace, justification, and righteousness (Rom. 5:12-21). John contrasts condemnation and the free offer of salvation with the text, "For God so loved the world that he gave his only Son, so that everyone who believes in him may not perish but may have eternal life. Indeed, God did not send the Son into the world to condemn the world, but in order that the world might be saved through him. Those who believe in him are not condemned; but those who do not believe are condemned already" (John 3:16-18). Jesus offers freedom from already-present condemnation.

Sin and judgment cannot be glossed over; they are experienced as fear, guilt, and shame, not to mention the impending anxiety of a final judgment. Correct diagnosis of the human condition must precede prescriptions for salvation.

Uniqueness of Christ

Jesus Christ is unique. The Old Testament stressed the unique claims of the God of Israel. The New Testament focuses on the self-revelation of the God of Israel in Jesus Christ. Chris Wright suggests, "In Jesus . . . the uniqueness of Israel and the uniqueness of Yahweh flow together, for he shares and fulfills the identity and mission of both."[1] The New Testament presents Jesus as Messiah, who represents and personifies Israel. As Messiah, Jesus completed the purpose for which Israel was placed in the world. The titles applied to Jesus were drawn from the Old Testament: Messiah, Son of Man, Son of David, Son of God, Lord, Prophet, High Priest, King, Redeemer, Savior.

At Jesus' baptism a voice from heaven declared, "This is my Son, the Beloved, with whom I am well pleased" (Matt. 3:17). John the Baptist witnessed concerning Jesus, "He must increase, but I must decrease" (John 3:30). At Caesarea Philippi, Peter confessed Jesus as "Messiah, the Son of the living God," and Jesus endorsed his statement (Matt. 16:16-17). When Jesus was transfigured, standing in continuity with the law (Moses) and the prophets (Elijah), a voice from heaven again exulted, "This is my Son, the Beloved; with him I am well pleased; listen to him" (Matt. 17:5).

The apostle John attests to the uniqueness of Jesus by presenting him as the way, the truth, and the life (John 14:6), one with the Father (John 14:9-10), and the one who with the Father provides eternal life (John 17:3; 1 John 5:11-12). Seven "I Am" sayings of Jesus appear in the Gospel of John: the bread of life (6:48); the light of the world (8:12); the door (10:7); the good shepherd (10:11); the resurrection and the life (11:25); the way, and the truth, and the life (14:6); and the vine (15:1). They link Jesus to Yahweh, the "I Am" of the Old Testament. George A. F. Knight writes, "The 'with-ness' of the I AM with his world in covenant is what we ultimately call the Incarnation."[2]

Jesus claimed, "The Father and I are one" (John 10:30). "Whoever has seen me has seen the Father" (John 14:9). Jesus did not make himself God; God became flesh in the person of Jesus (John 1:1-18). Jesus' statements concern his very essence, his being (ontological understanding); it is not just a confessional understanding.[3] Jesus claimed pre-existence by declaring, "Very truly, I tell you, before Abraham was, I am" (John 8:58). Christ is unique, not because God made him man, but because he is divine. The Son, coming among humans, made known the Father (John 1:14, 18). He is the ultimate revelation of God. Jesus as divine life-giver invited people to believe in him (John 7:37-39) and promised to forgive sins (Matt. 9:2).

Jesus and the Kingdom

Jesus inaugurated God's kingdom. In Jesus we have the proclamation and presence of the kingdom. The kingdom has a name and face. There is no kingdom without the King—Jesus. Jesus' words and works witnessed to the kingdom "at hand" (Matt. 4:23; 9:35; Mark 1:14, 15; Luke 4:43). The kingdom arrived in Christ; it will come in fullness when Christ returns. Jesus will be the judge in the kingdom (Matt. 25:31-46). Jesus proclaimed the kingdom. The early church proclaimed Jesus.

Those who do not come under the rule of God are part of a competing kingdom, the kingdom of darkness, the kingdom of this world. There is an ongoing struggle between God's reign and the kingdom of darkness, but principalities and powers will eventually be judged and give way to God's kingdom.

All are eligible to become citizens of the kingdom of God. Jesus modeled concern for a great variety of people. From the time of Jesus' infancy, Simeon said concerning him, "My eyes have seen your salvation, which you have prepared in the presence of all peoples, a light for revelation to the Gentiles and for glory to your people Israel" (Luke 2:30-32). John the Baptist quoted Isaiah concerning Jesus: "All flesh shall see the salvation of God" (Luke 3:6).

Luke's genealogy begins with Adam (representing of all humans), not just Abraham (Luke 3:23-38). Jesus sent out the Seventy to proclaim the message of the kingdom (Luke 10:1-12). This was symbolic of his concern for all nations (Jewish tradition counted seventy Gentile nations). Jesus praised the good Samaritan (Luke 10:33-37) and welcomed the poor, crippled, blind, and lame, inviting them from the roads to participate in his movement (Luke 14:21-23). Jesus showed generosity to sinners at the table (Luke 15:1-2), spoke of joy over one sinner who repents (Luke 15:6), expressed concern for the lost sons (Luke 15:11-32), and accepted the repentance of a tax collector (Luke 18:9-14).

Jesus complimented a Roman centurion (Matt. 8:5-10), declared that Jews and Gentiles will come into the kingdom (Matt. 8:11), and commended the faith of a Canaanite woman (Matt. 15:21-28). Jesus took time to converse with the Samaritan woman about issues of faith (John 4:1-26). He said the good news of the kingdom would be proclaimed throughout the world as a testimony to all nations (Matt. 24:14). Not all who encountered Jesus became believers, but Jesus' relationships were inclusive. The New Testament is forthright; God desires the salvation of *all*, and salvation is in *Jesus* (Matt. 11:28; John 12:32; Rom. 5:18; 2 Cor. 5:15; Titus 2:11; 2 Pet. 3:9; 1 John 2:2).

Uniqueness and Universality

The New Testament combines the uniqueness of God specifically revealed to Israel and in Christ with a universal concern for all people. God has not withdrawn from humanity. Humanity, like a lost son, has withdrawn from God, but God comes seeking. These two themes, uniqueness and universal concern, must shape the church's attitude toward people of other religions. Knowledge of God is not limited to Israel and the church, but God's disclosure in Christ was considered unique and final. Christ becomes the normative reference point in the midst of the relativities of human experience. We confess Christ with confidence, not arrogance. As Vinay Samuel says, "God's grace affirms that the chosen people can make no exclusive claims for themselves."[4]

The New Testament confidently confesses the lordship of Christ over all nations and cultures. The message of salvation is a *universal* offer, but it is through the *unique particular* Christ. The relationship between the universal and the particular has been a subject for much debate. Religious pluralists emphasize the universalistic texts and deemphasize the particularistic texts.

Yet it is important to note how the universalistic and particularistic texts are held together in the New Testament (emphasis added below). John declares that God loves the *world* and sent the *Son* (John 3:16-17). "God sent his *only Son* into the *world* so that we might live through him" (1 John 4:9). The "Father . . . sent his *Son* as the Savior of the *world*" (1 John 4:14). Paul says that God was reconciling the *world* through *Christ* (2 Cor. 5:19). God desires *everyone* to be saved and come to the knowledge of the truth, but there is *one mediator*, Jesus Christ, who gave himself a ransom for *all* (1 Tim. 2:4-6).

The early church declared the uniqueness and universality of Jesus Christ for Jew and Gentile. After Jesus' resurrection and ascension, the disciples waited in Jerusalem for the coming of the Holy Spirit. The experiences of the Spirit at Pentecost reversed the scattering at the Tower of Babel. People from the Jewish Diaspora heard the proclamation of Jesus Christ in their own languages. When they asked how to respond to the convicting message, Peter replied, "Repent, and be baptized *every one of you* in the *name* of *Jesus Christ* so that your sins may be forgiven; and you will receive the gift of the Holy Spirit" (Acts 2:38, emphasis added). Peter and John were harassed for healing the lame man and asked by what name they had done it. Peter declared, "There is salvation in no one else, for there is no other name under heaven given among mortals by which we must be saved" (Acts 4:12).

Those who became disciples of Christ formed a new community. Members of this new community shared the gospel with Jews, Samaritans (Acts 8:1-25), Ethiopians (Acts 8:26-40), Cornelius (Acts 10, a God-fearing Gentile), pagan Gentiles at Lystra (Acts 14:8-20), and sophisticated Gentiles at Athens (Acts 17:16-34). The gospel encountered multicultural and multireligious communities such as Philippi, Thessalonica, Corinth, Ephesus, Colossae, and Rome.

Paul, in the context of Corinthian idolatry, declared that Christ is the one foundation (1 Cor. 3:11). There is one God the Father and one Lord Jesus Christ (1 Cor. 8:6). In Philippians 2:5-11 the uniqueness of Jesus was asserted in the midst of the religious pluralism of the Greco-Roman world. Paul declares, "At the name of Jesus every knee should bend, in heaven and on earth and under the earth, and every tongue should confess that Jesus Christ is Lord, to the glory of God the Father" (Phil. 2:10-11). The author of the letter to the Hebrews reminds his audience that God, who spoke previously by the prophets, now speaks through the Son, who is the definitive self-revelation of God, has the imprint of God's being, reflects God's glory (Heb. 1:1-4), and has become the pioneer of salvation (Heb. 2:10).

Cultural Pluralism and Religious Pluralism in the New Testament

The New Testament affirmed cultural pluralism as the gospel was translated into the many cultures of the Roman empire. Christians who confessed the lordship of Christ had to understand what Christ's lordship meant in particular situations. The apostles interacted with Greco-Roman religion as well as Greek philosophy, literature, sports, and education. The gospel transcended its Hebrew context; it found expression in Greek thought forms. Though Jesus came as a Jewish Messiah, the movement he began was more than a messianic sect defined by circumcision. The gospel was not culturally imperialistic but did encounter the conflicting ideas of religious pluralism.

Though cultural pluralism was affirmed, religious pluralism was rejected. Hellenistic religions did not understand the exclusive demands of the gospel made by Christians, who were completely committed to Jesus. For Christians, there was no other Lord, neither emperor nor pagan deity. They based their confidence in Christ alone. Jesus alone was Lord of all people, all cultures, and all nations. People were invited to submit to him. Hellenistic religions were never exclusive. One could belong to one of the religions, perform ancestral worship, and do obeisance to an ancestral shrine, all at the same time. The options were many: mystery religions, magic, gnosis, astrology, philosophy. Allegiance to one did not supplant another but supplemented it. Syncretism (combining religions) was the mood.

Christians resisted a tolerance that would place their faith merely on the same footing as other cults of the Roman empire. They refused idol worship and objected to making offerings to the Roman emperor. They held to the oneness of God and to God's moral and ethical norms. The letters of Paul show that Christians contended with many lords and many gods. The first century was a time of struggle against pervasive religious pluralism. Many of the epistles were written to counter religious heresies. Some of these were not an outright denial of Christian faith but a mixture of revealed truth and pagan Greek thought (such as in the developing Gnosticism). The New Testament faced two dangers, narrow isolation and syncretism.

God-Awareness in Other Religions

While indicating that Jesus is unique, Scripture also shows that humankind has awareness of God through what is sometimes called general revelation. We have seen God's special actions in the era before Abraham and in specific persons such as Melchizedek, Jethro, Balaam, and Job. We have noted that the wisdom tradition of the Old Testament was related to some degree with wisdom in surrounding cultures. Was there something in the culture of the wise men, which together with the appearance of a star, pointed them to Palestine (Matt. 2:1-12)? These examples of general revelation raise the issue of the extent to which God's self-disclosure is limited to covenant people. The New Testament presents additional perspectives.

Logos (Word): John 1:1-18

The prologue of John's Gospel (1:1-18) begins with the creation of the world and the creation of all people, emphasizing the universality of God's purpose in Christ. The universally significant creative Word (Logos) became incarnate in Jesus Christ. The Word was light for all people, shining in the darkness, and the darkness did not overcome it (1:4-5). The universality of the Word finds expression (emphasis added): "*All* things came into being through him" (1:3); "so that *all* might believe through him" (1:7); "the true light which . . . lightens *everyone*" (1:9); "*all* who received him" (1:12); and "from his fullness we have *all* received" (1:16). Jesus was not only for the people of Israel; he was for the *world*. "He was in the *world*, and the *world* came into being through him; yet the *world* did not know him" (1:9-10).

In the second century Justin Martyr developed Logos theology. He suggested that all people participate in the universal cosmic reason, the eternal divine Logos. According to this view, the Logos appeared in all its fullness in Jesus Christ, but the "seed" of the Logos was spread over all humankind long before it manifested itself in Jesus. Every human being possesses a little seed of the Logos, particularly patriarchs, prophets, and pagan philosophers (such as Socrates). Justin believed pagan philosophy could be used to bring people to Christ. He had little respect for pagan religions as a whole. His interest focused on individual people who lived in accordance with the Logos.

Some of Justin's ideas have been revised in recent theological thinking. Theologians suggest that Christ as the Logos (Word) of God is not limited to the New Testament or the Christian community but has spoken in and through other holy people in a more hidden way.

Because of the manifestation of the Logos, persons understand aspects of God, give reverence to God, and live ethically.

How are we to respond to John's prologue and to Logos theology? If the light created the world and the world did not know him, yet darkness could not overcome the light, I believe we can expect to find universal light because word and light are before the incarnation. Everyone has received some illumination; none is wholly in the dark. Light illumines the intellect, intuition, quest for truth, memory, and conscience. All have received common grace. The light causes us to have a desire for God that nothing else can satisfy.

Though the light shines upon all people, how it is received or understood varies. How do we understand this in relation to other religions? Can one acknowledge that there are vestiges of an original revelation preserved in all religions so that the non-Christian religions "echo" a primeval revelation? Other religions, for example, have stories of alienation and the need for sacrifice. Our common capacity for religious and moral experience and our ability to create religious language is itself evidence of God's shining into our broken world. If everything is created by God through the Word, then there already lies within the creation an address to people, for the fact that everyone is created means that each person has a link with God.

Other religions are not merely human fantasy. There is something of God in them. That which is good, beautiful, and true has its origin in God even if people are ignorant of that origin. In particular circumstances, religions are human responses to the universal religious quest of humankind, which is itself a gift or enlightenment from God. It is necessary, however, to distinguish between profound spiritual impulses which are the moving of God and the local clothing in which such impulses appear. The light is reflected with varying degrees of brightness as the moon is reflected differently in a mud puddle, the sea, or a clear mountain lake.

We do not wish to deny that God is sovereignly active beyond the borders of synagogue and church. We acknowledge that God's light shines everywhere, sometimes dimly, sometimes brightly. This does not imply that other religions are equally valid revelations from God or alternate ways of salvation. Human religion often dims the light of God and keeps people from coming to salvation.[5] People fail to live according to the light they have.

Some suggest that if all receive light from the cosmic Logos, they are already in a saving relationship with God through Christ, whether they are conscious of it or not. According to this argument, since the

Christ-light is already present in all people, it is not necessary to share Christ's offer of salvation with people of other faith traditions. One should be prepared to meet Christ, who is already present in that religion. This represents a misunderstanding of the Logos. Instead, Jesus Christ is the normative expression of the Logos, the light that has come into the world.

We must not underestimate or overestimate the function of the Logos. Jesus is the way, the truth, and the life (John 14:6). But this is not a denial of the Logos enlightening everyone coming into the world. On the other hand, to say that God is at work in other religions is not to say that this is equal to God's work in Christ and thereby discount Jesus as the way, the truth, and the life. A universal light is not necessarily sufficient light or automatically a saving light. The emphasis of John's prologue is that the Logos became flesh. If enlightenment means that all have a sufficient knowledge of God, why did the light become incarnate? The gospel is concerned with the enfleshment of the light. If all people are redemptively enlightened by the Logos (the non-incarnate Christ), why do some people reject the light of the incarnate Christ? Why do they prefer darkness, which leads to judgment (John 1:10-11; 3:19)?

John said, "And the Word became flesh and lived among us, and we have seen his glory, the glory as of the father's only son, full of grace and truth" (1:14). Logos separated from the incarnate Christ easily becomes an abstraction. The historical Jesus then becomes merely the Christ-principle.[6] To avoid abstraction, the incarnate Jesus must more fully define and illumine the Logos.

Goldsmith reminds us that we cannot separate the creative Word and the light of God from the Word made flesh. Light must be connected with the birth, life, death, and resurrection of Jesus. Jesus came into the world so people would receive him by faith and become children of God. Through the Word becoming flesh, we can see the glory of God and receive the fullness of God's grace (John 1:16).[7]

When that happens, common grace becomes saving grace. The light of the Logos can lead people to the incarnate Jesus. The function of Christian witness is to help make that connection.

Cosmic Christ: Colossians 1:15-20

Colossians 1:15-20, perhaps an early Christian hymn, praises the cosmic Christ and is the core of Christology in Colossians. Christ is presented as the "image of the invisible God" and the "firstborn of all creation" (1:15). All things in heaven and on earth—visible or invisible, thrones, dominions, rulers, or powers—have been created by and for Christ (1:16). Christ who is before creation is the source, agent, and goal of creation. Subject to Christ are the four classifications of celestial hierarchical powers: thrones, dominions, rulers, powers. As the preexistent one, Christ sustains the created order; he is the controlling and unifying personal force in creation (1:17).

Christ, in addition to his role in creation, has a role in the new order of redemption. He has not only *cosmological* (for cosmos, world, universe) significance but also *ecclesiological* (for the church) and *soteriological* (for salvation) significance. He is the head of the body, the church. He creates a new spiritual community by supplying life, control, and direction for the church. He was the first to rise from the dead (others were raised but died again), thus becoming the firstborn in creation and resurrection. The life which animates the church is his risen life. In this new order of creation, Christ is also preeminent (1:18). Through Christ, in whom the fullness of God dwells, God reconciles all things on earth and in heaven, bringing peace through the blood of the cross (1:20; 2:9).

On the basis of this passage, a cosmic Christ theology developed which emphasizes Christ's cosmic role in all the world. This theology believes Christ is not only head of individual believers or the church but also related to humanity as a whole. God through Christ is active in every facet of world history. Christ is said to bring light to all cultures and religions, whether or not people know of the incarnation.

According to this view, Christ is present in the best of religious traditions and should be discovered there. Since Christ is thought to be larger than Jesus, it is proposed that an understanding of the cosmic Christ enables us to affirm religious plurality by being more inclusive, whereas Christologies that are incarnation-centered tend to be more exclusive. Cosmic Christ theology makes a closer connection between creation (world history) and redemption (salvation history), rather than making a sharp distinction between world history and salvation history.

How shall we respond biblically to these speculations? If Christ is the head of the universe and present in world history, and if he is the creator of humanity, we should not be surprised to see Christlike values in other religious traditions. We expect to find such values. We should not deny them; we can affirm them. Allegiance to Christ doesn't obligate us to deny goodness in other religions and cultures. Instead, we test such goodness by the Word made flesh. Sometimes we find evidence of Christ's stirring and beckoning among people. Often people from other religions who have become followers of Jesus indicate that Christ was there, drawing them.

However, a biblical view of the cosmic Christ is not just an abstract principle referring to the most noble concepts in other religions. Not everything good, kind, or beautiful in another culture or religion is Christ. He is not just culture's best. He is not whatever we make him. It is too easy to assume that all nice people are followers of the cosmic Christ. Even if Christ is present in all things, his presence is not always legible, and the awareness of Christ varies. To understand the fullness of God in Christ, we need to look at Jesus. Instead of speculating about the cosmic Christ, we should concentrate more on holding the cosmic Christ of creation together with the incarnate Christ, who as head of the church provides reconciliation. From Colossians 1:15-20 it is clear that creation, incarnation, and redemption are all part of Christ's life. They cannot and should not be separated. They are not separated in Colossians or in John 1.

The New Testament moves from the universal and active presence of Christ to the particularity of Jesus, who was incarnated, died on the cross, and is head of the church. The emphasis is not so much on the invisible as the visible. In the New Testament, the cosmic takes form in the incarnation, not the other way around. Christ who lived on earth, who died and rose again, is the one who was before all creation, preexistent, and cosmic. Whatever is previously understood about God has received fresh illumination in Christ, not only in regard to salvation but also in relation to creation and history (Eph. 1:10; 1 Cor. 15:24-28). The cosmic work of Christ is grounded in historical existence, not simply in metaphysical speculation. It is precisely in the incarnation, crucifixion, and resurrection that we discover how Christ is cosmic. Christ intends to effect complete reconciliation—with heaven and earth. Our understanding of the cosmic Christ must be determined by all that he is and does.

Cornelius the God-Fearer

In the New Testament, the Roman centurion Cornelius represents a group known as God-fearers, those from a non-Jewish background drawn to monotheism and to what God was doing in Judaism (Acts 10:2, 22; 13:16, 26). Cornelius is known as a "devout man who feared God with all his household; he gave alms generously to the people and prayed constantly to God" (Acts 10:2). He is described as an "upright and God-fearing man, who is well spoken of by the whole Jewish nation" (Acts 10:22).

Cornelius, a man of faith who is not a Jew or a Christian, seems to have a positive relationship with God. He is given instruction by God through an angel telling him, "Your prayers and your alms have ascended as a memorial before God" (Acts 10:4). He is to make contact with Peter. After Cornelius and Peter meet, Peter speaks of his own transformed perspective: "I truly understand that God shows no partiality, but in every nation anyone who fears him and does what is right is acceptable to him" (Acts 10:34, 35). After Peter witnesses to him concerning Jesus Christ, Cornelius receives the Holy Spirit and was baptized.

Cornelius is an example of one who models God-awareness, devotion, and ethical sensitivity. Some use Cornelius to suggest that God accepts without favoritism sincere followers of other religions who believe in God, worship God, and live ethically, though ignorant of Christ. The argument is that Cornelius was a "saved" person before his contact with Peter. There is no indication that Cornelius was rebuked for his religious sensitivity or for his religious quest; in fact, he is to be complimented.

However, does this narrative indicate that sincerity by itself can bring one into a right relationship with God without knowledge of Christ when the whole point of the story is just the opposite? Cornelius' piety, generosity, and prayers represent the best that Gentile religion and his exposure to Judaism could offer. Though God connected with his religious experience and search, Cornelius still needed to hear the gospel and the facts about Jesus so he could more completely respond in faith. God sent an angel to Cornelius and a vision to Peter. Because of this divine initiative, Cornelius experienced forgiveness (Acts 10:43), the gift of the Holy Spirit (Acts 10:44-47), salvation (Acts 11:14), repentance, and life (Acts 11:18).[8]

God knows the hearts of pious God-fearers. God will be their judge. Though God treats them with respect because they are earnestly seeking and are moving in a right direction, they are not complete simply because they express interest in God. If we interpret "God shows no partiality, but in every nation anyone who fears him and does what is right is acceptable to him" (Acts 10:34-35) as God's unconditional approval of sincerity, we miss the primary point. It was not the piety of Cornelius but his response to the knowledge of Christ that brought him fullness of joy, salvation, and life.

Rather than affirming the validity of all religious quests, the emphasis is on the availability of the gospel for all people. It seems more faithful to the text to conclude that God shows no partiality concerning who should hear and respond to the salvation provided by Christ. This is the lesson of witness that Peter needed to learn and that the church needs to continually learn.

God-Awareness at Lystra and Athens

Paul and Barnabas modeled acceptance of valid religious insights in the context of religious plurality. They recognized the religious awareness of rural pagan Gentiles at Lystra (Acts 14:8-18), even when they were worshipers of Zeus and Hermes. The apostles acknowledged that God, as Creator of the world, is present in creation and the cycles of nature and witnesses through nature: rain, harvests, food. God providentially cares for the world, satisfies human needs, and brings joy to their hearts (Acts 14:15-17).

However, the apostles did not stop with affirmation of religious awareness; they engaged the religious worldview of Lystra. People were asked to "turn from these worthless things to the living God" (Acts 14:15). Though there was some religious common ground, idolatry was criticized. They understood something of God, but the key issue was what they didn't understand. The apostles witnessed to something more.

When Paul arrived at Athens (Acts 17:16-34) with its more sophisticated religious-philosophical environment, he was distressed to see that the city was full of idols (17:16). He took the occasion to interact seriously with the Epicurean and Stoic philosophers (17:18). Epicureans believed that the gods were distant, lived in perfection, and cared little for human beings. They thought everything happened by *chance* and death ended it all. Epicureans would have agreed with Paul that the gods needed nothing and certainly do not live in temples made by hands. Epicureans were indifferent to the gods, agnostic, secularist, materialist. Since everything happened by chance or random, judgment was a strange idea to them.

Stoics were pantheists, believing that everything is God and God is in everything. Stoics emphasized the Logos as the rational principle that ordered the universe. God was the soul of the universe, not distinct from it. God was identified with eternal matter. For pantheists, God is immanent and humans are a fragment of God. Stoics had some understanding of God's providence, but they thought of God's providence in an impersonal way, as *fate*. The Epicurean and Stoic systems represent two alternatives to personal God, *chance* and *fate*, both of which are hopeless.

Paul connected with the religious sensitivities of Athens by referring to their being "extremely religious" (Acts 17:22) and by mentioning an altar with the inscription, "To an unknown god" (17:23). Paul quoted their poets approvingly when they spoke the truth (17:28). Paul had a clear understanding of their religious convictions, literature, and philosophies. He met them at their best, accepting some of the truth and values in their religion. He started where they were and built bridges between the gospel and their ideas. Though he saw some continuity between Christian faith and other faiths, he also differentiated between their religious concepts and the Christian gospel.

Indeed, Paul criticized their religion both directly and indirectly in his presentation of the gospel alternative. He was disturbed by their false religiosity, expressed in material images. He declared that "God who made the world and everything in it, he who is Lord of heaven and earth, does not live in shrines made by human hands, nor is he served by human hands" (Acts 17:24-25). Deity is not like gold, silver, stone, or images formed by the creative art and imagination of human beings (17:29).

I recall traveling on a plane in India some years ago. A Hindu seatmate asked me, "Is God everywhere?"

I thought a while and replied, "Yes."

He responded, "Then God is in the image."

However, the problem with the image is that God cannot be confined to time and space. Idols reflect ignorance of the all-pervading presence of God. Human manipulation of images does not gain God's favor. God wants to move humans beyond the ignorance of images to a fuller revelation.

Paul used the altar to the unknown god as an occasion to make God more fully known. Though beginning with the unknown god, Paul did not commend all their religious conclusions; he criticized their shrines and those who served in them. Though they were religious, they were ignorant and confused. Paul explained that God the Creator, Lord of heaven and earth, created everything that exists and is the source of all life and breath. God is Maker, not made; nothing humans do can reinforce God's life. God is the one who controls nature, history, and destiny. God made all human beings and acted providentially in the history of the nations, allotting their times of existence and geographical places of residence (Acts 17:26).

By calling God the Creator of heaven and earth, Paul was refuting the Stoic doctrine of eternal matter. By affirming God's intimate concern for people, he corrected the Epicurean idea of distant and uncaring gods. Yet he acknowledged common ground with the Stoics by teaching that God preserves and guides all of life, and that God is immanent in the world. Human beings were created to seek God and find God. Yet God is not far away, even as their own poets affirmed (Acts 17:27-28). God is not absent from life but is involved deeply in all of life. God as Creator is present everywhere, but humans often fail to find God. Humans instinctively long for God but grope in ignorance and search the shadows. Athens, having not found God, created their own gods.

Paul responded to their ignorance (Acts 17:23, 30), not by merely calling for further enlightenment, but by inviting them to repentance (17:30) and warning of coming judgment (17:31). The chasm between their religion and Christian faith was so great that repentance was required. Ignorance and disobedience must give way to conversion. Religious philosophers like ideas but often distance themselves from commitment and repentance.

Paul presented Jesus and the resurrection. Greeks accepted immortality but not resurrection. God-awareness could not teach them about Jesus and the resurrection. As Andrew Kirk says, "It was the message of the resurrection, rather than the 'creation theology' of the main part of Paul's address, which many of his hearers rejected."[9]

Paul was not just affirming or congratulating Athens. He was not merely offering acceptance to the "extremely religious." He said they were worshiping what they didn't know (Acts 17:22-23). Their sincerity had not led them to understand the fullness of God. Their worship indicated religious thirst and aspiration, but Paul said that despite their religiosity, they still didn't adequately know the true God. He called on them to turn away from idols to the true and living God, made known in Jesus. The call to conversion indicated that more than sincerity was needed. To understand God, one needed to understand Jesus.

Several themes emerge from the Gentile audiences at Lystra and Athens. Paul doesn't quote the Old Testament but engages the hearts and minds of different audiences by starting from their religio-cultural understandings and pointing toward a fuller revelation. In respect to the natural order, God is the one who created and providentially cares for the world (Acts 14:15; 17:24). God acts in creation so that people will seek and find God (17:27). In respect to the nations, God is in charge of all nations; nations are not under the patronage of different deities (14:16; 17:26-27). Paul criticized pluralist understandings of deity, whether Zeus, Hermes, the "unknown god," or gods of gold, silver, and stone (14:15; 17:23, 28-29). Conversion involved the rejection of other gods. God-awareness should stimulate people to seek and hopefully find God.

From Lystra and Athens, we learn the importance of assessing one's hearers, acknowledging correct understandings already present, and addressing the crucial faith issues. Paul sought to contextualize the message. He showed appreciation for the truth the gospel had in common with the hearers' culture, though even their highest truth didn't go high enough. He did not discount aspects of that truth or exaggerate it, nor did he romanticize the beauty of their religions. He was bold but not arrogant or sarcastic; he did not ridicule. Though respectful and gentle, he clearly rejected their idolatry and invited them to conversion. Paul did not bless them as they were or call for a synthesis of the gospel and their religion. The gospel was more than a new theory of religion or new ethical system. It was the good news of Jesus Christ.

God-Awareness at Rome

Romans 1 and 2 recognize the religious knowledge people have because of creation and conscience. Romans 1:18-32 indicates that those who don't have special revelation from God are not totally ignorant; they know God through general revelation. Creation testifies about God, bearing witness to God's eternal power, invisible qualities, and divine nature (1:19-20). General revelation is visible because God made it visible to them; nature discloses something of God's power and character. Paul's teaching is similar to the Old Testament, which attests God's communication to every person through the heavens, sun, moon, stars, light, sea, hills, and mountains (Ps. 19:1-6; 104; 148:9-11; 150:6). Through intuitive reflection on creation, some knowledge will be accurate. People perceive God's deity by looking at what God created. We often hear people say, "When I look up at the stars, I know God exists."

However, according to Romans, humans have failed God. By their ungodliness and wickedness, they have suppressed the truth (1:18). People are therefore without excuse, for though they had some knowledge of God, they didn't honor or give thanks to God. Instead, they became futile in their thinking, and their minds were darkened (1:20-22). They became fools because they exchanged the glory of the immortal God for images resembling mortal human beings, birds, animals, and reptiles (1:23). They worshiped created things instead of the Creator. Humans repressed their intuited and inferred knowledge of God. Instead of a Godward movement, there was spiritual degeneration. Human beings created substitutes for the living God.

Such religious distortion leads to God's wrath (1:18). Because humans have rejected the knowledge they had, God abandoned them to lust and passion. Three times Romans says they "exchanged" the truth of God for a substitute: they traded the glory of God for images (1:23), the truth of God for a lie by worshiping the creature instead of the Creator (1:25), and sexual morality for sexual immorality (1:26). Three times we are told that "God gave them up"—to lust, impurity, degradation (1:24), to passion and immorality (1:26), and to a debased mind (1:28). Because truth was confused with falsehood and good was mistaken for evil, judgment and condemnation resulted (1:32).

Creation testifies to the presence of God, but more communication is necessary. Though creation presents a partial image of the Creator, that image is insufficient. God is not identical with the world; God transcends it. People tend to misread creation when calamities occur. How is God to be understood when there are earthquakes in India and Los Angeles, or a flood in the Mississippi River valley?

One reason creation alone is not adequate for religious knowledge stems from the impact of the Fall upon creation. Nature groans under the burden that has come upon it (Rom. 8:19-22). But basically, people misread creation because they have spurned the knowledge available to them. Instead of living according to the knowledge they have, they distort that knowledge by preferring darkness more than light. Distorted knowledge results in restlessness and condemnation. The acquired knowledge is not untrue; it is imperfect because of the darkening effects of sin.

It is important to distinguish between what is a search for God and what is a rebellion against God or a flight from God. Those who believe in gods and spirits and bow before images, show that they are touched by God and that God is seeking them. But at the same time, they are suppressing what is necessary for them to come to God. Bavinck identifies the problem: "The aerial of man's heart can no longer receive the wave length of God's voice, even though it surrounds him on all sides."[10] The human mind creates its own myths and projects its own ideas of God. Images of God reflect human images. Yet humans are constantly confronted by God's existence, even when they try to escape God.

Romans 2:12-16 focuses on God-awareness among Gentiles because God has placed the law within their heart and conscience. Gentiles have moral sensitivity; they are aware of God's ethical demands. Gentiles are responsible to God for the light they have, and some do what the law requires (2:14-15). Whenever they obey the moral law, conscience approves. But when they act contrary to moral law, conscience rebukes them (2:15).

Some suggest that God will grant eternal life to those who by doing good seek glory, honor, and immortality (Rom. 2:6-7, 10). If Gentiles who do not have the law respond faithfully to the revelation within their hearts, they can fulfill the law by trusting in the God of creation. They will be judged on the basis of the revelation they received in their hearts (Rom. 2:15). The argument is that Paul assumed their conscience would "accuse" them but allowed the possibility that conscience might also "excuse" them (Rom. 2:15). Gentiles, it is said, can fulfill the law by trusting the God of creation. The God of creation works for salvation before the coming of Christ. Christ is then the climax of God's revelation for salvation, God's normative disclosure.

Some who have difficulty with the foregoing argument raise serious questions. Can people be saved by doing good things? Can ethical behavior defend one on the day of judgment? If Scripture recognizes that good deeds and partial knowledge of God are possible apart from Christ, is God's action specifically limited to Christ? Can people be saved without explicitly responding to the gospel of Jesus Christ (Rom. 2:16)?

Such questioners recognize that all people exhibit some good behavior, and that such goodness should be celebrated wherever it is found. But to suggest that the passages above indicate that one can be saved by works seems to contradict what is said elsewhere in Romans. Romans is emphatic that justification is not by deeds (Rom. 3:20) but by faith apart from the law (Rom. 3:28). Though moral goodness has its origin in God, is moral goodness the basis for redemption? Therefore, if one concludes that Jews and Gentiles alike are under the power of sin (Rom. 3:9), one has difficulty concluding that it is the enlightened, sincere, or devout who are saved.

However, those who are more optimistic about salvation apart from Jesus do not suggest that people by morality earn their salvation. *Faith* in the heart expresses itself in obedience (Rom. 2:4-7, 14-16; 3:28-29). Works righteousness is excluded, but obedient response to God's grace is not. Emphasis is on *trust* more than *action* or *knowledge* of *truth*. Gentiles who know God through the created order can trust God. Yet just as those who have received special revelation can refuse to trust God, those who know God only by general revelation can also refuse to trust God. According to this view, saving faith is not primarily dependent on the type of knowledge one has (whether Jewish or pagan) but on the way one trusts God. Since Christ is the norm, witness is still important so people might know the fullness and blessing of the gospel.[11]

Our response to these opposing viewpoints will be conditioned by our view of general revelation. We must be careful not to overestimate general revelation but to hold it in tension with fallenness. Whether one knows God by special revelation or general revelation, it is clear that all have sinned (Rom. 2:12) and are "without excuse" (Rom. 1:20). This is true whether one is a Jew who has the law of Moses, or a Gentile who has the law in the heart. Because the natural order and the human conscience have been corrupted by the Fall, revelation is mediated through imperfect channels. Gentiles did not always follow general revelation (Rom. 1:18-20; 2:15; 3:11), and Jews did not always follow special revelation (Rom. 3:11, 23). Because sin is universal, justification can only be provided by Christ, who removes sin (Rom. 2:9; 3:9, 29-30).

God has given to all humanity a revelation in creation, but humans often reject what could be known and rebel against God. God is available to us, but we are not available to God. We do not make use of the knowledge available to us. Paul in Romans shows the failure of sinners adequately to respond to God's general revelation in order to show why Jesus, God's special revelation, had to come. Humanity cannot be saved apart from the work of God in redemption.

Negative Aspects of Religion
Jewish Perversions

Though religion can be an expression of God-awareness, human beings often use religion to exert themselves, deny God, distort God's will, or supplement the revelation of God in Christ. Jesus was critical of certain Jewish religious leaders because they misused ritual, displayed piety, and exerted power by seeking status or titles. He rebuked them because of their preoccupation with externals and their legalism, calling them hypocrites and blind guides. Jesus considered their piety an impediment to those who sought genuine faith (Matt. 23:1-37; Luke 11:37-52). Religious leaders were the ones who called for the crucifixion of Jesus.

Years later, Saul (Paul), zealous for religion, needed to be converted (Acts 9:1-22). On the way to Damascus, he learned that he was called into mission so that people's eyes would be opened, and they would turn from darkness to light and from the power of Satan to God

(Acts 26:18). Paul wrote that certain Jewish leaders had an unenlightened zeal for God (Rom. 10:2).

Magic and Occult

Magic and occult activity is a perversion of religion. When Philip confronted evil spirits and magic at Samaria, people converted from magic to Jesus Christ and received the Holy Spirit. When Simon sought to manipulate the Holy Spirit through magical power, he was rebuked for thinking that he could obtain God's gift with money and told that his heart was not right with God. He was commanded to repent because he was chained by wickedness (Acts 8:9-24). Paul confronted Bar-Jesus (Elymas), a magician and false prophet, who tried to obstruct the faith: "Son of the devil, you enemy of all righteousness, full of all deceit and villainy, will you not stop making crooked the straight paths of the Lord?" (Acts 13:6-10).

At Philippi, Paul met a slave girl who had a spirit of divination and made money for her owners by fortune-telling. When Paul cast out the spirit, the girl's owners retaliated by seizing Paul and Silas, accusing them, flogging them, and putting them in prison (Acts 16:16-24). At Ephesus, the confrontation with magic led to the destruction of magical paraphernalia (Acts 19:11-20). There was spiritual warfare between God and the religio-magical powers of evil.

Idolatry and Spiritism

In the New Testament, the gospel confronted idolatry. At Ephesus, the gospel came into conflict with Artemis, the Greek goddess, daughter of Zeus and sister of Apollo. Artemis functioned as a fertility goddess. She was considered a savior, cosmic queen, and lord. She mediated between individuals and their fate through astrological power because she was in close contact with demons and magic. People supported this cult because they feared persons who could be manipulated by the goddess. Mystery, vision, and prostitution were part of the worship of Artemis. The temple of Artemis, one of the seven wonders of the ancient world, attracted many pilgrims. Worship was closely linked with the economy. Silversmiths took advantage of this pilgrimage by manufacturing and selling silver shrines of Artemis.

Paul said clearly that gods made by hands are not gods; a choice needed to be made between Jesus and the gods (Acts 19:23-41). In the midst of the religious pluralism, Paul did not emphasize revelation in their religion. Instead, he called upon all to abandon their futile religion and turn to Christ.

In his letter to the Ephesians, Paul gives a negative assessment of their former religion. Ephesians 1 alludes to their religious background, but the primary emphasis is on the unique role of Christ. There are thirteen references to Christ in the opening sentence (1:3-14). Ephesians 2 refers to the pre-conversion domain of the powers of sin. Believers formerly followed the "ruler of the power of the air, the spirit that is now at work among those who are disobedient" (Eph. 2:2). Paul says that before conversion they were "without Christ, being aliens from the commonwealth of Israel, and strangers to the covenants of promise, having no hope and without God in the world" (Eph. 2:12). The word used for "without God" is *atheoi*, from which comes the English term *atheist*. They didn't lack religion, but their religion lacked God. Their humanly constructed religion did not lead them to God but away from God.[12]

The inferiority of idolatry is reinforced by Paul's writing to the church in Thessalonica. He describes Christian believers as those who "turned to God from idols, to serve a living and true God" (1 Thess. 1:9). Paul also says that the Galatian Christians had been "enslaved to the elemental spirits of the world" (Gal. 4:3).

On several visits to Corinth, I have discovered how numerous and how pervasive were the religions of that city. First Corinthians 8–10 discusses how Christians should live in the midst of religious pluralism, specifically idolatry. The Corinthian Christians were concerned about food offered to idols. Paul insists that in contrast to idols, which have no real existence, "there is no God but one" (1 Cor. 8:4). He admits that "there may be so-called gods in heaven or on earth." But even if there are many gods and many lords, "yet for us there is one God, the Father, from whom are all things and for whom we exist, and one Lord, Jesus Christ, through whom are all things and through whom we exist" (1 Cor. 8:6). Jesus is Lord over all other lords and powers, many of which functioned as gods in other religions.

First Corinthians 10 warns against falling into idolatry, as Israel did (10:7, 14). Earlier Paul said that idols are nothing (1 Cor. 8:4), but later he said that food offered to idols is sacrificed to demons (10:19-20). For many worshipers, idols become gods. Christians who participated in meals with pagans engaged in idolatrous activity, shared in the worship of demons, and risked provoking the Lord.

Brian Rosner notes, "Amidst the pressures to be open, tolerant, and accommodating to other faiths of the early Empire, some Corinthian Christians were quite unaware of the real danger of becoming guilty of idolatry by association."[13]

False Gospels

The Corinthians were warned of another danger. There were super-apostles who could lead them astray by proclaiming another Jesus, a different spirit, and a different gospel (2 Cor. 11:3-5). They are called "false apostles, deceitful workers, disguising themselves as apostles of Christ" (2 Cor. 11:13). This is not surprising, since Satan himself can act as an angel of light, and his servants pretend to be servants of righteousness (2 Cor. 11:14-15). Religion is not necessarily positive. Religion can deceive, enslave, and blind. In Galatians 1:6-9 a similar theme occurs, warning against a "different gospel," a gospel contrary to what Paul proclaimed. Christians must always be alert to the kind of gospel that is being promoted.

Syncretism

Syncretism (fusion of religions) was a problem in the New Testament. Colossians gives us the most direct encounter with syncretism by addressing a Gentile church in danger of succumbing to religious syncretism in a pluralistic environment. There are many allusions to their "pagan" past and few references to the Old Testament.

Though most of the believers were from Gentile background, the environment of the Colossian church was a meeting place where the free-thinking Judaism of the dispersion and the speculative ideas of Greek religions were in close contact. From this interchange and fusion, there emerged a syncretism which tried to add Christ to a spiritual hierarchy, and which advocated specific kinds of behavior (ceremonialism and asceticism) consistent with that worldview.

The "Colossian Heresy" was subtle; it both compromised and denied the gospel. This false teaching seemed to combine Jewish ritual practices, angel worship, and Greco-Gnostic speculations, though it was less developed than the Gnosticism of the second and third centuries. This heretical teaching considered God to be remote and inaccessible except through a long chain of intermediaries; Jesus was demoted to only one of these. The intermediaries (spirits or angels) needed to be worshiped or placated because cosmic reconciliation was a model for personal reconciliation. Followers of this religion sought mystical illumination and higher knowledge of things heavenly; redemption was understood as the ascent of the soul to the higher world. Though such syncretistic mixing of religion was common, it was denounced because Christians began to rely on a variety of alien powers.

The theme of Colossians is the complete adequacy of Christ in contrast to the emptiness of human philosophy. The Colossian syncretism was human tradition according to the elemental spirits of the universe. But there was no need for elemental spirits because the incarnate Christ embodies the fullness of deity. Jesus did not simply have divine qualities; instead, all the divine essence was within him. Since believers were already filled with Christ, the one in whom the fullness of deity dwells, they should not regress to inferior religious experience. They were delivered from the kingdom of darkness to the kingdom of the Son (Col. 1:13).

Paul argues that Christ and the gospel are not deficient. Indeed, since Christ is the head of all rule and authority, whether celestial orders or angels, every rank of spiritual being is subordinate to him. Many Colossians worshiped the powers so they wouldn't be harmed. But why should believers either fear or cultivate relationships with the spirits of the universe in order to guarantee their security? Why should they be intimidated by such spirits or feel subject to a fate determined by astrological usurpers? They need not be helpless victims in a hostile universe if they trust Christ, who controls the powers. Believers were buried with Christ in baptism and raised with Christ by the power of God. Death, burial, and resurrection have joined them in a living bond with Christ (Col. 2:8-23).

We must increase our awareness of the negative aspects of religion. In writing to Timothy, Paul warns that in the last days, people will be holding to an "outward form of godliness but denying its power" (2 Tim. 3:5). Peter reminds us that judgment begins with the household of God (1 Pet. 4:17). Six of the seven churches of Asia heard words of judgment (Rev. 2-3). All too frequently, error and corruption exist under the guise of religion, even in the practice of Christian religion.

6

Theological Issues Concerning Religious Plurality

Several years ago a friend of mine returned from a visit to Thailand, quite impressed with Buddhists. Because Buddhist people were much nicer than expected, my friend questioned traditional Christian answers concerning Christian faith and other religions. Relationships challenged theological understandings.

Though congenial relationships with people of other faith traditions are crucial for understanding, our evaluation of religions must go beyond relationships, feelings, or intuition. Since plurality of religions has led to a plurality of theologies, it is essential that we learn to think biblically and theologically about the religions. When one examines the multiple responses to religious plurality and surveys biblical perspectives on religions, several important theological issues emerge.

General Revelation and Special Revelation

A survey of the Bible provides convincing evidence that human beings have awareness of God because they are in the image of God (internal awareness) and live in a God-created world (external awareness). Humans are created to respond to God; they are God-oriented. Religious impulses are natural if human nature has God's imprint upon it. It is not surprising that creation should witness to the Creator.

This awareness of God outside of Judeo-Christian revelation is frequently called *general revelation* (preferable to *natural revelation*, which overemphasizes human nature and rational power). Revelation through the Bible (Old Testament and New Testament) and Christ is regarded as *special revelation*. General revelation is universally available because of God's involvement in the world, whereas special revelation is God speaking to specific people at specific times.

According to this understanding, there are two kinds of revelation and two kinds of knowledge. Some experiences, however, are difficult to classify as general revelation or special revelation. Was the revelation to Melchizedek or to the wise men general or special revelation? Are there modern Melchizedeks today? How are we to regard dreams and visions? Are they general or special revelation?

Evidence of General Revelation

We have already seen evidence of general revelation in the chapters on the Old Testament and the New Testament. The Bible indicates that humans through general revelation understand that God exists (Ps. 19:1; Rom. 1:19), is Creator (Acts 14:15), sustainer (17:25), universal Lord (Acts 17:25), transcendent (Acts 17:24), immanent (Acts 17:26-27), eternal (Ps. 93:2), majestic (Ps.8:3-4; 29:4), powerful (Ps. 29:4; Rom. 1:20), wise (Ps. 104:24), good (Acts 14:17), righteous (Rom. 1:17), sovereign (Acts 17:26), has standards of right and wrong (Rom. 2:15), should be worshiped (Acts 14:15; 17:23), and will judge evil (Rom. 2:15-16).[1]

I am not surprised to discover people with profound religious insights that resemble revelation in the Bible. Since persons have religious capacities, I expect to find them questing for spirituality, having moral sensitivities, and creating religious language. Humans perceive aspects of God through created nature, providence, history, conscience, latent memory of God, reason, intuition, yearning for spirituality, quest for truth, and the common grace and light of the cosmic Logos. Other religions are more than human fantasy; there is something of God in them. God's voice can be heard in any culture. Religions can echo God's activity in the world because the reality of God lies behind the religious quest.

The study of religious systems confirms that many people have a rudimentary concept of God and respond religiously. They infer the existence of God intuitively and by rational reflection on the created universe. Humans have a sense of cosmic relationship and acknowledge a superior power that governs destiny. Humans have a vague sense that there are religious norms and that God expects obedience; certain things are obligatory, and others are to be avoided. There is often a sense that the relationship between human beings and the supreme power has been disrupted and needs to be reestablished (e.g., the many examples of sacrifice in other cultures). There are dreams of a better world and craving for some kind of salvation which transcends death.

Relationship of General Revelation and Special Revelation

General revelation is incomplete and ambiguous; it is not always legible or reliable. Few would debate that all people have God-consciousness. Yet the value one places on general revelation is a key theological issue. We wish to find a balanced and fair understanding between the wisdom present through the universe and that present through Judeo-Christian revelation. We should not try to limit the light; we can rejoice in the light wherever we see it, even when it is a mere gleam in the surrounding darkness. To despise such light disparages the witness of God's created world, God's image in all human beings, and God's wrestling with the world. We can expect to find goodness, beauty, and truth, even in a fallen world. The image of God has been marred but not destroyed.

In understanding general revelation, we must beware that the immanence (closeness) of God does not swallow up transcendence (distance). Some theological pluralists emphasize theologies of creation, nature, and immanence and thus shift away from transcendence, sovereignty, and authority. General revelation does not supplant special revelation as the primary means by which God is known. God cannot be fully known by humans except as God provides fuller revelation. Though John, Peter, and Paul recognized the constant activity of God in the world, including the religious world, general revelation was for them a beginning, not the final word.

General revelation does not make special revelation unnecessary. It is not a second or alternate revelation; it is the prerequisite and foundation for special revelation. Special revelation did not come down from heaven without antecedents. Special revelation is the necessary supplement and interpreter of general revelation. Special revelation uses the light of Christ, who is the fullness and pinnacle of revelation, to discover and unveil what is hidden in other religions. In this light, general revelation is tested and corrected. Christian theology should connect whenever possible with the data of religion, while keeping Jesus in focus in conversation with other religions.

Through general revelation, God has paved the way for acceptance of special revelation and prepares people to hear the gospel. Don Richardson speaks of God putting eternity in the hearts of people who have not yet heard of Christ. He calls general revelation the "Melchizedek factor" and special revelation the "Abraham factor."[2] God has prepared people for the gospel (general) and the gospel for people (special).

The fact that the gospel can be communicated in all religio-cultural settings indicates that there has been preparation. We can be positive toward general revelation when it provides real and authentic truth about God. But when general revelation is misused, it becomes an obstacle to special revelation.

General revelation is revelation; it is not a false revelation but a fragmented or incomplete revelation. General revelation should not be ignored, but neither should it be overstated. Because general revelation is partial and provisional, a fuller and more complete revelation is needed. General revelation never precludes the unique revelation through Jesus Christ.

Religions: Alternate Special Revelations?

If there is light and truth in other religions, how are we to understand the revelation found there? Some move beyond the concept of general revelation to suggest that different religions are each separate special revelations from God. Insights from the Buddha or Confucius are then considered alternate special revelations. This raises the issue of how special revelation is defined. Is God disclosed partly to some and partly to others? Is there more than one self-disclosure from God?

We must proceed with caution in defining the relationship between general and special revelation. How sharp shall the distinction be made? If God is at work in the history, culture, and religion of other people, there is clearly revelation. Aspects of this revelation may even be complementary to biblical revelation rather than contradictory.

However, to suggest that this revelation is an alternate special revelation is problematic. Knowledge of God in other religions does not imply that each religion is a different revelation from God. We have redefined special revelation if we use it to refer to alternate special revelation outside of salvation history in Israel (Old Testament) and Christ (New Testament). The understandings of Buddha and Confucius are better categorized as general revelation rather than as alternate special revelations.

Even if we were to assume that each religion is an alternate special revelation from God, the religions are not equally valid or effective in dealing with human sin. Sin is the point on which the religions divide. The purpose of God's revelation in Christ is to show God's mercy, goodness, and compassion, and God's desire to overcome alienation so a relationship can be restored. The revelation of God in Christ is a normative revelation. What God has done in Christ increases our awareness of what God has done in general revelation.

The degree of human fallenness and frailty affects our evaluation of general revelation. We must not forget that nature can conceal God as much as it reveals God, that parts of creation are in rebellion, and that human beings through sin and perversity have obstructed and corrupted the knowledge available to them. General revelation is not untrue. But humans can misuse the revelation that God offers by inverting truth into a lie. Goldsmith said that humans are "cracked mirrors which reflect and at the same time distort the image of God."[3]

Persons who believe in gods and spirits and bow before images, sense that God is seeking them, but at the same time they are afraid to encounter God and either avoid or flee from God. Fractured relationships keep people from being receptive to God. But despite distortion, general revelation is not completely obliterated.

General Revelation: Alternate Plan for Salvation?

How God is at work in other religions is a crucial matter. Some ask whether general revelation has salvific value, whether other religions are instruments of salvation, or whether Christ is savingly involved in other religions. Does God work because of religion or in spite of religion? What is God's providential working, such as through the role of Assyria and Babylon in bringing judgment upon Israel or the role of Cyrus of Persia in permitting Israel to return from exile? What is God's redemptive work?

Some argue that the Creator of the whole human race will offer salvation to the whole human race. General revelation, it is said, can not only enlighten but can enable salvation. The idea that saving grace is only available through special revelation is questioned. More attention is given to God's universal self-communication. But though, according to this view, salvation is universally available, it is not universal salvation because not all accept it.

General revelation does not make redemptive revelation unnecessary. Nowhere in the Bible is knowledge by itself, whether from general revelation or special revelation, equivalent to salvation. General revelation lacks a full understanding of redemptive grace. God in grace may lead people toward Jesus Christ through general revelation, but not all respond positively to such rays of grace. Some become aware of new dimensions of grace but turn their backs on it. God can providentially work in religions, though other religions are not God's alternate providential plan to bring redemption.

Luther called general revelation God's "left hand." General revelation provides some knowledge, but it is not the knowledge of personal encounter, as in Judeo-Christian revelation. There must be response to God's initiative. Revelation, whether general or special, does not save; Jesus Christ saves.

If general revelation were fully adequate for salvation, why would the incarnation, crucifixion, and resurrection of Jesus Christ be so important? General revelation prepares the human heart. But the gospel is able to interpret human longings, unfulfillment, and distance from God, and in grace the gospel of Christ offers salvation. Even though there are hints of grace in other religions (such as the scapegoat theme), it is precisely the grace offered in Jesus Christ that remains unknown or vague in other religions.

Surprised by Witness

Though religions often reflect the drama of the divine approach to humans and human rejection, either through repression or exchange for something inferior, God sometimes intervenes in extraordinary ways to encounter people. Perhaps this accounts for gradations in the history of religions. We meet people in other faiths with whom God seems to have wrestled in a particular way. Some have abandoned their religion in search for something more satisfying, have expressed their joy upon hearing about Christ, and have confirmed that he was the answer to their religious quest.

When Christians come into contact with followers of other religions and speak about the gospel, we can be sure that God has been concerned with those persons long before our contact with them. We need to be clear that God, whose eternal power and deity has been revealed, now addresses such persons in a new way. The Logos who radiated light now appears with greater brightness as the incarnate Jesus. Ignorance, suppression, or substitution of the truth now give way to a fuller understanding as one surrenders to Christ.

In one sense every part of the created world and all human beings are already related to Christ through the Logos. The presence of Christ is not confined within the area where he is acknowledged. Recognizing that the light which shines in the dark has not been overpowered by darkness, Christians must bear witness to the light. The

Christian confession of Jesus Christ as Lord does not involve any attempt to deny the reality of the work of God in the lives, thoughts, and prayers of people outside of Christian faith. We can appreciate and rejoice in that work. Sometimes when persons make a decision to follow Christ, they intimate that they are not adopting another God but that the God they formerly worshiped is now more fully known to them. I asked a friend, formerly Muslim, why he became a believer in Jesus. He replied, "The God I knew as Allah came close in Jesus Christ."

World History and Salvation History

When Joseph Sittler introduced the concept of "Cosmic Christ" in New Delhi, he pleaded for a closer connection between creation and redemption, arguing that redemption should be as inclusive as creation. By his specific emphasis on God's activity in creation and every facet of history, he abandoned the distinction between world history and salvation history, between the world and the church.[4]

Important to any discussion of a theology of religions is God's activity in *world history* (creation, history, and providence) and its relationship to *salvation history* (God as Savior). God created all people and is Lord of the whole world. God is not a tribal God, a God only of Jews and Christians. We explore the implications of creation, the universal covenant with Noah, and the particular covenant with Abraham. In that exploration, we discover that God's work in creation and the world, and God's work in redemption, both converge in God's concern for the nations.

If God as Lord of the world is at work in the various cultures of the world, religions lie within the orbit of God's concern for the world. God's call to Abraham and the people of Israel does not mean that God has abandoned non-Abrahamic people throughout the centuries. Beeby says, "Salvation history is . . . not a history alongside history; it unfolds in history."[5] Salvation history must not be quarantined by world history nor absorbed into world history. Salvation history intervenes in world history.

In the Old Testament, creation is not independent from but subservient to the theme of redemption. The New Testament also preserves the inseparability of creation and redemption as well as their distinctiveness. When Christ was born, a star announced his birth: at his death, light was withheld. Miracles within creation were associated with Christ's redemptive activity. Christ's creative and redemptive tasks are linked (Rom. 8:19; Eph. 1:10; Col. 1:15-20). Christ was the agent of creation and the agent of the new creation.

We have seen in chapter 3 that the name Yahweh emphasizes God's uniqueness, yet Yahweh was sometimes connected with El. We have also noted that Christ is present in world history; he is the cosmic Christ of creation and redemption (John 1:3, 10; Col. 1:15-20; Heb. 1:2). It is this relationship that must be probed. Christ is head of the cosmos as well as head of the church. But it is only in the church that his headship is acknowledged and confessed. The church and the world are not the same. The church is Christ's body; the world is not. Creation must not be confused with redemption, but creation and new creation should be held together and engage one another. If God in Christ was present in the creation of the world and of humanity and is involved in the historical process, can we not assume that God contends with the world religions as humans search for life's meaning?

More attention should focus on discovering God's definitive revelation in Jesus Christ for redemption than on discerning the work of God in world history. If Christ enlightens all persons (John 1) and the Spirit anticipates the church's ministry, divine power and grace is to some extent present in creation, history, and providence. But God's presence there should not be used to minimize God's place in redemption. God is Lord of the world's history. But God sent Jesus into the world precisely to disclose the meaning of the history of salvation. As Braaten said, "The Lord of the church is . . . the Savior of the world, and the Savior of the church is the Lord of the world."[6]

What does it mean that Christ will unite all things in himself (Eph. 1:10; Col. 1:20)? Is this happening now, as Christ works in other religions, or does this occur when people accept him as Savior? Some argue that Christ is united with each person through his incarnation and resurrection, even if persons are unaware of it. All religious longing is validated by Christ. Or they say that the Spirit is carrying out God's design in history and is guiding all to the fullness of the truth.

However, is it enough to discern where God in Christ or through the Spirit is working in world history without adequate reference to God's plan for salvation through Christ's death? By emphasizing speculative interpretations of incarnation and resurrection more than atonement, sin is diminished. Humans are promised salvation through a rich variety of manifestations of Christ and the Spirit, manifestations separated from Christ's unique work at the cross. The Ephesian and Colossian passages should be seen in the context of Christ's redemptive work and the church. God purposes the salvation of all, but that purpose is not accomplished in ways that bypass Christ, by whom it was revealed and effected.

Uniqueness, Universality, and Universalism

A question that arises in a theology of religions is the understanding of the uniqueness of the Christian faith in relation to universality of faith. How does one understand particularism (the one) and universality (the one for all). We read in Scripture that Jesus *alone* is Savior. We also read that he is the Savior of *all*. Uniqueness and universality are kept together. Paul Clasper contends that understanding uniqueness and universality is like walking on two legs—the two legs must be coordinated to make possible an effective, poised, and gracious movement.[7]

Universalisms

The concern for universality (that Christ offers salvation for all) should not be confused with universalism (that all will in some way be saved). Many religions claim a kind of universality (they have the answer for all) or promote a variety of universalisms. *Four* understandings of universalism are identified here to illustrate the theological issues involved.

One form of universalism is the belief that all people will eventually be saved through their own religions. God is considered absolute, but the idea that God's self-disclosure is absolute or that biblical faith can be absolutized is rejected.

This form of universalism is closely identified with religious pluralism. In chapter 3 we noted the impact of Arnold Toynbee, Ernst Troeltsch, William Ernest Hocking, Wilfred Cantwell Smith, and John Hick on religious pluralism. Here we see their impact and the impact of others on universalism.

Toynbee believed it impossible that so great a mystery should be reached along only one path. Troeltsch understood religion as a meaningful expression of its own culture and accepted Christian faith as an absolute religion only for the West. Hocking said religions should not compete with each other but compete to understand each other. Paul Tillich, who did not want a mixture of religion or the triumph of one over the other, believed that when one reaches the core of one's own religion, it transcends itself. Gandhi regarded the soul of religion as one, but with that soul encased in a multitude of forms; therefore, all the religions are fundamentally equal. Hick believes Jesus is only one of the many ways. Smith would like to see religions emphasize personal faith instead of their cumulative traditions (doctrine, rite, myth, cult).

In this form of universalism, religions are regarded as one, with variations according to culture and temperament. By emphasizing the mystical elements of religion (attitude, spirit) rather than dogma or practice, one is able to understand their unity. According to this view, one should not persuade Hindus, Buddhists, or Muslims to become Christians. Instead, one should encourage people to discover the fullness of salvation in their religious traditions. Hindus are to become better Hindus, Buddhists better Buddhists, and Muslims better Muslims.

This form of universalism is based on human feeling and argument more than on a close examination of God's self-disclosure. We should not criticize universalism from a desire to see sinners condemned. But neither should we conclude that God makes decisions on the basis of what we feel is right, thereby ignoring biblical history and the normativeness of Christ.

A second form of universalism suggests that the covenant people are the means of God's self-disclosure, but they are not the limit on such disclosure. It is suggested that there are two phases of salvation. The first phase began at the time of the creation of the human race and continues wherever Christian faith has not yet reached. The second phase began with Abraham and climaxed in Christ. C. S. Song believes Israel was not the only nation through which God's redeeming love was mediated. Instead, Israel is a symbol of how God would also deal redemptively with other nations.[8]

In another version of this universalism, Donald Dawe suggests that Christians may affirm God's creative and redemptive presence in other religions and affirm the legitimacy of responses to God through other religious traditions. But that does not mean that all religions are equally true. He argues that the covenants of the Bible were not simply for the purpose of securing the particularity of certain communities. Instead, those covenants were the means of expressing the universality of God's sovereignty. Dawe says that covenant particularism is not the saved against the damned, but the particularism of a people given a vision of God by which the world would be illuminated. For Dawe, the new covenant in Jesus does not replace the covenant with Abraham, as the Abrahamic covenant does not displace the covenant with Noah. Rather, we are to see how God works in the larger covenant of salvation. The church's duty is then to point to the saving work of God throughout all creation.[9]

Thus this form of universalism says that God's action in the covenant with Israel is basically symbolic. But such universalism does not give adequate attention to the way God works through the historically particular with certain people, at certain times, or in certain places as an invitation to all. How did the Old Testament regard the gods of Egypt, Canaan, and Assyria? How did the New Testament regard the gods of Greece and Rome? Were these religions part of a larger covenant of salvation? We can affirm the positive values of other religions, without accepting them as adequate instruments of salvation.

A third form of universalism is based on the universality of Jesus Christ as found in the New Testament (1 Cor. 15:22-28; Eph. 1:9-10; Phil. 2:10-11; Col. 1:19-26; 1 John 2:2). Jesus is regarded as unique because of his universal significance; he is the Savior who will eventually be universal Savior. People will not be saved through other religions but through Christ as expressed in other religions. Aspects of this view parallel inclusivism, but inclusivism opens the possibility of being saved through Christ as known in other religions. Inclusivism does not necessarily conclude that all will be saved.

This form of universalism suggests that because Christ who redeems creation will redeem other religious systems, Christians should be open to exploring what other religions can contribute to our understanding of Christ. Since the apostles and church fathers could find anticipations of Christ in the Old Testament, we have a right to expect similar things in the texts and traditions of other religions. We can discover Jesus as the ancestor of Africa, the *avatar* (appearance of God) in India, or the liberator in places of oppression. The fact that titles for Jesus can be drawn from each culture is considered evidence that Christ is present in each culture. Humanization is regarded as the work of Jesus, even though the name of Jesus is not specifically known or confessed. Jesus then becomes synonymous with every expression of new being. According to this form of universalism, there is only one way, one savior, and one salvation because all will eventually be united in Christ. But Christians should not make Jesus Christ their possession.

This form of universalism, by preferring the cosmic Christ to the historical Jesus, raises the question of our understanding of Christ. We must exercise caution so we do not de-emphasize the historical Jesus. How can we regard so many things as Christ and give so little attention to the incarnate Jesus Christ as presented by the New Testament? The New Testament invites an explicit confession of faith (Rom. 10:10,14-15) in Jesus Christ.

A fourth form of universalism is specifically concerned with the destiny of the unevangelized. This view is sometimes held by those who subscribe to an evangelical faith but don't want to restrict salvation only to those who have heard of Jesus Christ and have explicit faith in him. It is suggested that those who have not heard of salvation in Christ will not be condemned but, under certain conditions, saved through Christ. These universalists argue that God desires all to be saved (1 Tim. 2:4; 4:10; 2 Peter 2:9), that the atonement of Christ is unlimited (2 Cor. 5:19; Titus 2:11; Heb. 2:9; 1 John 2:2), that there are indications of the universal atoning work of Christ (John 10:16; 12:32; Rom. 5:12-19; 11:32; Col. 1:16, 20), and that all people are finally redeemed (Phil. 2:9-11). If there is punishment, it will be temporary; eventually all will come into the kingdom of Christ. These universalists are close to inclusivists. But again, inclusivists open up the possibility of salvation for all without insisting on salvation for all.

The theological arguments related to this view of universalism are concerned with how one understands God's love, power, and justice. It assumes that if God *can* save all, God *will* save all. If God cannot, God is not sovereign. If God does not, God is not totally good. Because God's love and justice are considered identical, punishment is seen to contradict God's love. But God's power does not swallow human freedom; God works with people until they freely accept redemption.[10]

When this form of universalism argues that all will eventually be saved, it minimizes personal decision-making and too easily assumes that salvation is automatically conferred upon people. When we confess that Jesus Christ is Lord of *all*, we do not say that *all* recognize him as Lord. God's grace can certainly overpower ignorance or even rejection. But the biblical story shows us that God's love is sometimes thwarted by human freedom. It is important to find a balance between confidence in God's love and grace, and the recognition of God's power to judge.

Particularity and Universality

When Christians proclaim, "Jesus Christ is Lord," they claim universality for the particular Jesus, the one for the many. Yet Christians are often nervous and defensive about Christian particularity. However, they are not fair to the Christian tradition when they argue for a generic God or generic revelation devoid of the particular. Though people are often offended at the scandal of particularity, the Bible indicates that God works through the historically particular. When they enshrine the principle of an imagined universalism at the expense of the universality of the particular Christ, they confuse universalism for the truly universal.

The covenants of the Bible are particular but are the means of expressing universality. The covenant made with Abraham had its setting within the larger universal covenant made through Noah, by which God entered into covenant with all humankind. The covenant with Abraham is a constant reminder that election to covenant was for the potential blessing for all. Universality and particularity do not contradict one another; instead, they require and complement one another. We can hold to particularity without violating universality, but particularity is false when it is robbed of its universal intent.

We need to recall that the particularity of God's revelation is always linked to the universality of God's sovereignty (Exod. 3:13-15). But we cannot assume that universal sovereignty automatically means universal salvation. A universal view of humanity need not de-particularize faith. Biblical faith is universal in scope but particular with respect to belief and commitment. God wishes to save everyone, but that doesn't mean that all recognition of God is in essence one unitary faith.

Universality and particularity must be kept in tension. Some biblical texts envisage a universal intent in the atonement (John 4:22; Eph. 1:7-10; 1 Tim. 2:4-6; 1 John 4:14). Other texts focus on a more particular purpose in Christ's death (Matt. 1:21; John 10:11, 15; Eph. 5:25; 1 John 3:5). Romans emphasizes the universality of grace (Rom. 3:21-23) and the particularity of response (Rom. 4:1—5:21). In Ephesians 1:3-14, universality and particularity are brought together. First Timothy helps to resolve universality and particularity by stating, "We have our hope set on the living God, who is the Savior of all people, especially of those who believe" (4:10). The particular savior of each believer is the potential Savior of all humankind. It is important to distinguish between salvation *objectively* offered and salvation *subjectively* received. Salvation is universally accessible to those who hear the gospel, but God does not override human freedom.

While we struggle with the question of pluralism and universalism, asking whether God will save all people irrespective of their religion, this was not the primary question of the New Testament. The early church was concerned with *universality*, not *universalism*. They asked whether the God of Israel was the God of all people and whether Gentiles could believe in Jesus without accepting Jewish culture.[11] The early church understood that cultural universality developed from a faith particularity. The confession "Jesus is Lord" was a new universal particularity.

Relativism and Truth

As we have seen in chapters 1 and 3, pluralism frequently leads to relativism, which rejects claims to ultimate truth. In this section we will look further at the implications of relativism and truth.

Pilgrims on faith's journey are often encouraged to reject the notion of final truth amid the finitude of history because particular truths are only partial truths. Such relativism is the mood of modern Western culture with its secular, privatized, and pluralistic values. Relativism grows out of the diversity in cultures and religions and finds expression in one's beliefs and values. Relativism is a cultural, intellectual, and theological issue. Its impact is all-pervasive. As Andrew Kirk says, "The relativistic outlook has descended on us like a blanket of fog."[12] Relativism can be described in three broad categories.

Kinds of Relativism

Cultural relativism, when used in connection with religion, considers each religion an appropriate response to its cultural environment because it meets the needs of its members. Cultural relativism, when used to describe variety in cultures, encourages greater appreciation for cultural diversity. This is also known as cultural pluralism. But a problem emerges when one is asked to move from a descriptive relativism to a normative relativism, where right and wrong are determined by the cultural norms (e.g., polygamy is acceptable if the culture approves; infanticide is legitimate for cultural reasons).

Epistemological relativism (concerning the nature and ground of knowledge) denies that one can know the absolute truth. We know truth only insofar as it is valid for us. No religion is regarded as the truth. Instead, all religions contain aspects of the truth and are therefore true for their adherents. Christian faith may be true for Christians, but they should not assert that it is valid for all people, because no one is in a position to make judgments about another religion. Epistemological relativism takes a functionalist approach to religion. Whatever belief system works is valid.

Since no single religious tradition can have a monopoly on the truth, relativism operates on the principle of complementarity in arriving at the truth. The sum total of particular truths is said to be greater than any one truth. Religions hold different but mutually enriching truths, or truth expressed in a different style of language. Truth is found in consensus or synthesis. If each religion gives expression to a particular aspect of truth, one is asked to renounce intolerance, cultivate openness, and give up claims to exclusivity and uniqueness.

Theological relativism suggests that all religious forms and systems are merely approximations of the truth. God alone is the truth; truth is one. Though one can understand God to some degree, that understanding is partial, colored by a particular history. Even when the soul apprehends truth, human language limits expression of the truth. Since religions are historically and culturally conditioned manifestations of the Absolute, no religion can claim to be absolute or definitive. Human understanding of the truth is determined by where one was born; religious beliefs are human constructions. Each religion is an authentic response to God and an equally valid path to salvation for its adherents. To speak of a "uniquely saving truth" is considered arrogant, as though one monopolistically possessed the truth. Such relativists say a closed, rigid, or narrow understanding of the truth limits the work of God to one time and to one history. Hence, humans are asked to remain in their own religion, but with the realization that no one has a preferential claim to God's truth.

The problem with *cultural relativism, epistemological relativism,* and *theological relativism* is that they all make absolute statements about *relativism.* These claims don't honestly look at real differences among religions or at the full consequences of relativism.

Truth and Experience

As we have seen in chapters 1 and 3, relativists prefer to place more value on *experience* and *action* than on *belief.* Wilfred Cantwell Smith gives primary emphasis to the inner faith experiences of religious believers rather than to beliefs, rites, practices, institutions, or scriptures.[13] When experience is the primary focus, religious belief statements are not understood or evaluated on the basis of external norms. The significant issue then is not belief but what belief points to, just as the finger is important only as it points to the moon. Focusing on doctrine is mistaking the finger for the moon. Beliefs and doctrines are considered inadequate pointers toward the Ultimate.

In his critique of this view, Vinay Samuel noted, "Questions of truth are . . . secondary to the search for universal values found in religious experience. Values are separated from the facts of religion. Values and meaning are not dependent on historical facts."[14] Relativism encourages individual freedom in the choice of values, an approach to truth described by Os Guinness as the "Smorgasbord Factor."[15]

Those who recommend *experience* or "personal truth" as the basis for truth-seeking, suggest that there is often convergence in multiple religious experiences. When one reaches the heart of one's own religion, one has reached the heart of the other also. But are religious experiences that similar, and are experiences good in themselves? Standing in reverence before Yahweh is radically different from mystic unity with nature deities. A compulsion to kill for one's faith is a quite different experience from laying down one's life for the faith.

The immediate and the existential must never become more important than truth. A relativism is inadequate if it is only willing to speak of "truth for me," and not consider "truth for all" or "what is true." Subjectivity easily undermines belief; so long as faith is sincere, one doesn't ask if it is true. Personal experience should not displace certainty; "meaning of faith" must not ignore "truthfulness of faith." Many evaluate truth statements by the number of people who believe the statements. But truth is at risk if matters of faith are determined by majority opinion. Some things are true irrespective of consensus of opinion.

Though it is important to acknowledge human experience, human experience by itself must not be allowed to occupy the center of theological authority. We believe there is objective revelation, a word beyond ourselves, which provides the norm for truth. Subjective experience, listening to ourselves or to others, is important, but not to the exclusion of truth objectively revealed.

One sometimes hears that God is revealed in personal terms but not in propositional terms. However, this is an unwarranted dichotomy (John 1:7; 14:9). Andrew Kirk argues, "Truth is both personal and propositional; truth is both received in the mind and carried out in action by the will; truth both comes to us from an independent source outside and is made ours in our own experience."[16]

Truth and Action

One frequently hears that truth is discerned best in *action*. Religion is considered true if it supports morality and human welfare. Ethics then becomes the major criterion for truth rather than experience or belief. We are asked to open our eyes to Christlike behavior in people who follow other paths (Buddhist compassion, Gandhi's nonviolence). The morally exemplary lives of Buddha and Gandhi are considered evidence that their teaching comes from God. Some suggest that people are saved by Christ because of their Christlike behavior. I heard one person say that he knows some atheists who are generous and peace loving. He believes God will accept them because the Scripture says that peacemakers are children of God (Matt 5:9).

Orthopraxis (right action) is given more emphasis than orthodoxy (right belief). The greatest need is said to be justice, the standard by which all truth is tested. All religions seem to agree that true religion requires justice. But is justice the primary criterion for truth? How is justice defined? Religions do not always agree concerning "just" practice.

Where do we get the motivating power for justice, given the gap between what we know to be right and good, and what we actually do? How do we integrate personal morality and social justice? Can justice be the new absolute standard, the universal criterion for determining the truth and falsehood of religion?[17] Martin Goldsmith says, "If we stress right practice rather than true doctrine, then there is no longer any division between those who believe in Jesus Christ and those who reject him. The division lies rather between those who practice justice and those who support the status quo."[18]

We do not doubt that God is concerned for ethics. Believers are expected to *know* the truth and *do* the truth. The truth of the gospel must be matched by the integrity of discipleship. Truth of proposition and truth of character must be kept together. Fresh understandings should lead to fresh applications of truth. The Anabaptist tradition nobly emphasizes discipleship, ethics, and behavior. Christians applaud doing the truth, but truth is not limited to deeds. A good moral life is not itself validation of one's claim to be from God or of one's teaching. Christ's lordship involves more than following ethical prescriptions. His lordship is inseparably linked with his total ministry. Belief, experience, and action must all find their center in the truth manifest in Jesus.

Truth and Belief

Relativism has undermined the importance of belief as part of truth-seeking. Can we speak of "Hindu truth," "Muslim truth," and "Christian truth" as if all are equally valid, no matter how much they differ? Hindus understand God theistically and nontheistically, personally and super-personally. Are both true? Honesty forces us to admit that religions begin at radically different points and go in different directions. For Christians, belief is crucial. Unfortunately, belief has sometimes become dogmatic or hardened into legalistic prescriptions. But errant dogmatism does not invalidate authentic belief.

Critique of Relativistic Understandings of Truth

All-pervasive relativism calls Christians to a renewed commitment to truth. From a Christian perspective, the most important question is not what a religion does for society but whether what it affirms is true. Christians must respond to issues of truth with discernment rather than from fear. When religions disagree, which is right?

On what basis does one discern truth? The starting point must be the authority of Scripture and its witness to Christ. Christians accept God's revelation as the criterion by which to evaluate other beliefs. Biblical truth is not truth by consensus. Truth is not merely the product of the human quest but the result of God's search for humans. The human quest for truth is important, but the truth found in Jesus is foundational to the human quest.

A biblical perspective, by holding to the finality of truth in Jesus, critiques relative truth. The gospel is not one opinion among many; it is true. But people are not convinced of the truth of biblical revelation simply by assertion; there must be recognition. Such recognition is enabled by the Holy Spirit. Our task is to witness to the self-authenticating Christ and to trust the Spirit. Christians claim the truth of the gospel, but the gospel commends itself as truth in the face of alternative truth claims. People must be invited to recognize the truth; they are not argued into Christian faith. We need to introduce them to Jesus.

Other religions must be approached honestly without forcing them to fit some common denominator. There are real differences between religions. Relativism does not enhance conversation if it ignores real differences. If all beliefs are equally good because they are culturally conditioned responses to the divine, what is there to converse about? Relativism discourages one from making judgments. But how is one to be discerning in the midst of conflicting options? Either God exists or does not exist; God is either personal or impersonal; God is either loving or not loving. There is truth and falsehood in religion. But relativism emphasizes only the truth and thereby prevents one from confronting falsehood and evil. On what basis does one critique apartheid, child sacrifice, or witchcraft? Relativism erodes ethical guidelines.

If something is considered true, is not that which contradicts it untrue? Many find this kind of judgment offensive because human subjectivity is said to limit one's perspective. But are all value judgments then to be suspended? Hebrew prophets criticized prophets of Baal. Jesus criticized abuses of religious leaders. Muhammad denounced polytheism on the Arabian peninsula. Christians who believe in the Trinity are critical of Muslims and Jehovah's Witnesses when they deny the Trinity. The issue is not whether we should make judgments, but what criteria we should use to do so.

If truth is defined by what people happen to accept, then judgments about religion, whether positive or negative, need to be suspended. Some insist that all religion is equally good, so they can refrain from making a judgment. Yet by that affirmation, they are making a judgment. Christians consider the Shinto understanding of *kami* (the divine) inadequate because it is incompatible with the biblical understanding of the eternal creator God. Christians deem the Buddhist understanding of the human predicament misleading, because it excludes sin as rebellion against a holy God, and because its notion of rebirth contradicts the biblical teaching of eternal life or resurrection (John 3:16; 5:29).[19]

In our critique of other religions, we need to balance conviction with sensitivity and tolerance. Tolerance shows respect without compromising truth; tolerance need not be indifferent to truth or morality. We attempt to understand the background of the Hindu caste system, but tolerance does not demand that we approve it. Openness and tolerance must not be allowed to blind our eyes to truth-seeking.

Some believe that an assured faith in God's revelation in Christ as uniquely true is arrogant intolerance. They argue that since truth is forever beyond our reach and finite humans cannot grasp the truth perfectly, our understanding is tentative. For any religion to claim sole authority from God is considered a sign of intellectual or emotional insecurity.

However, if the Bible is God's Word, and if Christ is the Word incarnate, Christians have a standard for evaluating other truth claims. Is it arrogant if one attempts to be a steward of the truth of God's revelation? Or are we not arrogant if we reject it for our own definitions? It would be arrogant indeed to claim the truth on the basis of our search or to assume that our understanding of the truth is equivalent to God's revelation. We must recognize that as finite beings we do not know truth absolutely; we have a limited grasp of the truth. But that does not excuse us from truth-seeking on the basis of God' communication to us (John 1:17; 14:6; 17:17; 18:37; 2 Cor. 4:2; Eph. 1:13; 2 Tim. 2:15).

Andrew Kirk aptly says, "If truth comes ultimately from God, it is not arrogant to believe; rather, it is arrogant not to believe it."[20] Our fear of being labeled arrogant or dogmatic often causes us to overlook the dogmatism of other religions: Judaism is dogmatic about monotheism; Islam is dogmatic about the finality of prophet Muhammad. Relativists who scorn absolutes have themselves become absolutist. They are absolutely sure their position is correct. It is as dogmatic for relativists to insist there is not just one truth as to claim that truth is found in Jesus.

In the context of religious pluralism and relativism, Christians will need to give more attention to the truth of the gospel. When we are clear theologically about the truth of the gospel of Jesus Christ, only then can we encounter with empathy and clarity the other religious options. Affirming the sovereignty of God as expressed in Jesus Christ, we confess that in Jesus truth was made present in the midst of the relativities of cultures and religions. This is a countercultural affirmation that is seriously questioned by the relativistic mood of contemporary culture. Clark Pinnock characterizes the contemporary mood: "Christ cannot be sole mediator between God and humanity, not because he did not claim it, not because the church has not confessed it, but because in the present cultural mood, such a belief has become unthinkable and intolerable."[21]

Religious pluralism and relativism assume that religious truth is inseparable from culture, and that the cultural configuration of religion constitutes religious reality itself. Cultural conceptions become theological conceptions. Clearly, religion is part of culture, and no religious belief is without implications for cultural perceptions. Yet cultural formulations of God and the character of God are not identical. Culture can be used to represent God, but God is always greater than cultural manifestations. From a Christian perspective, God is in culture but also above culture.

Christians must wrestle with questions of truth in the face of philosophical doubt and cultural suspicion. There is much skepticism about the possibility of knowing the truth. In a culture where the controlling dogma is relativism, we need to hold to the gospel which we believe to be normative and universally significant in its engagement with religions. We can avow that what God did in Christ is truth for us and for all people. On this basis we hold that it is possible to know the truth. But we witness to the universal truth of the gospel with sensitivity to contextual realities.

When Christians witness to the truth in Jesus, this does not mean that they possess all truth. Truth is much more than anyone can grasp or verbalize. There is always more truth to be discovered. No person, community, or tradition can claim to have infallible knowledge of God. Those committed to Jesus Christ can be open to correction and revision of their understanding of truth. Yet Christians who have been entrusted with the truth, attempt to be faithful to what they have been given. Stewards of the truth are cautious that truth not be negotiated away. If what they have been given is true, they want others to know about it. As they share, they begin to understand more of the truth when others confess Jesus as the truth.

Christians should not insist that all truth worth knowing is to be found in Christian faith. We insist, however, that all truth, regardless of where it is found, is God's truth and is compatible with God's revelation in Scripture. Sometimes other religions are a rebuke to us as they remind us of aspects of our faith that we have neglected (meditation, spirituality). We confess that our grasp of the truth is imperfect and our practice flawed. But when beliefs of other religions are incompatible with God's revelation in Christ, they cannot be accepted as truth.

As Christians, we have chosen to follow the way by which we know the truth. We seek the truth as learners under the guidance and discipline of Jesus, the one who embodies the truth. We do not claim to know exhaustively, but we claim to be on the way. We do not hesitate to invite others to join us as we press toward fuller understandings of the truth. We are not detached seekers; we have a faith commitment and a faith community. God meets us in our search as the truth is verified through the Spirit, not through our own subjectivity or rationality.

Jesus is the truth, but not everything that Christians have claimed is true. Christians have often been nearsighted and parochial or have married truth to power and have become oppressive. We deeply regret that some of what Christians have presented as truth is distorted. But limited knowledge or distortion should not cause us to slip into an easy relativism which debunks what is valid. Not all that we believe is distortion.

We may assert that since the truth is greater than anyone can grasp, one should give up all claims to discern the truth. But that would be false humility. True humility acknowledges that we have not grasped the whole truth but profess to have a valid perspective for beginning our understanding. The only way we can reject invalid interpretations of truth is to have an acquaintance with that which is valid. Truth must be based on reality, not on changing values. We believe in the reality of God's revelation in Jesus Christ, to whom the Scriptures bear witness.

7

Assessment of the Religions

I was at the traditional site of the upper room in Jerusalem for an ecumenical prayer service. In conversation with a seminary student from Germany, I mentioned that I teach world religions.

He asked, "Are you a person of faith?" He continued, "Most people who teach comparative religion are not persons of faith."

Many teachers of comparative religion think they cannot be objective if they are committed to one of the faiths. None of us is completely objective, of course. But is faith a disadvantage to understanding other faiths, or can it be an asset? Standing within a particular faith commitment, one can, I believe, be open to explore and evaluate other traditions.

Christian love suggests that we should be interested in others' beliefs and experiences. Those who are religious should develop sensitivity to other religious people. Belief in Jesus Christ should not cause us to develop a rigid narrowness toward other religious ideas or to distance ourselves from persons of other faith traditions. Christians can listen to and learn from others, recognizing God's hand in some though not all their religious expression. We take people of other religions seriously even if we don't accept all their beliefs.

Perspectives on Religion
Historical Perspectives

For some people, religion has a positive meaning, but for others religion is negative. Karl Marx saw religion as a cover for oppression, and Sigmund Freud considered religion an illusion. Dietrich Bonhoeffer believed religion exploited human weakness rather than affirming human dignity. Karl Barth saw religion as unbelief; for him, religion was a human attempt to save oneself, a bridge to close the gap between humans and God. He contrasted religion with faith, suggesting that God's revelation in Christ was not a new religion but the abolition of old religion.

Both Barth and Hendrick Kraemer made a sharp distinction between revelation and religious reflection, between God and humanity. They believed religion, including historic Christianity, is a human construct which is under judgment of God. Whereas religion is human effort to reach God, revelation is God's movement toward us. Kraemer, like Barth, believed there is discontinuity between Christ and religion, including Christian religion. But he admitted that in all religion there is a response to what God is seeking to reveal.

Karl Rahner, an inclusivist, had a more positive view of religion. Rahner tried to find continuity between Christian faith and other religions. He understood religion as a product of human response to the divine; humans, by nature of being created in God's image, seek to reach beyond themselves to the true and the good.

Is Christian Faith a Religion?

Some want to make a sharp distinction between Christian faith and religion. They insist that Christian faith is not a religion. Here careful analysis is required. From a functional perspective, the development of Christianity as a social-historical movement has religious characteristics—structure, beliefs, rituals. But the Bible does convey that there is a rupture between biblical faith and religiosity.

Christianity has characteristics of religion. But we must distinguish between revelation and religious reflection, between Christ and religiosity, and between genuine encounter with God and religious tradition. We should not claim that Christianity as a religion is superior to other religions. When we are inclined to criticize other religions, can we also admit that our own faith is too often closely identified with national, cultural, and social ideologies? Christianity as a religion must acknowledge its imperfections and sinfulness because it is a human response to revelation in Christ. Christ judges all forms of idolatry, including those of Christianity. Jesus Christ offers salvation which is beyond all religions, including Christianity.

Religion as Belief, Worship, and Ethics

In the study of religion, it is important to look at three aspects of religion: *belief, worship,* and *ethics.* Personal and corporate belief, individual and collective worship, and ethical behavior—all these are significant. These three components play a significant role in every religion. Yet religions differ in the emphasis they give to each and in the way the three are related to each other.

When Christians emphasize concepts and doctrinal statements, they readily reject other religions whose concepts and doctrines differ. If Christians emphasize worship, a distinction is often made between the worship of one God and the worship of multiple gods, or the way one understands God. If the emphasis is put on ethics (an Anabaptist concern), Christians often feel a close relationship to people of other religions who have similar ethical concerns about peace, justice, and ecology.[1]

There is a tendency to focus on commonality in ethics to cultivate more positive attitudes toward other religions. Differences in doctrine are then regarded as irrelevant dogmatism, and differences in worship as excessive ritualism. One's attitude to another religion is to some degree determined by its moral and social effects, but this should not be the only criterion. Broad criteria are needed for evaluation. Belief, worship and ethics must be seen as a whole.

Objective and Subjective Criteria in Religion

Religions are also evaluated from perspectives that are *objective* (cumulative tradition, institutions, worldview) and *subjective* (faith, piety, fear of God). Objective belief can cause one to lose sight of the commitment of the heart. But subjective faith needs objective faith as its reference point so that experience does not become its own norm.

An objective approach can concentrate excessively on religion as a system, thereby detracting from focus upon God. God is then lost behind the moral order which God has established. The moral order becomes an independent entity, and God is either made an appendage to the moral order or excluded from it. Buddhist *dharma* (the eightfold path), Confucian order and harmony, Jewish Torah, Christian ordinances, or Islamic law—any of these can easily replace a relationship with God. In the Bible, instruction (law) is placed in the context of a covenant relationship. Bavinck warns against the danger of eclipsing God: "God who extends his arms in Jesus Christ to this world is pushed aside, . . . hidden under duties and commands."[2]

Positive and Negative Aspects of Religion

When religions are viewed historically, one observes *positive* and *negative* aspects of religion. Human religious systems may be a positive response to God's desire to interact with humanity or to the human quest to transcend oneself. But they may also suppress God-awareness. Religions respond positively to God's challenge when they search for meaning and help illuminate the universe. Religions provide personal identity and social cohesion. Religious concern for morality (including justice and peace) indicates that humans reflect the image of God and seek God's will for the world.

However, religion can also be a negative factor. Religions may express reaction against God, disobedience to God, and flight from God. Truth is trivialized. Error and darkness assert themselves. Religions can be obstinate, fanatical, blind, unbelieving, escapist, destructive, inhumane, deceptive, hypocritical, power-seeking, and oppressive. Elijah opposed Baal at Mt. Carmel because Baal was not a true God and also because of the perverted social and economic system which Baalism promoted.

Religion can be self-deceived, self-righteous, and idolatrous. Jesus confronted religious professionals and liberated people from oppressive religion. The shadow side of religion is obvious when zeal becomes hostility. Instead of getting rid of vice, religion can incite vice. Mystical experience can lead to delusion, inspired by another spirit. Religion may repress God's signals and conceal the human need for God. Some want to count themselves as God, or to use God rather than serve God. Such prefer independence to dependence on God.

The dark side of religion can enslave, darken the mind, distort perceptions, corrupt the will, and harden the heart. Religion can be cruel and savage. Religion can include demonic elements: omens, curse, magic, fatalism, holy wars, inquisition, burning heretics, licentiousness, temple prostitution.

The darkness of religion manifested itself in human sacrifice among the Aztecs, Voodoo in Haiti, caste system in India, crusades against Muslims, and Islamic intolerance for those who forsake Islam. Religion is the source of conflict and tension between Catholics and Protestants in Northern Ireland, Hindus and Muslims in India, Hindus and Sikhs in Punjab, Hindus and Buddhists in Sri Lanka, Muslims and Christians in Sudan, and Muslims, Christians, and Jews in the Middle East. I heard an Israeli Jew criticize the way some Christians defend particular religious/eschatological views about Armageddon in which the Jew is regarded as no more than "cannon fodder."

Identifying Good and Evil in Religion

If religions are good and evil, we need objectivity to recognize the good and evil in religion. When humans are addressed by God, they answer positively and negatively. No religion is without the holy, but none is the holy. Humans long for divine light but pervert the light. Humans tend to filter out divine reality and reduce it to forms with which they can cope. They invent gods they worship instead of God. They display God's image and distort God's image. They manifest superhuman and subhuman qualities. Humans reach out for the transcendent, but they sin. Religion can be true or false, a stepping stone or a stumbling block, creative or destructive, liberating or oppressive, loving or aggressive. Religion can inspire saints and rogues.

Religion can teach the primacy of God, cultivate detachment from self, promote justice, encourage prayer and fasting. But it can also lead to unbelievable cruelty: sacrifice of children, burning of widows. Religions are a mixture of spirituality and superstition, mysticism and money, grace and sin. On one occasion in Africa, I tried to convince a seriously ill neighbor to let me take him to the hospital. He resisted because a witch doctor had told him that he would die if he were taken to the hospital. Some religions reduce love and holiness to fate and capriciousness, or turn freedom into bondage to laws.

No one can deny that elements of truth are found outside of Christ, but they are often mixed with alien elements. In Africa, I've seen rainmaking ceremonies in which the desire for rain arises from good intention but with a distorted worldview. Islam is noble in rejecting idolatry and polytheism. But its perception of human disorder is inadequate. Islam speaks of instruction more than salvation and fails to provide reconciliation for those alienated.

The Bible describes humankind as being in rebellion against God and hiding from the judgment of God. Humans not only blunder; they also express hostility against God. There is the stark reality of evil in the world. Religions are often against God instead of letting God be God. Religions are used as a shield or shelter from the judgment of God. They take the good things of God and make them into darkness.

Often religion emphasizes human effort rather than the grace of God. Goodness and piety degenerate into self-justification, self-redemption, or self-sanctification. Noble and ethical elements in other religions are frequently considered the basis for salvation and used to justify resistance to Christ. But the best of spiritual and moral experience does not impress God. In chapter 5 we noted that Ephesians 2:12 regarded those separated from Christ and from God as atheists. The Ephesians had some knowledge of God or gods, but they worshiped many gods and not the one God. In spite of the splendor of their civilization, they were atheists.

Religion often keeps people from believing by attempting to use or placate God rather than entering into fellowship with God. Religion easily becomes an enemy of God. Often those who are closest to the truth are bitter opponents of the gospel. Religious people put Jesus to death. But his death on the cross was God's judgment on all religiosity.

Avoiding Generalizations

When evaluating other religions we need to guard against making general statements about "world religions." This requires realism about religion. Uninformed praise or condemnation of another religion is not warranted. We are most credible if we are honest and fair in evaluating other religions, so followers of those religions recognize themselves. It is so easy to distort the religious views and practices of others. Yet a lie in defense of truth remains a lie.

There is also the tendency to compare the lofty ideals of Christian faith with the inferior practices of other religions. We need rather to compare ideals with ideals, and practice with practice. It is important that we listen carefully to what is going on in other religious communities and in lives of people who adhere to other faiths.[3] It is necessary to converse with people and not just study religious systems. We are not only concerned with Buddhism or Islam, but with the Buddhist person and the Muslim person. Since religions are dynamic rather than static, we can expect that religions will change or that adherents of other religions may have insights that transcend their particular religion.

In religion, given the combination of the positive and negative, light and darkness, careful discernment is required to avoid resolving the questions in categories too simple. We oversimplify if we suggest that all religions come from God, that one is as valid as another, and that each provides a way of salvation. Some consider religions merely as human constructs devoid of truth. Others believe everything good comes from Christ, and they want to make good people "anonymous Christians."

One needs to balance criticism of religion with understanding of religion. That which is valid and true can be affirmed, such as the ethical ideals of Buddhism, or the Islamic generosity in almsgiving. Good should not be called evil; but neither should evil be called good. The Bible teaches us that even good things can function in negative ways (Matt. 23; Mark 7:1-23). Careful discernment helps us avoid hasty judgments.

There is continuity between other religions and the gospel, but there is also discontinuity. Awareness of God is present in other religions. But though certain aspects of religion might reflect the biblical understanding of God, religious systems as a whole (including Christianity as a religion) do not fully comprehend God. We should not therefore overidealize other religions.

Christ as Norm

Since Christian faith is based on the historical reality of Christ, not on a philosophic system or mythology, we evaluate other religions from the perspective of Christ. The light of Christ opens our eyes to what God is doing in the world. Braaten suggests that as we can only read road signs at night when headlights shine on them, so when the light of Christ shines on other religions, we see meaning there which we would not understand without Christ. He believes, "We should avoid making any sweeping judgments about what can be known of God in the world religions apart from his self-revelation in Israel, Jesus, and the church."[4]

We can believe in the finality of Christ and still value positive aspects of other religions. We can be open to other religions and share Christian faith with other religions. In the study of other religions, we discover that they are more different from and more similar to Christian faith than we had thought. *Discontinuity* is evident when one looks at the unique revelation in Jesus in comparison to the whole range of non-Christian experience. But there is also *continuity* between God's activity in Christ and God's activity among all persons everywhere. Jesus is then crucial, normative, and definitive.

Gerald Anderson believes that discontinuity and continuity must be affirmed and maintained, though that is "difficult to do when some persons affirm continuity with doubtful uniqueness and others affirm uniqueness without continuity. What is needed in our theology of religions is uniqueness *with* continuity."[5]

Discontinuity: Religions Are Not the Same
Differences in Religion

The language of pluralism is misleading when it suggests that all faiths are forms of a *common essence* with different outward expressions. Some realize that it is difficult to find *objective unity* among the beliefs of religions. So they suggest there is an *experiential unity* in which people have common subjective, mystical, or intuitive experiences but speak of them differently.

Others argue that there is *ethical unity* among religions. John Hick understands the great world religions as different responses to the same divine reality. He regards differences in belief, ritual, and structure as a result of cultural and psychological factors. Though a theological core is lacking, Hick argues that there is a common ethical ideal.[6]

It is inadequate merely to emphasize a common essence of religions, as religious pluralism tends to do. The differences in doctrines, institutions, experiences, and practices are real. Even what appears to be similar, can have a diverse meaning when one goes beneath the surface. For example, the grace offered by Amida Buddha of Japan is without atonement, different from the grace of Christ. Similarity of ideas is often superficial. Clearly, there is not a common essence in terms of doctrinal content. Religious experience, by nature diverse and vague, is hardly a criterion for identifying what religions have in common.

Religious experience has to be understood in relation to a particular perception of divine reality. Thus the experience of divine reality by Hindu devotees is vastly different from the devotional experience of Sufi Muslims to one God. Common ethical ideals are more observable, but here too divergence is apparent. Thus interpretations of Judaism emphasize one's duty to punish evil, in contrast to Jesus' teaching to turn the other cheek. We should not focus only on the contradictions between religions. But we should frankly acknowledge that attempts to find commonalities are often forced or illusory.

Differences in religion are not just complementary; they are frequently contradictory and conflicting. Hindu *moksha* (release), Buddhist nirvana (release), Christian heaven, and Islamic paradise—these are not the same in understanding the final goal of life. While I was visiting a variety of Hindu temples in India, I discovered that our understandings of God had little resemblance. In conversations with Buddhists, I perceived that our analysis of the human problem is vastly different. From Muslim students, I've learned that, though we believe in one God, our understanding of the character of God diverges. I agree with Mark Heim: "The idea that all existing religious beliefs and symbols are expressions of some reality, which is filtered through all these contradictory masks, makes of that reality a cosmic zero."[7]

It is an illusion to believe that all religions are walking hand in hand to one destiny. Religions are frequently going in different directions. Religions are different, often irreconcilably different. Comparing religions is comparing different worlds. Their divergence concerns core issues, not just peripheral issues. Religions need to face each other with their particularities, not as watered down. We are not fair to one another if we reduce faith to the lowest common denominator. Difference must not be ignored or minimized.

Sometimes Christian faith has been generalized to make it harmonize with other religions, but in the end it is diluted. There is a qualitative difference between Christian faith and other religions, a difference in essence, spirit, and ethos. Christian faith and other religions are often more different than alike, though there are more similarities among the monotheistic religions. There is not total discontinuity but there is radical discontinuity.

We should candidly admit our basic differences. Candor and gentleness are preferable to assuming that all are on the same pilgrimage together. Given the basic differences, such an assumption is false and shows that we really don't respect the other.

Religions not only face in different directions, they also ask different questions. The basic question for Hindus is how to be released from the cycle of rebirth. The main concern for Buddhists is how to reach a state of detachment from suffering. For many Africans, the aim is to strengthen "life-force" by living in harmony with the high god, deities, spirits, and "living-dead" (ancestors). For Muslims, worship of Allah and submission to his revealed laws are the goal of religion. Each religion has its own axis around which it moves.[8]

Religions differ over issues of great importance. What some religions confess, others omit or deny. The confession of one religion is sometimes an offense to the other. Not all pieces of religion belong to the same puzzle; some elements of religion belong to one framework of belief, some to another. As Heim noted, "There is no reason to presuppose that Christianity is just another religion alongside others, as there is no reason to suppose that Hinduism is just another religion alongside others."[9]

Not only do religions differ from one another, but in each religion there are a variety of religious expressions. In Islam there are Sunnis and Shiites, in Buddhism there are Mahayana and Hinayana traditions, and in Hinduism there are numerous paths and many deities. In Judaism the Orthodox, Conservative, and Reform traditions vary in their interpretations of Torah. The divisions and disunity in Christianity are known. Each of these religious communities has particular responses to faith issues.

Religions provide strikingly different answers to basic questions of existence: nature of the religious ultimate, nature of the human predicament, mystery of life, challenge of death, agony of suffering, purpose of history, knowledge of truth, nature of beauty, structure of society, meaning of freedom, nature of hope. Discussed below are important religious categories with selected illustrations which help clarify issues and compare religions.[10]

Discontinuity Illustrated

Cosmos, Time, and History. Hindus believe time is cyclical, like an ever-turning wheel. Jews, Christians, and Muslims understand time as linear. Hindus believe that what is seen is not real but illusion (*maya*). For Hindus, history belongs to the world of the less real, without clear purpose or direction except for the cause and effect of karma.

I remember my visit to a Hindu temple the day following the airing of the film *The Day After,* which described the danger of nuclear annihilation. Hindus were not so concerned about this potential disaster because of their belief in the succession of yet other worlds. In Judaism and Christian faith, God is the Lord of history, which is the setting for God's self-revelation and salvation.

Deity. Hinduism is often described as impersonal pantheistic monism, the oneness of all things. While Hindus sometimes speak of personal deity (Brahma, Vishnu, Krishna, or Shiva), the personal is considered of lesser importance, an inferior level of understanding or a preliminary stage in spiritual pilgrimage. Hindus prefer to think of God as cosmic consciousness or a mysterious ocean of existence, yet many of them worship personal deities in image forms. Jews, Christians, and Muslims are monotheists who understand personality as an indispensable quality of God.

Buddha, who made no explicit reference to God, could be considered agnostic. But years later Amida Buddhism developed a belief in a personal deity and savior figure, Amida Buddha. The Chinese consider heaven as impersonal and worship many local deities. One wonders whether such developments in Buddhism and Chinese religion suggest that humans long for a personal understanding of God. In Shinto the definition of *kami* (god) is vague, with no clear distinction between the natural and supernatural realm or between kami, humans, animals, and natural objects. There is no place in Shinto for an absolute, eternal, self-sufficient Creator or self-revealing God. Traditional Africa believes in one high god but also reveres lesser deities, spirits, and living-dead (ancestors). I have watched rainmaking ceremonies where a lesser deity was given offerings so that he might beseech the remote and inaccessible high god to send rain.

Though Jews, Christians, and Muslims are all monotheists, their understanding of monotheism differs. Jews and Muslims object to the Trinity and to Jesus as the incarnation of God. Jesus is reverenced in the Quran and accepted as Messiah, Son of Mary, Messenger, Prophet, Servant, Word and Spirit of God. Yet Islamic understandings differ from Christian interpretations. Muhammad understood Son of God as physical generation, and Trinity as Father, Son, and Mary. In Judaism there are many understandings of Messiah, but Jesus is clearly not Messiah or Son of God for most Jews. Christians insist that accepting Jesus as Son of God and Messiah does not threaten the oneness of God but fulfills it, since they understand Jesus Christ to be God's self-characterization.

Revelation. Judaism, Christianity, and Islam are most explicit about revelation, yet Christians and Muslims define revelation differently. Muslims believe Muhammad was inspired of God to receive a verbal revelation of God's will; God sent the revelation down. Islam stresses submission to the will of God more than acquiring a personal knowledge of God. Christians understand the Bible as a revelation of God's person and will, and they believe God was revealed supremely in Jesus. God not only sent but came.

Some religions understand revelation more as the musings of philosophers and mystics, such as Confucius or Hindu gurus. Buddha's insights are revered, but he made no claim to having received revelation from God. Shinto has no accepted canon of scripture, carefully defined creed, or systematic theology, nor do most primal religions. In my teaching of African primal religion, I needed to learn the religious practices to comprehend the African worldview.

Humans. Hinduism makes no basic distinction between human life and the life of animals or vegetation. Since everything is part of one cosmic existence, and because of their belief in reincarnation, there is movement between the different categories of life. One's *karma* (moral law of cause and effect) determines whether one ascends or descends on the scale of existence. One's form of life and one's caste is determined by one's behavior in a former life. For the Hindu, soul is more important than body. Buddha, reacting against Hinduism, retained karma and reincarnation but objected to the notion of soul. For Judaism, Christianity, and Islam, soul and body are not so easily divided but form one complete entity. Jews, Christians, and Muslims believe in the freedom of the human, though Islam, stressing God's power, tends to see humans as somewhat more determined.

Judaism, Christianity, and Islam have a high regard for the goodness of humans as God's creation while at the same time recognizing the human potential for evil. Yet Christian faith is more pessimistic about human nature than modern Judaism or Islam. Christians have spoken more of original sin, depravity, and rebellion than of weakness and ignorance. Judaism and Islam reject original sin. A rabbi explained to a group of us that human frailty produces a mistake; it does not make one a criminal. Judaism and Islam teach that the potential for good or evil in humans is more equally balanced; they stress the need for instruction. Christians believe humans are more likely to do evil in spite of instruction and therefore need assistance outside of themselves: a redeemer, savior, mediator.

Salvation. All religions claim some kind of salvation-enlightenment-liberation, but how this is understood is dependent on the definition of the human predicament and how it can be resolved. It is totally misleading to assume that all religions share a common salvation but differ on the means to obtain it.

In Hinduism salvation is not deliverance from the guilt and power of sin but release from rebirth to mystical union with the Absolute. One can obtain salvation through multiple paths: knowledge, meditation, works, devotion. Hindus have little sense of a holy God, and forgiveness has little place in Hindu theology. I recall a conversation with a Hindu in India who insisted that he didn't believe in a "charge account for sin." I was uneasy with his limited grasp of the meaning of Christian forgiveness (and recognize that my grasp of other religions may be similarly limited).

In contrast to the offer of fullness of life in the gospel of Christ, Buddha taught the vagueness of nirvana. Buddha understood salvation (enlightenment and liberation) as release from desire and rebirth. According to Buddha, one could obtain salvation through comprehending the Four Noble Truths and following the eightfold path. Buddha believed that human beings were responsible for their own salvation. Buddha was not a savior but a pioneer who showed others how to achieve nirvana. Later Mahayana Buddhism developed the concept that help is available in one's search for nirvana. Pure Land Buddhism taught that one could obtain salvation by responding appropriately to the grace of Amida Buddha. On the other hand, Zen Buddhism teaches that *satori* (insight) comes through meditation.

Indian Jainism seeks salvation through rigorous self-discipline. Japanese Shinto has little concept of salvation because there is no concept of sin as willful rebellion against a holy God; evil is thought of in terms of pollution. In Japan I learned that humans can polish them-selves. Since humans are basically good, there is no need for radical transformation of character. One's task is to create a better world by faithfulness to the ancestors and to kami.

The Quran is silent about redemption. Muslims don't believe in original sin and have a more optimistic view of human nature than Christian faith. Islam speaks of education, not redemption; God is merciful but not redeeming. Because Muslims believe that no one can bear another's sin, salvation by faith is rejected. For Muslims, salvation depends on God's power and on human action. By repentance and self-effort, one can receive God's mercy. Muslims struggle with bal-ancing God's power and God's love. They insist that God as love should not reduce God's power, which increases God's vulnerability. Islam does not emphasize fellowship with God or discuss how God forgives and provides eternal life. Salvation focuses on the next world, but one cannot be fully assured now of eternal salvation.

Christian faith believes that sin breaks not just the law of God but the heart of God, resulting in alienation and hostility. Yet "in Christ God was reconciling the world to himself" (2 Cor. 5:19). We believe that humans need salvation and that the Savior, Jesus Christ, fully hu-man and divine, has provided atonement. Salvation is personal salva-tion and has important social implications.

Ethics. In ancient Greek religion, ethics was associated with phi-losophy more than with religion. In Shinto, deity is not the basis for moral order. There is no clearly defined ethical system or foundation for moral judgment. In African primal religion, ethics is defined by the particular religious community. For Hindus, ethical expectations vary according to one's caste, but service has not been a Hindu ideal except in some of the Hindu reform movements. In contrast to Hinduism, the Buddhist eightfold path is strong in ethical content, and Sikhs have noble ethical ideals.

Judaism, Christianity, and Islam have high ethical expectations based on an understanding of revelation from God. For them, loving the neighbor and doing justice cannot be divorced from faith in God.

In a conversation with Mother Teresa on a Saturday morning in Calcutta, I asked what motivated her concern for the destitute. She in-sisted that it was the compassion of Christ. Her simple confession was so meaningful because of the relative lack of ethical sensitivity in Hinduism.

Destiny. Religions do not invite us to the same destiny; the goals are different. Hindus hope, after many reincarnations, to be united with the Absolute. Buddhists are not seeking heaven (Amida Buddhism is an exception) but nirvana, ultimate enlightenment. Hindus and Buddhists believe that one's destiny is determined by *karma*, good or bad deeds which determine one's next life. In East Asian religions, one hopes to become an ancestor. In African primal religion, the goal is to become part of the living-dead (ancestor). Zoroastrians, Christians, and Muslims believe in resurrection, judgment, and final destinies of reward or punishment.

Religious Experience. In recent years there has been a revived interest in spirituality. In India I've seen many Westerners on a spiritual search. I am impressed with aspects of the spiritual search in Hinduism and Buddhism. However, there clearly is a vast difference between Eastern spirituality and Christian spirituality. Eastern spirituality is frequently characterized as mysticism. Christian spirituality explores the covenant relationship with God through Christ. It's important to open ourselves to divine reality. But the understanding of that reality differs as does our understanding of the place of faith, prayer, meditation, and fasting in relating to that reality.

Suffering. Most religions attempt to justify God in the face of undeserved suffering and the randomness of human disorder. Buddha wanted to get rid of desire, the cause of suffering. Christian Science wants to deny the reality of suffering, disease, and death. Judaism has taught us that one cannot always escape suffering but that suffering can be redemptive. Christians believe that Christ models the suffering, vulnerable God, and that only a suffering God can help us with our most profound problems. Yet the cross of Christ, the symbol of a suffering God, is a stumbling block to Jews and Muslims. Muslims insist that Jesus did not suffer on a cross because a powerful God would not abandon a prophet to death. Islam offers the kingdom of God without a cross.

Particularism and Universality. Hinduism is not exclusivistic; all religions are equally valid in their respective contexts, but none is universally valid. Buddhism, Christianity, and Islam seek to propagate the faith through "missionary" activity. Christianity and Islam both claim uniqueness and universality. Jews, through the covenant with Abraham, understand Judaism as mainly for Jewish people but teach that under certain specific conditions, non-Jews are accepted by God through the covenant with Noah. Shinto is an ethnic religion, limited to Japanese people. Likewise, African primal religions and Native American religions are meant for specific ethnic communities.

Discontinuity: Summary Observations

From the foregoing survey, it is clear that religions are not the same. Nor are differences always complementary; their radically different perspectives are often in conflict. It is impossible to reconcile these divergences. They cannot all be authentic human responses to one divine reality. It is a partial truth to explain differences as simply the relativity of human response. If we insist on the essential unity of religions, we ignore significant data and come to have a distorted perception of those religions. The world of faith is not a single lock with many keys; there are many locks with many keys.

Continuity: Preparation and Fulfillment

Similarities

Though all religions are not the same, as evidenced by the examples of discontinuity, they are not in total conflict. Some similarities, parallels, and correlations provide continuity between religions and the Christian faith. Confucius was concerned for the moral order of the universe and for moral conduct. That concern resembles Jesus' teachings in the Sermon on the Mount. There are parallels between the Chinese sages and the book of Proverbs.

In many cultures, traditions of a "lost book" have prepared people to accept Christian Scripture. There is an amazing correlation between the Old Testament and African ways of life and thought. For example, most of Africa is aware of alienation and the need for sacrifice. Islamic concern for the sovereignty of God, who provided revelation, is similar to the Christian understanding of God and revelation. Buddha's deep concern for the world's sorrow, and the Hindu concern for the priority of devotion and spirituality—these resemble aspects of Christian compassion and spirituality. Hindus have devotional literature and parables that are similar to themes in Christian Scripture.

Continuity should not surprise us in light of universal religious consciousness through the image of God in humans and the footprints of God in history. Similarities make comparative religion possible and enable religious communication. Whenever we witness, we can be sure that God has already been at work preparing people for the gospel. As Augustine said, "God places salt on our tongues so that we might thirst for him." Ideas, experiences, and ethical values can be "points of contact." Some doctrines and practices can be refashioned to communicate something of Christ.

Fulfillment Theory

In the history of Christian theology, fulfillment theories focused on understanding religion in light of its history as an effort to preserve what is true and holy. Attention was given to the light of Christ, which beams faith everywhere, and to the rays of truth that enlighten all people. Christian faith, it was said, must build connections with pre-Christian or extra-Christian revelation. Fulfillment assumes that the good elements of other religions and the uniqueness of Christ can be brought together. We can accept the signs of God's grace in other religions without abandoning Christ. Fulfillment suggests that God can prepare people in their religious context and bring them to the threshold of salvation. When they are converted to Christ, some aspects of their religion are brought to full flower. According to this view, when a non-Christian becomes a believer in Christ, the former religion is not destroyed but fulfilled. The mission of the church is to redeem and liberate what is already Christian.[11]

Historically, the concept of fulfillment and continuity has taken a variety of forms. Justin Martyr believed that before Jesus was born, those who lived according to reason were Christians. J. N. Farquhar, missionary to India early in the twentieth century, developed a more sympathetic view of religion. He recognized the elements of truth and beauty in Hinduism but considered Christian revelation the pinnacle of true religion. He believed that the good in Hinduism parallels the Old Testament in leading people toward fulfillment through Christian faith. Christ then became the "crown" or "goal" of Hinduism.

R. C. Zaehner developed a similar approach by suggesting that Christ came to fulfill all other religions.[12] Some have spoken of the "living presence of Christ" in Hinduism, of Hinduism as the "vestibule of Christianity," or of the "hidden Christ" in Hinduism. William Temple taught that whatever is noble in other religious systems of thought, conduct, or worship, that is the work of Christ on them. As noted in chapter 2, Rahner affirmed truth-seeking in other religious persons by making them "anonymous Christians." Paul Tillich considered them as part of the "latent church." According to these views, the Christian's task is then to unveil Christ, who is already present in other religions.

However, David Bosch warns that we can overstate the premise that Christ is working mystically, cosmically, and anonymously in other faiths to fulfill them.[13] Some criticize fulfillment because it is patronizing toward other religions. Hindus and Buddhists see it as a slightly more sophisticated form of imperialism.

Need for Discernment

Continuity and fulfillment should not be overemphasized by the easy assumption that points of contact are theological common ground. The meaning of a particular doctrine, practice, institution, or experience is interconnected with the meaning of all the rest. As total systems, the major religions are not easily compatible with Christian faith because they usurp the place of Christ. I remember a student who had practiced Transcendental Meditation before conversion to Christ. Soon he discovered that TM belonged to a Hindu system and was incompatible with his new faith.

Many elements of religion are common only if separated from their specific contexts or if parallels are based on selective data. Resemblances in form must not be allowed to obscure great differences in content. The dying and rising saviors in mystery religions, for instance, were different from the death and resurrection of Christ. Jesus as Servant of God in Islam differs from Jesus as Savior. While to some extent religious ideas are points of contact or stepping stones to Christian faith, continuity must always be held in tension with discontinuity. Israel's religion was not in complete isolation from other religions. There was continuity between Yahweh and El. But though Yahweh took on some of the characteristics of El, Yahweh was essentially unlike the other gods.

The relationship between the religions and Christian faith is paradoxical. There are stirrings in the hearts of non-Christians that can only be explained as the stirrings of God. There is the image of God in humans, but there is also sin and its resulting blindness and perversion. We can expect to find parallels and correlations along with dissimilarities, omissions, denials, and antagonisms. Our understanding of the extent to which the image of God has been lost through sin, influences the amount of continuity that we see. Do humans have a wounded nature or a fallen nature? Are repentance and conversion necessary? Optimistic views of religion often fail to take seriously rebellion against God and the radical nature of the gospel. Do we help people to discover Christ's presence in their religion, or do we witness to the gospel?

If, as we believe, Jesus came both to judge and to fulfill other religions, we can say no and yes to other religions. We do this because in creation God said "Yes" to the whole human race. God's yes was not retracted but was confirmed by another yes to Abraham and a yes to Jesus. We counter whatever counters God's yes in Christ, but we open our eyes to any preparations in other religions. Continuity and discontinuity are focused in Acts 14 and 17. There the gospel is presented in the context of people's past, but it is also clear that a break with the past is needed.

Other religions hold truth about God and creation which are common to biblical faith. We respect the compassion of Buddha and the insights of Confucius concerning interpersonal relations. We admire Muhammad's criticism of idolatry, his belief in one God who is the Creator and Sustainer of the world, and his insistence that humans live responsibly before God. We need to preserve religious values that are in harmony with the kingdom we serve. At the same time we recognize that some aspects of religion cannot be accepted because the gospel calls for transformation.

Don Richardson holds that there are "redemptive analogies" (analogies illustrative of the meaning of redemption), evidence of God's grace, in every culture. These analogies make the gospel accessible. Traditions like the lost book, scapegoat themes, religions of grace (Bhakti Hinduism and Jodo Shinshu Buddhism) can point to the gospel. We should not be uneasy about these analogies but expect to find them. Perhaps one can regard these as preparations for the gospel and declare as Jesus said in Mark 12:34, "You are not far from the kingdom of God." Though God is at work in other religions, seekers need to find fulfillment in Christ.

Preparation and Fulfillment

Fulfillment is possible because special revelation fulfills general revelation. Goldingay and Wright noted, "Merely listing the many common beliefs between biblical faith and other religions can never dissolve the primary uniqueness of the Bible as witness to the unique events by which God has acted to restore creation."[14] We need to take seriously what human beings have experienced and believed about God prior to and apart from hearing the gospel. But that appraisal need not distract from the revelation in Christ because Christ supplies fuller revelation, justification, and reconciliation. The real difference between Christian faith and other religions is Christ.

To what extent, therefore, should we integrate into our theology insights and values from other religions? Tom Finger urges us to place the other religions in a Christocentric perspective. He says, "If their various religious insights and practices can be loosened from such claims and directed toward Christ, many such features will not only prove compatible with but will even enrich empirical Christianity."[15]

A careful look at preparations in other religions which are fulfilled in Christ can assist us in dealing with continuity. Religious questions, glimpses of truth, yearnings, anxieties, symbols, and ideas—these can be preparation for the gospel. If persons are searching for forgiveness and peace with God, they can find fulfillment in Christ. We should seek to discover general revelation and use it as a starting point in communication.

The Old Testament used the language and thought forms from its environment, and the New Testament used language and thought forms from the Hellenistic world. The understanding of Yahweh did not develop in a total vacuum but was linked to an already-existing knowledge of God. The biblical writers used indigenous names for God and made use of ideas, values, and practices that were compatible with the worship of one true God. The very existence of other religions makes it possible to convey biblical revelation. We are able to share the gospel with non-Christians because religions provide a sounding board for it.

Dialogue is possible because of universal religious consciousness. People use religious language and have words for God. If there were no points of connection between other religions and biblical faith, Bible translators would have an impossible task. If Christian faith is presented as an annulment of all religious understanding, cultural identity would be threatened. This is true because it is impossible for humans to have a faith that is not expressed in cultural settings. The gospel fulfills and perfects whatever God-given insights are embodied in other religious paths. Those parts of religion that reflect light are elevated.

There is then a sense in which Christ fulfills aspects of religions rather than abolishing them. Partial insights are corrected and completed by the gospel. Christians in Japan suggest that religious paths lead part way up the mountain, but only Christ leads the whole way. Those from an Islamic background who become Christian confess to new understandings of God. Many African Christians see Christian faith as fulfilling the yearnings in African religion. No religious truth need be annulled, no moral message unfulfilled, no ideas remain empty or forgotten. Grace, rather than abolishing nature, perfects and fulfills it.

Religious Systems Not Fulfilled

The gospel can fulfill the religious aspiration of people or reinterpret certain practices of religion, but the gospel does not fulfill the whole religious system. Furthermore, because there is good and bad in other religions, we should not speak of the fulfillment of religions as a whole system in the way aspects of the Old Testament found fulfillment in Christ. Other religions are not tutors or midwives preparing the way for Christ as the Torah was. Nor should we quickly assume that people in other religions are saved in the way Old Testament saints were. The Old Testament had a unique role in relation to Christ and the New Testament.

In India I heard a Christian theologian suggesting that Hindu or Buddhist scriptures might function in place of the Old Testament in that setting. However, I am not ready to replace the Old Testament with Hindu scriptures because the worldview of Hinduism is so radically different from the theological understandings of the Old Testament. We need to be very cautious when we suggest that other scriptures can help us penetrate more deeply the mystery of Christ, or that such scriptures be used in liturgy alongside the Bible. Non-Christian religions can be used as a bridge to the gospel but do not provide the same preparations for the gospel that the Old Testament does.

Negative Preparation

When we speak of preparation and fulfillment, a word of caution should be noted. Religion can also distort the biblical message and misrepresent God. Religions are then "negative preparation." Questions are asked which are different from God's questions. Many elements of world religions are not compatible with biblical faith. Thus sometimes sin is considered ignorance instead of rebellion, and salvation is something achieved rather than a gift. But even when there is a deep gulf between Christian faith and the religions, we can regard religion as a "negative preparation" and use it as a base from which to start because Jesus fulfills the truth which religions have sought in vain.

E. Stanley Jones described India as "the land of the almost."[16] Christian faith fulfills what is good in Hinduism but also responds to the vacuum in Hinduism. The experience of Paul is mirrored in the lives of many people who come to Christ from other religious backgrounds. At a point of crisis, the cross exposed the deficiency of their religious worldview but also met their need. Jesus appeared to them as someone who threatened all that was sacred to them. But in the light of Christ, they afterward look back and see that he fulfilled it all.[17]

8

Who Is Christ?

Caesarea Philippi is a favorite spot of mine. It is twenty-five miles northeast of the Sea of Galilee and near the slopes of Mt. Hermon. This area was a center for ancient Syrian Baal worship. The Greek god Pan, god of nature, was also worshiped there. Part of the complex was a temple built by Herod the Great, dedicated to the godhead of Caesar.

When Jesus went to Caesarea Philippi with his disciples (Matt. 16:13-28), the area was littered with temples to Syrian gods. Images of the ancient Greek gods looked down from their recesses on the cliff, and the temple of Caesar stood as witness. Jesus asked his disciples, "Who do people say the Son of Man is?" They mentioned Jewish persons, prophets. Then he asked, "But who do you say that I am?"

It is as though Jesus deliberately set himself against the background of the world's religions in all their history and splendor. He demanded to be compared with them and to hear the disciples' verdict. Their verdict as spoken by Peter was emphatic: "You are the Messiah!"

Where Jesus asked this question is important. The population was mainly non-Jewish. At first Jesus did not ask the question directly. He led up to it by asking about popular opinions. Some thought he was John the Baptist; others suggested Elijah or Jeremiah, certainly a prophet. These affirmations were complimentary. Elijah was one of the greatest prophets and anticipated as the forerunner and herald of the Messiah (Mal. 4:5-6). Jeremiah was among the best-known prophets.

Jesus was given a high place but not the highest place. The answer that Jesus is a prophet received no commendation from Jesus. Jesus is more than a prophet. Peter said it right: Jesus is Messiah.

Human categories, even the highest human categories, are inadequate to describe Jesus. People place Jesus in the highest categories they can imagine; they deal with Jesus politely. He is considered the best of those who have spoken for God. People lavish tribute upon him—but that is not enough. Jesus is the Christ; Jesus is Messiah!

Jesus let people discover for themselves who he was. Likewise, our discovery of Jesus Christ must be a personal discovery. "You— what do you think of me?" Our knowledge of Jesus cannot be second-hand. We need personal conviction that Jesus is the Christ.

Jesus Christ is the foundation of the church's belief and action. He is the one who has the keys to the kingdom. He guarantees that the gates of Hades will not prevail against the church. What kind of Messiah is Jesus? What is the newness that separates him from the prophets? It is the person of Jesus that distinguishes him from the prophets: his life, suffering, death, and resurrection.

Nevertheless, the Peter who made the great discovery and confession also misunderstood. He was still thinking of a conquering Messiah, a warrior king to drive Romans out of Palestine, perhaps a military leader like Judas Maccabaeus. How can one understand a suffering Messiah? When Jesus spoke of his death, Peter declared, "It must not and cannot happen to you." Jesus replied, "Get behind me, Satan!" Peter's words reminded Jesus of the force of temptation which he earlier faced and would again encounter.

While confessing Christ, Christians too quickly pass over the suffering Messiah. We look for a powerful Christ who deals with frustrations, fears, and enemies. We forget that there is suffering before resurrection (Matt. 16:21). Only after resurrection is a new power released in the world, climaxed in Jesus' coming again (16:27). We easily say Christ is the Son of God, then misrepresent or reinterpret him. How we understand Christ is as important as our confession.

Misrepresentation of Christ
The Church's Failure

The Christian church has often misrepresented Christ. How can we *portray* Christ and not *betray* him? How do we live and teach all that Jesus is? We need humility, acknowledging that we might confuse the truth with our grasp of the truth. At the very point of Peter's confession of the truth, Peter became an agent of Satan. He grasped the truth but immediately made it an instrument of falsehood.

Like Peter, the church has often preferred a sovereign king (messiah) without the suffering servant. Belief in a powerful messiah, separated from the suffering Messiah, led to the Constantinian Christ, the Crusading Christ, the Colonial Christ, and the Anti-Semitic Christ. The cross was turned into oppression for Jews, as it later was for Native Americans and African-Americans. At one of Hinduism's most holy sites in India, I met a French psychiatrist who admitted he was drawn to Hinduism as a reaction against Christian and Islamic wars.

We betray Jesus when we equate his kingship with ruling ideologies, elitist power structures, wonder workers, or when we make him a guarantor of success. But it is equally wrong to emphasize his suffering servant character without his kingship.

Other Religions Reinterpret Christ

Christians are not alone in misrepresenting Christ. In many religions, Jesus is not disregarded but takes on different meanings according to the adherents' worldview. New Age thinking speaks of "Christ consciousness," "Christ idea," or "Christ principle." Members of the Bahai religion insist that Jesus has returned as Baha Ullah. Followers of Moon, in the Unification Church, believe that Christ provides partial salvation and that another messiah is needed. On a visit to the Unification Church in Washington, D.C., I heard a Jewish man who had joined the Unification Church say that he had seen the face of Jesus. He had room for both Jesus and Moon in his worldview.

Jehovah's Witnesses describe Jesus as "*a* son of God." Hindus have no problem with Jesus as a guru, yogi, spirit master, or one of many emanations from God. He is easily incorporated into the Hindu pantheon. When I visited an ashram along the Ganges River in India, I noted that Jesus' picture was on the wall along with Hindu deities. I heard a Hare Krishna member at the Hindu Temple in Washington, D.C., say that Jesus had led him to Krishna.

Gandhi, a Hindu, said that he accepted Jesus as a lord but not the solitary Lord. He saw Jesus as one of many teachers or prophets. One of Gandhi's favorite songs was "When I Survey the Wondrous Cross." He liked the poor, suffering, gentle, loving, patient, and forgiving Jesus. He saw Jesus as a martyr and the cross as a model for the world. Jesus' example of suffering informed his nonviolence. However, he rejected atonement and forgiveness through Jesus Christ, believing there was no miraculous virtue in Jesus' death on the cross. He regarded grace as moral license. For Gandhi, the Sermon on the Mount and Jesus' ethics were most important.

Buddhists regard Christ as a kind of Christian Buddha or "enlightened one" but cannot accept the voluntary suffering of an innocent man for others. Jesus and the Buddha are compared in terms of their teachings, stories, parables, proverbs, and disciples. The Muslim Quran, which contains explicit teaching about Jesus, honors Jesus as a miracle worker, prophet, messenger of God, word of God, servant of God, and truth of God, but denies his deity and crucifixion. Yet Islam, which accepts the death of Muhammad, believes that Jesus is currently alive. Judaism accepts Jesus as a moral teacher, prophet, healer, exorcist, or righteous one. A rabbi friend of mine called Jesus a "smart rabbi." Many Jews suggest that Jesus is for the salvation of Gentiles, not for Jews, because Jews find God through the former covenant and Torah. Jesus of Nazareth is both a link and a point of division between Jews and Christians.

Reverence for Jesus in other religions often does not result in commitment to him. People cannot dismiss Jesus, so they reinterpret him. Jesus' identity is the crucial issue. Which Jesus do we talk about? Certainly Jesus is a great moral teacher, a rabbi, a prophet, a liberator, and a miracle worker—but he is more than these. Jesus is a model for piety and morality but also more. Some want to make him into a mystic, an unorthodox rabbi, or a subversive political leader. Many have exchanged belief in the atonement of Christ for the idea that Jesus' death was simply to manifest God's self-giving love. Most religions revere Christ as a teacher, spiritual leader, or mediator of revelation. Yet Christ often becomes no more than a pioneer moved to the leading edge of the religious quest.

Nearly every religion has a special place for Jesus in its hierarchy of sacred names and symbols. Even when Jesus is considered a great or perhaps the greatest religious leader, he often remains in the same category as other great leaders. Thus religions assert that while God was present and active in Jesus, God was also in Buddha, Muhammad, or Confucius. None can therefore claim to be universally normative. The meaning of Jesus is often defined by one's own experience, self-understanding, moral idealism, or philosophical system, rather than by letting one's thought patterns come under the scrutiny of Jesus. Carl Braaten says, "From the sublime to the ridiculous, Jesus is pictured as the perfect model of what each group understands itself to be. Like plastic surgeons making over the face of the patient in their own image, Jesus becomes a prisoner of our fads and fashions."[1]

As Christians, we recognize that there are diverse understandings of Christ in the New Testament, but diversity does not sanction deviation from central norms. The doctrine of salvation and the cross separates Christ from other religions. We understand Jesus Christ to be the particular presence of God for all people, but religions often reinterpret the scandal of Christ's particularity.

Christ's Uniqueness

I've been enriched by the testimonies of believers from other cultures. Jewish believers are discovering the Jewishness of Jesus. Muslims are often attracted by Christ's offer of forgiveness.

When I taught at Union Biblical Seminary in India, I interviewed students who were first-generation Christians to discover why they came to Jesus. One from Sikh background saw Jesus as the answer to his fear of death and reincarnation. One from Hindu background replied, "Krishna came to kill sinners, but Christ came to die for sinners." Another from Hindu background spoke of finding "peace in Christ." One student was on the verge of suicide from despair and saw Christ as the answer to his "spiritually orphaned condition." A woman, formerly Buddhist, said, "Buddha is regarded as the light of Asia, but Christ is the light of the world." She continued, "Buddha was never sure of his salvation, but Christ provides assurance."

In India, the impact of the historical Jesus is a powerful motivation for peace-and-justice activity. In Latin America, Christ is the suffering one and the liberator. In Africa, Christ is welcomed as mediator, victor over evil powers, healer, exorcist, and the sacrifice for sins.

The illustrations cited above express people's experience of the uniqueness of Jesus. When we combine the special attractiveness of Jesus at a personal level with a biblical perspective, the uniqueness of Jesus can be summarized under several categories.

Incarnation and Revelation

I am writing this within sight of Bethlehem, where Christians remember that God became flesh. Jesus Christ is unique because he defines the reality of God. This is in stark contrast to the "monistic" language of religious pluralists who refer to God as the "mystery" or the "absolute."

Jesus is the Word who was with God and is God (John 1:1). The one who has seen Jesus has seen the Father (John 14:9). Jesus is described as "in the form of God" (Phil. 2:6), the "image of the invisible God" (Col. 1:15), the "reflection of God's glory and the exact imprint of God's very being" (Heb. 1:3). In the incarnation, God is directly and personally revealed. God can be known apart from Jesus Christ, but

God's love is most fully revealed in Christ.

This contrasts with Islam, which speaks comparatively little about the love of God. It also contrasts with Buddha and Confucius, who were not sure that God exists. Carl Braaten says, "God is never more divine than when he becomes human and never more self-revealing in his true essence, love, than in the death and resurrection of Jesus."[2] In knowing Christ, we know God in a way not available in any other revelation. Founders of religions have explored the meaning of the divine, but Christ is divinity incarnate.

Part of the mystery of the incarnation is the historical particularity of Jesus Christ, in whom God is shown most fully. The historical person of Jesus is in contrast to the mythological *avatars* (appearances of God) in Hinduism. We do not, therefore, anticipate additional manifestations of God (as in Bahai) or continuing revelation (as in Mormon tradition). Jesus is the only Son of the Father, who does not share his glory with a multitude of divine incarnations.

Jesus Christ is God (ontologically, in being). Jesus didn't just show us God (functionally). While Jesus is the representative and instrument of God who operates in God's place, he is also God. The New Testament affirms that the man Jesus is the Christ of God. God was not only acting in Jesus; Jesus is God (John 1:1-18).

Jews and Muslims would only agree with the first part of this assertion. But God has not just *spoken* to humanity, as in Islam. God *came* to respond to the human condition. God came in flesh, not in a system of symbols or ideas; Christ is not a *principle* but a *person*. Revelation from God is not confined to a document, as in Islam; Christ is the "living word." In him we receive personal knowledge of God. Without the incarnation, our knowledge is deficient. The Bible witnesses to Christ in words, but the words point to the one who invites us into a relationship with himself. For Islam, the Quran is the message; for Christians, the Bible points to Christ, who is the *messenger* and the *message*.

Though Jesus was particular in a specific place and time, Jesus is the truth for all times and places. Because his universality is not merely abstraction but expressed in a particular way to each person and culture, he is able to identify more deeply with all humans. The God of Jesus is not a general God but one who relates to specific situations.[3] The ministry of Jesus was directed mainly to the Jewish people, but his significance is for all as seen in his care for the Samaritan woman, the Roman centurion, and the Syro-Phoenician woman.

Incarnation and atonement are linked. God's revelation in Christ is salvific because Christ bridged the rift between God and humans. God went the ultimate distance; God could not have come closer. Muslims have difficulty with the closeness of God; God is majesty, not Emmanuel, "God with us" (Matt. 1:23).

Jews also have difficulty with God becoming human. In a conversation between Jews and Christians, a Jewish friend of mine frankly admitted that he cannot accept God in a human body: "Incarnation is a scandal in my religion."

In the incarnation, God reaffirmed creation and history. Christ's coming is also God's response to the human condition. Jesus shared in flesh and blood and was made like us in every respect (Heb. 2:14-18). The self-emptying of Christ implies identification and solidarity with humankind. Mark Heim notes that "Christ not only decisively defines God, but decisively defines humanity."[4]

Salvation

I am writing this during Passover and Christian Holy Week in Jerusalem. I participated in the Palm Sunday walk from Bethphage, over the Mt. of Olives, and into Jerusalem. On Maundy Thursday I joined a group of Christians in Jerusalem for worship and the Lord's Supper, followed by a reflective walk from Jerusalem through the Kidron Valley to Gethsemane. On Easter Sunday I participated in the sunrise service at the Garden Tomb. Through these events, I've recalled again the significance of Christ's death and resurrection for our salvation. I believe the heart of the gospel is that God in Christ cared enough for us to suffer for our sins.

The gospel is good news because God acted in Christ to restore humanity to God. As Adam represents "fallen" humanity, Christ represents "new" humanity. Jesus' incarnation cannot be separated from his crucifixion and resurrection. Jesus came to bear our sins and destroy death. Christ did in his death what he could not do in his life; he became a sin offering for us (2 Cor. 5:21; Gal. 3:13). Jesus, as the one in our place and the one in God's place, saves us from sin and makes God's transforming power available to us (Heb. 2:14-18).

By his vicarious suffering, Christ models the vulnerability of God; in the cross, evil had to yield to love. The suffering servant who agonizes on "Calvary's Tree" stands in contrast to the Buddha who passively sits at the foot of the Bodi Tree. And Christ's willingness to suffer is radically different from Muhammad's flight from Mecca to Medina. Muslims reject Christ's death on the cross because they don't believe God is that vulnerable. They have no theology of redemption.

Our understanding of salvation must be predicated on a correct diagnosis of the human problem. The basic human problem is rebellion against God and alienation from God, resulting in death. Humans are in need of salvation from sin, alienation, and death. The Bible is realistic about the human condition. The human problem is not merely the lack of religious knowledge but the need for forgiveness and restoration of a relationship. Religions often stress the need for divine self-revelation, but more than revelation is needed: redemption is needed.

From a biblical perspective, salvation is what breaks the vicious cycle of sin and death. Salvation is how God has defeated death in the crucifixion and resurrection of Jesus, thereby liberating us for eternal life.[5] The heart of Christian faith is the centrality of Christ for salvation. Jesus Christ cannot be reduced from his position as Savior of the world to become a symbol for all truth in every religion. By providing salvation, Jesus' uniqueness is without parallel. No other religious leader claimed to forgive sins and invited people to find salvation in his person. Jesus provides the radical salvation which humans need. For the basic human sickness, there is one prescription: Jesus Christ.

Jesus' *particular* death has *universal* significance (John 6:51; Rom. 8:32; 2 Cor. 5:21; Heb. 2:9). His death was not merely the execution of a martyr. There is an "instead of" character to Jesus' death. The one who did not deserve death voluntarily offered his life for others, becoming the victim of sin. At the cross, sin pierced the Son of God, but by becoming the victim of sin and bearing its wounds, he was able to forgive sin. Jesus' death is universally significant because it is universally representative.[6]

The redemptive grace of Jesus contradicts the religious quest by undermining our self-confident behavior. Christ releases us from self-justification. In the presence of the cross, we confess, "There is none righteous, no not one." We do not find; we are found. We do not choose; we are chosen. Our salvation does not depend on the intensity of our search, our righteous life, or the strength of our faith. These things are important but are not the path to God.

We are dependent upon God's invitation in Christ to receive the free gift of salvation. God wants people to be saved, not to perish. Christ came not to condemn, but to deliver from condemnation. Jesus extends his gracious invitation, "Come to me, all you that are weary and are carrying heavy burdens, and I will give you rest" (Matt. 11:28). When Jesus asked his disciples whether they would desert him, Peter replied, "Lord, to whom can we go? You have the words of eternal life" (John 6:68).

Salvation has profound *personal* implications. Christ provides forgiveness of sins, release from condemnation (Rom. 8:1), abundant and eternal life (John 11:52; 1 Cor. 15:22), and reconciliation (2 Cor. 5:19). The gospel is not only about a theology of creation but about a new creation (2 Cor. 5:17); we participate in a new order. We are not only in the image of God; we are a new humanity (Eph. 2:13-15). We are members of the household of God (Eph. 2:19). Christ provides fellowship with God and assurance of salvation, in contrast to religions which depend on good works and whose adherents are therefore never certain of salvation.

However, salvation is not only personal. There are important *social* implications. The unity which many religions seek is made possible through the reconciliation of Christ. The lordship of Christ need not be a barrier to social unity or a cause for division. Instead, Christ's lordship actually becomes the basis for unity not otherwise achievable. By dealing with sin, Christ has dealt with the fundamental alienation of humankind. Christ is the one who breaks down walls and creates a new humanity. Christ reinterprets and reconciles gender, race, culture, and nationality. Can religions do better? If unity is based on God's creation of all humans and on redemption in Christ, the unity of people does not need to be invented but appropriated.

There are *ethical* implications for salvation. Jesus is Savior but also a Teacher-Prophet and model for saved and Christian behavior. In Jesus' life, words, and actions, the kingdom of God is revealed. God's reign is actualized when people respond in covenant obedience. Citizens of the kingdom commit to Jesus Christ in faith and discipleship.

Resurrected and Exalted Lord

Christian faith begins where other religions end—with the resurrection. The uniqueness of Jesus is confirmed by his resurrection. All other religious leaders died; Jesus was resurrected. Some doubt or deny the resurrection because they do not understand it. Even though we stumble over this mystery, we are not faithful to the biblical message and Christian tradition if we deny the resurrection. Resurrection transformed the apostles. The early church was so effective because the apostles and other believers were convinced that Jesus was alive.

Resurrection vindicated Christ's life and linked the incarnation with the ascension. By his resurrection, Christ broke the power of death and evil, enabling a new creation. As the disciples were transformed by the resurrection, we also experience the power of God for salvation and for transformed behavior. Because Christ's resurrection is a promise of our resurrection, the dread of death is diminished.

Christ's lordship is connected to resurrection, but lordship is triumphalistic if there is resurrection without the cross, victory without suffering, kingship without servanthood. Yet the resurrected and ascended Christ is exalted Lord and has a name above every other name. Christ is seated with the Father, and he is mediating between humans and God. As Lord, Christ is not only Savior but also Judge. As Judge, Christ exposes sin's destructiveness, inviting people to renounce sin and receive his love.

The resurrected and ascended Lord draws men and women to himself. While Islam denies that Jesus died on the cross and was resurrected, it is in fact the resurrection that attracts some Muslims to Jesus. When Muslims in Africa came to Jesus and were asked what attracted them, they replied, "Suppose you were going down the road, and suddenly the road forked in two directions, and you didn't know which way to go; and there at the fork were two men, one dead and one alive—which one would you ask which way to go?"[7]

Christians are called to be ambassadors of God's love in Christ in the interim between the ascension and Christ's return. When he returns, there is fulfillment: "At the name of Jesus every knee should bend, in heaven and on earth and under the earth, and every tongue should confess that Jesus Christ is Lord, to the glory of God the Father" (Phil. 2:10-11).

Implications of Christ's Uniqueness

At different stages of our lives or in differing cultures, we are attracted to differing aspects of Christ's uniqueness: Savior, Lord, Teacher, Prophet, Victor, Judge, Mediator, Liberator, Healer, Protector. These are all valid perceptions so long as we do not reduce Jesus to whatever we want. Jesus meets our needs, but he is more than a "need meeter." When we reduce Jesus to our preferences or particular experiences, we domesticate him, limit his sovereignty, and have a partial Christ.

On the other hand, there are some fifty names or titles for Jesus in the New Testament, as he is presented from many angles. Stephen Neill describes the many facets of Jesus as a prism which refracts the light in varied colors.[8] There is not only one model in the New Testament for interpreting Jesus. The message is contextualized in differing cultures to address specific needs.

For example, there are numerous models for Christ's atonement in the New Testament. John Driver identifies the following themes:

conflict and victory over evil powers, sacrifice, propitiation/expiation, ransom/redemption, vicarious suffering, reconciliation, justification/righteousness, adoption into God's family.[9]

The synoptic Gospels tend to emphasize the humanity of Jesus, while John's Gospel and the epistles speak more of his divine lordship. It is important that we accept all parts of the New Testament and let our understanding of Christ be expanded by the full range of views in Scripture.

We must be guided by the New Testament, which announces a new fact. In the ministry, death, and resurrection of Christ, God acted decisively to effect the possibility of redemption for the whole world. Though there are different ways of presenting redemption in the New Testament, the writers agree that Christ is decisively important for all people everywhere.

Clarifying Christology

Theological pluralists raise questions about aspects of traditional Christology, arguing that belief in the lordship of Christ stands in the way of appreciating other religions. They are critical of making Jesus Christ into a personality cult. Here I describe several reinterpretations of Christ which highlight the need for clarifying Christology.

Relationship of Cosmic Christ and Logos to Jesus

As we have seen in chapters 3 and 5, within theology there is much debate about the relationship of the cosmic Christ and the Jesus of history. Some propose that an understanding of the cosmic Christ requires Christians to modify their claims that the uniqueness of Christian faith is based on its historicity. They prefer to emphasize the cosmic Christ over the historical Jesus.

Raimundo Panikkar argues that the confession "Jesus is the Christ" is not the same as "Christ is only Jesus." For him, "Christ is Lord," but not "the Lord is Christ." He is critical of Christians who want to monopolize Christ.[10] But when incarnation is de-emphasized, "mythic" formulations soon make Jesus into a universal abstract Christ. Then the "Jesus event" is replaced by the "Christ principle."

Similarly when emphasis is given to the Logos (the divine power in all things), the Logos principle is identified with an ideal Christ who has little connection with the historical Jesus. The Logos who saves is said to be universally reflected in all religions. Jesus then bears witness to the Logos. The Logos may be incarnated in Jesus but not in a unique way; Jesus is Logos-Christ, but Logos-Christ is not confined to Jesus.

Some consider Jesus of Nazareth a *Christ-symbol*, a universal Christ who through multiple incarnations can bring revelation to different people through a variety of religious figures: Buddha, Jesus, Muhammad, Krishna. Jesus is regarded as unique and normative so long as one recognizes that there are other saviors who are also unique and normative.

There is danger in giving too much attention to the mystery of the cosmic Christ or Logos. Though there is much about the cosmic Christ or Logos that we do not understand, the emphasis of the New Testament is that the mystery has been made known in Jesus. Christ, the mystery hidden for ages, is not a universal generic person but a particular person. Jesus Christ is the center of the divine plan, the mystery of salvation (Rom. 16:25; Eph. 3:4; Col. 2:2; 4:3; 1 Tim. 3:16). Jesus Christ embodies the mystery; he is not just one manifestation of the Logos.

However, it is also empty to speak of Jesus without Christ. The mystery of the cosmic Christ must be demonstrated, not in Jesus without Christ, but in Jesus-the-Christ. If the cosmic Christ, the hidden Christ, the unnamed Christ, is at work in other religions, we test that work by Jesus-the-Christ.

Our interpretation of Christ must give priority to the incarnate Jesus of Nazareth, as the New Testament itself does. We give priority to Jesus defining Logos, rather than to Logos defining Jesus. The Logos must not eclipse the Jesus of history. We must remember that the Logos became flesh, and we must anchor the Logos in the historical Jesus. It was precisely the incarnation, crucifixion, and resurrection of Jesus that became a stumbling block to Jews and foolishness to Greeks. When the incarnation is de-historicized, the scandal of particularity dissolves and the stumbling block and foolishness disappear. But then the unique salvation in Christ also disappears. It was the historical incarnation of the Logos that the world did not know (John 1).

If we wish to be biblical, we cannot surrender the scandal of God's unique revelation in Jesus. It is refreshing to note that some people in other religions are fascinated with the Jesus of history. More Jews are exploring the meaning of Jesus the Jew. In India, it is not the mystical Christ but the historical Jesus that has had the deepest impact upon Hinduism.

We should not assume that some variant of the Logos principle is the most useful basis for conversation between the religions. Carl

Braaten states, "This concept of the larger Christ manifest in all religions is a way of co-opting them. It makes them appear to be mere
echoes of what we know already or seeds of the same stalk that grows
in our garden."[11] Braaten insists that a Logos Christology without its
particular basis and content in the historical Jesus is void of the gospel.
Christian faith loses its meaning when the link between the Jesus-
event and the Christ-principle is loosened, for Christians can only understand God meaningfully as defined by the human Jesus.[12]

Impact of Incarnation and Resurrection

Though incarnation is a distinctive core of Christian belief, it is
being questioned at many levels. We have noted earlier how some
theologians teach that the incarnation should be understood as *myth*.
According to this view, the language of incarnation is not meant to be
understood literally but as a parable, story, image, or figure of speech.
It is not descriptive language but designed to evoke a response of faith
and commitment. The incarnation is not then taken as factual history
but as a story designed to proclaim that the encounter with Jesus was
and is an encounter with God. Jesus was not God but a human being
who was open to the presence of God.[13]

Sometimes theologians speak of God's action in and through the
person of Jesus as a vehicle of God's purpose for the salvation of the
world. However, they downplay the unique focus of God's revelation
in the Word made flesh. Parallels are then drawn between Jesus and
the *avatars* or *bodhisattvas* of eastern religions. The suggestion is that
there is continuity between the Christ-event and experiences of grace
in other religions.

Great care must be taken when using the language of myth and
symbol. Such interpretations are ways to avoid the offense of Jesus
Christ by reducing his particularity. New Testament christological formulations are more than mythic descriptions of religious saving experiences mediated through Jesus. Jesus did not merely mediate transcendent religious experiences; he spoke with the authority of God
and promised a new kind of life. Promises are different from mythological insights. Jesus came to announce a historical fulfillment of
God's rule and to inaugurate something new. Jesus declared, in word
and action, that the way of the cross and resurrection is God's method
of working in the world.[14]

Some argue for a broader view of salvation based on the incarnation and resurrection of Christ. They insist that the incarnation sancti-
fies human nature. Through the resurrection of Christ, every human

has automatically become part of the new humanity. Salvation becomes possible as the resurrection permeates everything and everybody with the fullness of Christ.

Though the incarnation and resurrection are foundational to Christian understanding, I disagree with those who suggest that the incarnation and resurrection automatically guarantee salvation. Certainly the world has been profoundly impacted by the incarnation and resurrection, but God's power does not overwhelm human beings. Humans are responsible to choose for or against the incarnate and resurrected one. Furthermore, the cross links incarnation and resurrection. Apart from the suffering and death of Jesus, incarnation and resurrection fade in their significance. When we speak of suffering, cross, and death, we raise the issue of sin and lostness, along with the possibility of forgiveness and reconciliation. Theology must not bypass the reality of sin and Christ's dealing with it.

Reliability of Scripture's Witness to Jesus

The reliability of the New Testament documents in their witness to Jesus Christ is sometimes questioned. Some suggest that Scriptures like "Before Abraham was, I am" or "The Father and I are one" are not really from the mouth of Jesus (John 8:58; 10:30). It is argued that Jesus' actions and words were recorded according to the theological concerns of the writers, or that people read back into the New Testament the doctrines of later times. There are attempts to relativize the claims that Scripture makes for Jesus by insisting that Christology reflects the social situation of the church more than the essential nature of Jesus. It is said that Jesus belongs to history, but Christ belongs to the church. Ambivalence about Scripture is expressed by contrasting the religion *of* Jesus with the religion *about* Jesus, implying that Paul distorted the faith of Jesus by focusing on the person of Jesus.[15]

For example, Knitter believes that early New Testament Christians had a culturally conditioned understanding of Jesus. Their high praise of Jesus was an expression of love and devotion, not a truth claim; Jesus was relationally unique but not universally unique. He had a unique relationship with God but was not divine. The early church made him divine. Knitter insists that the language of the New Testament should not be taken literally but figuratively and mythically; it is language of confession and testimony, using symbols in that culture.

Knitter regards the New Testament titles for Christ as a *medium* rather than the *core* of the message. Thus he thinks that the absolute and exclusive quality of New Testament Christology reflects the social situation of the early church more than the essential nature of Jesus. Knitter believes that exclusiveness, normativeness, and finality need to be adapted. One can use such language to confess faith but should not understand the language factually. Jesus is unique, distinctive, and universally important, but he is not God's normative revelation for the whole human family. Jesus is Lord for Christian believers, but not everyone needs follow him.[16]

Can we trust the New Testament witness to Christ? Though some question the reliability of the New Testament documents as witness to Jesus Christ, I believe we must reaffirm our confidence in the New Testament as a reliable source for the deeds and teachings of Jesus. We need to question a view of the New Testament that undermines or alters significant affirmations of Jesus. One doesn't need to insist that all the words attributed to Jesus are exact quotations of Jesus. Yet we can believe that those words are authentic representations of what Jesus said or did. We should not try to separate Jesus' self-understanding from the church's understanding of him. We can regard the New Testament declaration of Jesus' words and deeds as true affirmations of his character, not just what the early church imposed on him to suit their purposes. Nor should we make a sharp division between the Gospels and the epistles, between Jesus and Paul, or between the historical Jesus and the "Christ of faith."

When Christians are criticized for failing to recognize that the New Testament has different Christologies, we must ask: What precisely is meant by different Christologies? Is the essence of Christ changed by the differing Christologies? Or is the essence of Christ presented differently in varied cultural contexts? Christology in the New Testament clearly varies according to cultural situations because Jesus is translatable in each culture. But all Christologies must be rooted in the biblical witness. Otherwise, we interpret Jesus for our own purposes. Contextualization of Christ must not discount his essential person and work.

Summary Perspectives on Clarifying Christology

How shall we respond to Christologies that we consider problematic? A fundamental issue in Christology concerns the relationship of God's presence in Christ with God's presence in the rest of the world. We believe Christ is the fullest expression of the salvific will of God in human history. Commitment to Jesus Christ need not be an obstacle to understanding other religions.

Chris Wright appropriately says, "Christian theology of other religions cannot really change to a more all-embracing stance without a corresponding change in the understanding of Jesus."[17] The uniqueness of Jesus remains at the heart of the debate with other religions. When we ask what we think of other faiths, we also ask what we think of Christ. Disputes in church history concerning Christology confirm this dynamic. Whenever the person and work of Christ recede in our consciousness or are not explicit in our theology, we easily succumb to a theological pluralism which either diminishes or redefines Christ. We need to articulate in fresh ways a Christology that responds biblically to the challenge presented by other religions. And preoccupation with a faithful Christology must be matched with our resolve to follow Christ.

Relationship of Christ and the Spirit

Trinity

A theology of religions must take seriously the mystery of the Trinity. An understanding of the Trinity guards against a theocentrism which diminishes the place of Christ, or against a "Jesus-ology" or "Christomonism" which neglects the place of God and the Spirit. According to the Bible, God is manifest through Christ and the Spirit. Therefore, we cannot satisfactorily speak of the Father without the story of Jesus; the Father is revealed in the Son. The Spirit discloses the riches of the mystery of God and illuminates the Son. The doctrine of the Trinity helps us understand God's rule over the whole world; God who is active in creation and history is also involved in the lives of each human being. It should not surprise us if God works either providentially outside of religious structures or within them. It is not our task to determine where God is not.

Spirit

Like the Logos of God, the Spirit of God is involved in cosmic revelation. God's Spirit broods over all creation and history (Gen.1:2; Ps. 33:6; 104:30; Job 27:3; 34:14-15) and impacts the religious quest. Though the Spirit works specifically in the church, the Spirit also works in the cosmos outside the church. The church cannot limit the work of the Spirit, for the Spirit is not the property of the church. But whether the Spirit works in the church or outside the church, the work of the Spirit is not in contradiction to the Father and the Son.

Since none of us knows all the ways of the Spirit, we need to be aware of the mysterious working of the Spirit and be open to the surprise of the Spirit. The Spirit acts and speaks beyond the areas where Jesus has been known or named. The Spirit may be at work in other religions, either through aspects of the religious tradition or in people's lives in spite of their tradition. God through the Spirit was drawing Cornelius to faith (Acts 10). Similarly, without our knowing it, God through the Spirit can lead men and women to the gospel. Genuine search for God, pleas for forgiveness, and abandonment of oneself to God's mercy within other religions—all these actions may be evidence of the Spirit's work.

I am impressed with many testimonies I have heard of people in other religious traditions who were drawn to Jesus Christ in dreams, visions, or divine appearances (significant in Muslim societies). Sometimes we meet people who had no knowledge of the gospel but who long for God, or who have light we cannot explain except to conclude that the "breath of God" is free to blow wherever it chooses (John 3:8). God through the Spirit has prepared people for the gospel, guiding them toward the light. When Philip contacted the Ethiopian official, he found the Spirit had already been at work preparing the way for his teaching ministry (Acts 8:26-35). Often when people make a decision for Christ, they recognize that it was Christ who was drawing them to himself through the Spirit. When we see the Spirit working outside the church, we should not simply say "Hallelujah" and leave it to God. As we witness, we should link the work of the Spirit to Jesus Christ.

The Spirit not only works beyond the church; the Spirit also works through the church. The Spirit guides and empowers the church in its witness and anticipates the church's witness. Peter declared, "We are witnesses to these things, and so is the Holy Spirit" (Acts 5:32). We discover that the Spirit works with the church, ahead of the church, and in spite of the church. The Spirit prepares human hearts for the grace provided by Christ; through the Holy Spirit, people come to faith.

Christ and the Spirit

While there is much about the Spirit that we do not understand, we should remember that the Spirit has a close identification with God and Christ (John 16:12-15). God works through the Spirit to renew and revitalize what God has done in Christ, and the Spirit centers on Christ. Because there is a general work of the Spirit and the focused work of Christ, the cosmic influence of the Spirit and the universal activity of the risen Christ must be kept together. We must recognize reciprocity between Christ and the Spirit, not separation. What the Spirit does is not in contradiction to what is revealed in the crucified and risen Christ. Christ is present in the person of the Spirit; the Holy Spirit is the Spirit of Jesus, pointing to Jesus and his teaching (John 14:18, 26).

The Spirit convinces the world of sin, righteousness, and judgment on the basis of what God has done in Christ (John 16:8-11). The Spirit of truth is the guide to truth, as the Spirit glorifies Christ (John 16:13-14). The Spirit bears witness to the Son and inspires the confession of Christ (1 John 4:2-3). As Paul says, "No one can say 'Jesus is Lord' except by the Holy Spirit" (1 Cor. 12:3). The function of the Spirit is to continue the work of Christ, to fulfill and extend his mission. The Bible emphasizes the renewing power of God's Spirit as the Spirit works in the world, moving people in a Godward and Christward direction. The Spirit unites human beings to Christ and creates new community (1 Cor. 3:16-17; Eph. 2:21-22).

Since we know about the tendency to stress the independent work of the Spirit, separated from Christ and the church, we need to be discerning about the work of the Spirit. The Spirit is freely at work outside the church. It is important to keep our eyes open for evidences of God's Spirit at work in the world and link such activity with Christ and the church. When we separate the Spirit from Christ, we are in a precarious position, for some confuse the Spirit with other spirits. Just as the Logos should not be separated from the incarnate Jesus, the Spirit should not be separated from Jesus Christ. The Spirit is recognized and tested by the Spirit's witness to Jesus and conformity to Jesus' teaching (John 16:13-14). We can be sure that God, Christ, and the Spirit do not act independently of each other but as a unity.

Trinitarian theology can assist us in probing the relationship between the particular and the plural and widen our horizons to premessianic occurrences of God's grace in other religions, but it should not displace witness to the normativeness of Christ. Carl Braaten reminds us, "The church does not move God around the world; God moves the church around the world through the ongoing activities of the three persons of the Trinity."[18]

9

Witness to Christ

Several years ago when I was teaching in Elderhostel (international noncredit program for seniors) at Eastern Mennonite College (now University), a lively religious debate emerged among the participants. In the midst of the discussion, a Jewish man (not a believer in Jesus) declared, "Well, I've read the New Testament, and it's clear the New Testament wants people to believe in Jesus."

I was surprised and somewhat puzzled. Had I heard correctly? He was right, of course, the New Testament wants people to believe in Jesus. But I was surprised by his willingness to admit that. Regrettably, I've met Christians who are less sure that the New Testament recommends Jesus for all people.

Called to Witness

Since the New Testament wants people to believe in Jesus, Christians have the opportunity to make Jesus known. Past failures or poor performance in witness should not cause us to forfeit the privilege of witness. Rather, the task is to share faith appropriately in ways that are neither triumphalistic nor relativistic. New Testament theology is a theology of witness.

Faith results in witness. "We declare to you what we have seen and heard" (1 John 1:3). Faith is to be shared; it is not a deposit to be placed in a bank or buried. Lesslie Newbigin writes, "The mystery of the gospel is not entrusted to the church to be buried in the ground. It is entrusted to the church in order to be risked in the change and interchange of the spiritual commerce of humanity."[1] If we wholly embrace faith, that must include sharing faith. Christian faith is not a solitary religion; others should be invited to participate in it. If it is not true for others, it is not true for us. Kenneth Cragg doubts that conviction is honest if not honestly commended.[2]

Witness is a response of love rooted in the nature of Christ and the gospel. Christ has instilled an indebtedness in the hearts of those who love him. Christ offers love to us, and we in love commend love to others.

Christ reveals the love of God in caring compassion, in the creative power of God in healing and peacemaking, and in the holiness of God in exposing sin and offering forgiveness. Stephen Neill notes, "In Jesus Christ the turning of God towards the human race, and the turning of the human race towards God, have perfectly met."[3] Christ offers grace, forgiveness, and peace. No other religion offers redemption and reconciliation through the death of an incarnate God. We witness to the passion (cross) of Christ with the patience of Christ, not by winning religious arguments.

Christians point to Jesus Christ as the clue to salvation, believing that in Christ we have been shown the road. But this is not a private matter that we keep to ourselves; it concerns all humanity. We want to share with fellow pilgrims the vision given to us concerning the route that leads to salvation.

Witness to Jesus Christ is not *against* religion but *for* people. That which we share we have received as a gift and offer as a gift. The one who has given the gift to us longs to give others the same gift.

We witness with certainty, but our confession should not assume an apologetic form that denigrates others. The tone of witness must commend faith. Definitions of faith must give way to discovery of faith; people must be permitted to discover the finality and normativeness of Christ.

We may have been conditioned to think that Jesus and the gospel are not attractive. Familiarity seems to have robbed us of the freshness of the gospel. Yet when we witness we discover that people are searching and that what Jesus offers is attractive as it meets their needs. Kenneth Cragg asserts, "What is given in revelation coincides deeply with what is longed for in the soul."[4] We should not assume that everyone is satisfied with their religion. Is it too much to assume that if Jesus is lifted up he will draw people to himself (John 12:32)?

I have been awed by persons from other religious traditions who are willing to take a fresh look at Jesus. It is unfortunate when Christians equivocate about Jesus while others are being attracted to him. I have friends in Ethiopia, persons from Muslim background, who have been drawn to Jesus because he has responded to the longing of their soul. A colleague of mine converted to Christ from Islam and spent more than four years in prison. He said, "If I had been able to see in a vision all that has happened, I would still affirm that it is worth being a Christian. The love Christ expressed in his incarnation and death is so significant that anything required of us is not too costly."

If Jesus Christ is the way for all people, the church needs to be a beacon of hope bearing witness to the world. Will the church provide a message of hope or be a victim of relativistic pluralism? If the church becomes an institution of accommodation rather than a bearer of witness, the gospel will be anesthetized.[5] J. Verkuyl, a missiologist from the Netherlands, writes, "Rather than extinguishing the fire, a theology of religions ought to do precisely the opposite. Any view which tends to justify Christian inactivity and paralyze the church's missionary endeavor is doing a disservice to both theology and the church."[6]

The gospel is not universally successful, but we should seek to make it universally accessible. We do not know the result of witness; we can only anticipate the unexpected, the surprises. Since the success of witness is not measured by numerical response, the result of witness must be left to God. We sow the seed and nurture the plants. The harvest is God's.

Confidence in Christ

We find in Christ the most compelling clue to God's purpose in history. We can find no one who is greater or more inclusive than Jesus Christ. If he claimed to be "the way, and the truth, and the life" (John 14:6), are we to accuse him of arrogance? Did the New Testament make a mistake by attributing such a statement to Jesus? Are we to create our own picture of Jesus and ignore the New Testament? The claims Jesus made for himself or which are attributed to him are not ours to deny. Jesus has not vacated the center of history, so let us not ignore him or seek to remove him.

Some claim that our belief in Jesus is a culturally conditioned faith commitment. However, if they deny the uniqueness of Jesus and suggest that all religions are variants of one central experience, they also hold a culturally conditioned faith commitment. Some want values such as justice, compassion, mercy, love, and unity. However, they accept these abstractly rather than as personal qualities modeled and taught by one who lived a concrete life in history. Such views are also culturally conditioned.

When Jesus is the norm, all other claims are relativized. We are not consistent if we claim the normativeness of Christ for Christians but not for all people. By claiming that Jesus is the norm, we stand with the historic claim made by Christians of all ages.

The normativeness of Christ is not based on our experience but upon God's revelation recorded in Scripture. Only by regaining confidence in the authoritative witness of Scripture to Christ can we challenge assumptions of any culture. The Bible has a vision for the world from creation to consummation. At the heart of that story is the incarnation, ministry, death, and resurrection of Jesus. That story has universal implications for human history.

It is important to try to understand the biblical message in light of modern (and postmodern) thought, but we must be careful that such thought not become the final authority. Attempts to make the gospel compatible with contemporary thought can distort the church's witness and credibility. We need, rather, to give more attention to understanding current thought in light of the biblical story and conform our thinking to the message of the New Testament.

Jesus did not fit completely into any of the categories of his day. Jesus Christ was God's personal message to humankind; he was more than a vague religious idealism. The gospel is primarily concerned with this person, not only principles. The church must ground its existence solely in Jesus Christ. "Apart from the person of Christ the church has no existence, apart from the message of Christ the church has no proclamation, apart from the call of Christ the church has no mission."[7]

Have Christians in the name of modernity or postmodernity given up the uniqueness of Jesus Christ by reducing him to one of the cultural options? Pluralism is not a new challenge to Christian faith. The New Testament was formed in the context of many religions and philosophies. The church in the first centuries faced other religious options. The Pantheon in Rome symbolized many gods and goddesses. Christ would have been welcome there, but Christians refused to compromise their faith. The early church chose instead to go into the world of religious diversity and call people to decide about Jesus Christ.

Who is Jesus of Nazareth? How do we name him? It is the task of the church to answer these questions by modeling and declaring the fullness of Christ. Unfortunately, the church has often confused the answer to these questions by recruiting Jesus for its needs and causes. The gospel of Jesus Christ includes atonement, reconciliation, healing, guidance, intercession, power, ethics, peace, justice, and human rights.

However, the center of the gospel is none of these. The center is Jesus Christ. Subordinate aspects of the gospel can easily be co-opted by ideological systems. Our commitment is not to a program but to Jesus. There is a profound difference between commitment to a cause and commitment to a person. Causes become ideological. Christian acts of liberation point to the Liberator; acts of justice point to the Just One. We need to relinquish our tendency to domesticate or manipulate Jesus. Carl Braaten reminds us, "Christology becomes so much clay that we model to make Jesus look like ourselves."[8]

Christ and Truth in Other Religions

Our task is to witness to Christ as the center of our faith, even when we don't recognize with total certainty where all the boundaries between faith and unfaith are. But when Christ is the center, there is a criterion for discovering what is genuine in other faiths. And we can be confident that Christ is the one who evaluates all the phenomena of religion (including historic Christianity) and of antireligion.

Multidimensional Aspects of Religion

Christians have varied opinions about the truth of other religions in relation to Christ. Some have suggested that religions are wholly false, and that Christians have nothing to learn from them. Others consider religions the work of the devil. For them, any similarities are demonic deception. Still others argue that religions, by revealing the deep longing of the human spirit, are preparations for Christ. Some focus on the values of other religions, such as Islam's emphasis on the majesty of God, Buddha's deep sympathy for the world's sorrow, Hinduism's desire to contact ultimate reality, and Confucius' preoccupation with the moral order of the universe.[9]

In chapter 7 we discussed positive and negative aspects of religion. This leads us to consider religions as multidimensional. Humans seek truth, attempt to explain the phenomena of life, reach out to ultimate reality, or construct systems of thought, behavior, and observance in an attempt to satisfy human need. But religion can also distort truth through blindness, unbelief, sin, and pride. Religions are God-seeking and self-seeking, prompted by both good and bad inclinations. Religions respond to supernatural impulses from God and are tempted by Satan the deceiver, who can appear as an angel of light even in religion—or perhaps especially in religion.

Evaluating Other Religions

Our evaluation of other religions impacts our attitudes and actions. We often react with defensiveness and fear when religions deny basic Christian understandings, such as claiming that Jesus is not God, Jesus did not die on the cross, a savior is not needed, or the Trinity is not true. And when threatened or afraid, we are too quick to call the whole system demonic. While some aspects of other religions, including expressions of Christianity, may be demonic, it is not helpful to label everything demonic. On the other hand, by idealizing other religions, some persons lose the significance of Christ.

We need to balance the negative and positive expressions of religion by holding in tension the two extremes, what is demonic and what is true. If we regard everything in religion positively, we ignore omissions, falsehood, and the demonic. If we dismiss other religions as totally demonic, we do not account for what is true in other faiths. In each religious system, there is a combination of evil and good, ugliness and beauty, untruth and truth.

We should gladly acknowledge the search for truth, rays of truth, or seeds of truth in other religions, evident in goodness, beauty, spirituality, and self-sacrifice. There are words and signs in other religions which Barth called "parables of the kingdom." We need not reject anything that is true. When light is already present, we focus it; we do not deny it.

However, the amount of emphasis put on seeds of truth is a significant issue because truth is often mixed with untruth. We welcome all the signs of God's grace in the lives of those who don't confess Jesus as Lord. Yet while some aspects of religions are a preparation for the gospel, other aspects are judged by the gospel. There are stepping stones and bridges, but there are also contradictions to Christ. We need to distinguish between seeking and finding in other religions. Where there is goodness, we agree with Thomas Aquinas that "grace does not annul nature but perfects it." The presence of truth in other religions calls us to relate that truth to Jesus; it does not negate the necessity of witness. Moral achievement and devotion are present in other religions. Truth in other religions is a manifestation of God's activity but is not an alternate way of salvation.

When we speak of God being manifest in other religions, we need to be more precise. Not all beliefs and practices manifest God. In what aspects of religion is God manifest? God is most fully revealed in Christ. By starting there, we open our eyes to see God's manifestation in other religions. God may also be manifest among non-religious people who have struggled against religion to promote humane values. Religious people are not necessarily more likely to touch the reality of God. In the New Testament, religious people were often the most blind. We must therefore be alert to blindness and untruth in religion. When religion denies aspects of God's revelation in Christ, it is not a manifestation of God. Speaking in general terms about God's presence can often be more sentimental than discerning.

As a reaction to the past, when negative aspects of religions were emphasized, recently there has been more overidealizing of religions. Past misunderstandings should not cause us to go to the opposite extreme of "canonizing" religions by focusing only on the good. If we were uncritically negative before, we should not be uncritically positive now. Our acquaintance with morally upright people in other religions is something to be highly valued. But that should not lead us to an unbiblical optimism about other faiths. The presence of evil in religion calls for careful analysis and discernment. When there is error, corruption, destruction, and deception, it must be exposed.

At the same time, since there are positive aspects in religion, we should not be totally negative. While religious systems are not a means of salvation, if we listen and observe carefully, we discover signals of God's activity in the human religious quest. In sacred books and religious practices, among monks and mystics, there are sayings and attitudes that surprise us. Religions are not simply unrelieved error and blindness. Everywhere God is known in part. Even in its most degraded forms, religion is evidence that God has not abandoned humankind and that awareness of God remains in human consciousness. Other religions sometimes correct our misunderstandings, blindness, and unfaithfulness. There are truths in other religions from which we can learn. Such truth provides a frame of reference into which the gospel penetrates. We should not exaggerate the worst nor the best in other religions, but let Christ be the final judge. Our task as bearers of the gospel is to identify where people are fleeing from God or searching for God, and then bear witness to Jesus Christ.

Religion and the Truth in Jesus

The truth of Christian faith casts a shadow on truth claims of other religions. Christ is confessed as truth, not as one option among many. Jesus as the norm for truth makes relative all other truth claims. If Jesus is the decisive manifestation within history and the most compelling clue to history, we need to understand his claim more fully. To hold that Jesus is the truth need not be arrogant; rather, it is the bulwark against the arrogance of every culture to provide its own criteria by which others are judged. Jesus as the truth rejected the arrogance of power; his power was manifest in weakness and suffering.[10]

Jesus is the way, the truth, and the life, but this does not deny the reality of the knowledge of God that people had before Jesus came, or the true knowledge which people have today where he has not been named. Jesus is the fullest manifestation of truth, but truth present in other places is not excluded. How can we affirm the ethical and spiritual truths in other religions while maintaining our conviction concerning Jesus Christ?

As Christians we applaud the search for truth. We also affirm that Jesus Christ is the truth. This stance does not mean that we know all the truth found in Christ, or that other religions bear no relation to the truth in Christ. But revelation in Christ is the norm by which truth found in other religions is evaluated. When we say that all truth is defined by Christ, we do not say that all truth is confined to him. All truth comes from God, but Christ is the personal embodiment of truth. Heim suggests, "Not all truth is given in Christ but, as the New Testament says, all truth hangs together in Christ."[11]

We must know enough about the truth in Christ to discern what is true and untrue in other religious systems. Religions are sometimes right in recognizing symptoms of the human problem but wrong in their prescribed remedy. For example, most religions assume that some kind of salvation is needed, but they vary widely in their understanding of salvation. Reconciliation at God's initiative is not known in most religions. This fact illustrates variety in the elements of truth found in religions.

In testing the truth in other religions with the truth in Christ, we must be careful that we are not simply comparing abstract religious ideas. It is misleading to detach ideas from the living experience that gives rise to them, because faith is experienced as a whole. Doctrines are conditioned and limited by the rest of the religious system. Since each religious system is a unit, parts lose their meaning when separated from the whole. Different religions turn on different axes. The questions which Hindus ask may not be the ones with which the gospel is primarily concerned. No two religious systems ask precisely the same ultimate questions, nor do their answers occupy the same proportionate importance within the whole. Thus Buddhists are not concerned for sin, Hindus are disinterested in eschatology, and primal religions are preoccupied with security.

Religious movements are not static but constantly changing. Is it possible that the God who is revealed in Jesus Christ is hiddenly at work in the religions? Does the kingdom of God impact other religions? The kingdom of God should not be equated with religious movements. Yet values of the kingdom sometimes seem to be present in other religions. Perhaps God is drawing individuals or groups within religions, or is directing and shaping changes in religions. As people are drawn in new ways toward God, their religious complexes may be refashioned to express something new.[12] Verkuyl believes that since the cross and resurrection have cosmic dimensions, we can expect signs of the kingdom in religious life outside the church.[13]

As God builds up the kingdom through the church or independent of the church, we may discover that other religions are practicing some of the same values of the kingdom: love, justice, freedom, peace, hope. But kingdom theology should not be equated with the best in world religions, nor should we use the presence of the kingdom of God to argue that witness in the name of Jesus is unnecessary. Jesus' contemporaries had a knowledge of God's mighty acts and were waiting for the kingdom of God. Yet when it came among them, they did not recognize it. Even the presence of the kingdom does not guarantee that those who observe it will be redeemed. They need to be specifically challenged to believe and follow Jesus Christ. Where Jesus is acknowledged, there the kingdom of God has come. It is not the lordship of some hidden and mystical Christ-principle which constitutes the kingdom of God. Instead, the lordship of the historical Jesus brings the kingdom (Acts 8:12; 28:23, 31).

Clark Pinnock insists that if Christ can transform culture (e.g., abolition of slavery, civil rights movement, demise of the Soviet Union), he can transform religious dimensions as well. He does this through his confrontation with the invisible spiritual forces (1 Cor. 15:24-46; Eph. 1:20-22; 2:1-2; 6:12; Col. 1:16; 2:15). Pinnock believes we are now in the midst of a cosmic struggle involving social, political, and religious dimensions. He says that Jesus Christ, who is Lord over all powers, including other spiritual powers, can challenge other religions.[14]

Within major world religions are movements like Sufi Islam, Bhakti Hinduism, and Amida Buddhism—movements which emphasize more personal aspects of God, themes somewhat similar to Christian faith. In addition to specific groupings within religions or changing religious movements, there are reflective individuals within other religious traditions who are drawn or pushed beyond their religious boundaries.

The history of Christian mission is replete with stories of individuals having a pre-Christian understanding who nonetheless sought God with a clearer vision of the light than their contemporaries had. A Chinese youth in Indonesia refused to dust the household idols because they didn't answer prayers. An Indonesian leader realized his charms and fetishes were the creation of his own hands and began to worship the God who created his hands. An African leader in Burkina Faso reported that God told him to put away his fetishes and wait for a message instructing him in the true way. In Laos, a female shaman prophesied about the coming of a messenger who would tell them of the true God.[15]

An Ethiopian friend reported to me that his mother had taken him to a Muslim witch doctor when he was ill. The witch doctor told her that her boy could only be healed by Jesus Christ. He asked me, "How could the Muslim witch doctor know that?" One could list many other examples of people within other religious traditions who, because of unmet needs or intense search, have through visions and dreams been drawn unknowingly toward Christ.

Christians should understand other religious systems but also be alert to shifts within religions and to adherents of those religions who are asking questions not posed by their religion. This calls for perception but also for confession of the truth. There need be no dichotomy between confession of Christ and truth-seeking. We believe God's truth cannot be divorced from Christ, but we also believe no religion is without truth. We don't "possess" Christ; he "possesses" us. We possess faith but never fully embody the truth. By faith we seek to understand and appropriate the truth and confess that Christ is the truth.

By insisting on the truth in Christ, we should not over-personalize or privatize our conception of religious truth. Truth in Christ insists that piety and discipleship are one. Truth must be believed and obeyed. As disciples, we concern ourselves with knowing, experiencing, and doing the truth. We grasp the truth as we follow Christ in life. Truth in theology must be balanced with truth in community.

The task of Christian mission is to interact with other religions so there can be an encounter with the Christian message. We know that God is always working above and beyond us, that the Logos is already active, and that the Spirit is working in the hearts of people prior to their hearing the good news. Such knowledge should motivate and encourage us. We can expect to find religious elements which anticipate the gospel of truth. Those who confess Jesus Christ have come from a variety of religious paths, but those paths have converged toward the way that leads to the one destination. Some have come from within their religious tradition as they moved toward a more personal understanding of God, while others have been drawn to Christ as they grasped more fully the significance of the gospel.

Truth found in Christ offers a quality of salvation which can be found nowhere else. When people receive Christ, they count their former values as "loss" or "rubbish" (Phil. 3:8). The point is not that those values are inauthentic, but that they are inadequate for salvation. Conversion to the truth in Christ brings a reorientation and purification of the spiritual and moral values present in other religions. It does not lead to the denial of any valid truth. New values are substituted for that which was error, but suppression of the former values is not total.

We must not regard followers of religions as enemies of the gospel. Our task is not to negate everything in their religion but to witness to Christ in such a way that their quest is answered by the gospel. We are concerned for how God is providentially preparing adherents of other religions to encounter Jesus, even beyond the boundaries of the church, and preparing the way for persons to receive him. If we believe that God's providence can work redemptively in other religions, that belief provides incentive to witness to Christ so that he can be acknowledged.

Lesslie Newbigin reminds us that the presence and work of Jesus is not confined to where he is acknowledged. There is light and there is darkness, but the light continues to shine in the darkness. There is something wrong when Christians think they need to belittle the manifest presence of light in those who do not openly acknowledge Jesus. Christians are wise not to major in pointing out the weakness in another religion and think thereby to commend the gospel.[16] Our task is to bear witness to the light and thus to commend the gospel.

Cultural Pluralism and Contextualization
Cultural Pluralism in the New Testament
Cultural pluralism welcomes different cultures as an enrichment to life. No culture is by definition considered superior or inferior to another. Neither does the Bible absolutize any culture as though one were inferior or superior to another. The Bible does, however, reject an uncritical acceptance of all cultural or religious values. The New Testament insists that the God revealed in Jesus Christ is for all cul-

tures and all people. The New Testament models respectful integrity in evangelism to other cultures and religions; its engagement is constructive and corrective.

After the resurrection Jesus told his disciples, "Repentance and forgiveness of sins is to be proclaimed in [my] name to all nations, beginning from Jerusalem" (Luke 24:47). Before Jesus ascended, his disciples asked him, "Lord, is this the time when you will restore the kingdom to Israel?" Jesus internationalized their understanding of the kingdom by replying, "You will receive power when the Holy Spirit has come upon you; and you will be my witnesses in Jerusalem, in all Judea and Samaria, and to the ends of the earth" (Acts 1:6, 8).

At Pentecost persons from "every nation under heaven" heard in their own language praise for "God's deeds of power" through Jesus (Acts 2:6, 11, 22). There were Jews from Palestine, Jews from the diaspora, and Jewish proselytes (2:5-13). The many tongues became channels for a word from God at Pentecost and thus affirmed God's acceptance of all cultures within the plan of salvation through Jesus Christ. Pentecost broke decisively from monoculturalism by affirming cultural pluralism for the church. The Jerusalem fellowship included Palestinian Jews (Hebrews) and Hellenistic Jews (6:1).

Stephen, a Hellenistic Jew, understood that the new Israel was to include all nations and could not be bound by Jewish cultural institutions, such as law and temple (Acts 6:13; 7:47-53). His life, teaching, and death were a door through which the gospel would spread to other cultures. Philip, a Hellenistic Jew, took the gospel to Samaria (8:4-25) and later introduced an Ethiopian (perhaps a proselyte or God-fearer) to Christ (8:26-40). In Acts 9, Saul, a diaspora Jew, was converted and commissioned to carry the gospel to the Gentiles.

Peter, while at Joppa (a Jewish city), was called to go to Caesarea (a Gentile city) to lead Cornelius (a Roman God-fearer nurtured in Judaism) and other Gentiles to Christ (Acts 9:36—11:18). Through Cornelius, Peter learned that God shows no partiality but is interested in all people (10:34-35). Peter was accused not only of taking the gospel to Gentiles but of violating Jewish law. But in the church Jewish culture had to give way to the impartiality of God; there could be no cultural exclusion.

Meanwhile, many followers of Jesus fled Jerusalem because of the persecution after Stephen's death. They traveled to Phoenicia, Cyprus, and Antioch to speak the word to diaspora Jews. But some who fled, followers from Cyprus and North Africa, spoke the word to Hellenists in Antioch. Later the church at Jerusalem sent Barnabas, who with Paul nurtured the believers in Antioch (Acts 11:19-26).

The church at Antioch was multicultural (Acts 13:1). It was this culturally plural church which sent Paul and Barnabas to the Gentiles. Their action represented a crucial break from Jewish cultural control. From Antioch, the gospel was carried to cities and provinces of the Roman empire, in Asia Minor, Europe, and Rome. The identity of the early missionary community was essentially Jewish, but the transition from Jewish to Gentile mission was part of the essence of the gospel.

Later, the Jerusalem Conference (Acts 15) formally recognized the acceptance of cultural pluralism within the church by acknowledging that Jews and Gentiles could have equal status in the church. The church learned that Gentiles as Gentiles, not just as Jewish proselytes, were to be part of the new community. But this was not without difficulty. The emergence of the Gentile church produced profound theological discussions. Tension over the status of Jewish cultural roots erupted because the Gentile breakthrough had cast a shadow over any claims for Jewish cultural absolutism.

The Bible models a radical pluralism by relativizing all cultures. The tension between Jewish cultural absolutism in the Jerusalem church and the Gentile breakthrough at Antioch gave way to cultural pluralism. This shows that God is sovereign over Jewish and Gentile culture. The Gentile breakthrough demonstrated that the gospel reinforces cultural pluralism. A new cross-cultural perspective was created as Christianity breached the Jewish walls and swept into the Gentile world. The gospel accepted Gentiles without excluding Jews; it couldn't be yoked to any one culture. Christianity relinquished Jerusalem as the geographical center of the new religion and developed new centers. There was no one cultural center but a multiple frontier, with God at the center.

The early church, by straddling the Jewish and Gentile worlds, is a paradigm for the church's missionary expansion. The Spirit was the actor, as illustrated by the surprise of human agents in that mission. The movements of God's Spirit were signs that Jesus is Lord of all. The church was becoming a home for people of all nations and a sign of the potential unity of all humankind.

Cultural Pluralism and Translatabilty of the Gospel

Cultural pluralism arises from God's faithfulness to all people. As the church's missionary journey reaches to all the cultures, fresh insights and new treasures are brought into the life of the church. The church in multicultural form is a home for people of all nations and a foretaste of the unity of humankind. The church affirms cultural pluralism with the conviction that the whole world needs to know who Jesus is.

Lamin Sanneh insists that the genius of the gospel, its birthright, is that it is translatable.[17] He contrasts the Bible, translated into hundreds of languages, with the Quran, considered most authentic in the original Arabic. Translation of the Bible assumes versatility as the gospel is expressed in indigenous cultures. The essence of the gospel becomes concrete in each culture; it is culturally and historically specific. This universality and particularity of the gospel assumes and fosters cultural pluralism. By assuming local rootedness and by moving beyond each localism, the gospel promotes cultural pluralism and creates worldwide multicultural fellowships. One Christ is confessed in many cultures.

Sanneh claims that Christian faith relativized its Jewish roots and destigmatized Gentile culture. God doesn't consider certain cultures inferior or untouchable; all are worthy of hearing the truth of the gospel. This is radical cultural pluralism, a pluralism which accepts the nonabsolute character and coequality of culture.

Since the gospel is translatable, it can be at home and flourish in a variety of cultures. The gospel does not destroy authentic values of culture but reorients them toward Christ. Christian witness seeks new forms for traditional content and makes fresh attempts to respond relevantly to the issues and questions raised in each culture.

Gospel Affirms and Critiques Culture

While the gospel affirms culture, it also critiques culture. Humans are in God's image but also fallen. They create culture which reflects image-of-Godness as well as fallenness. Since God does not accept all elements of human culture, we need to find our way between judgment of culture and accommodation to culture.

In the past, judgment was often excessive. But we must also be wary of too much accommodation, which holds Christ captive. We understand the gospel through our culture, but we must also understand our culture through the gospel. The gospel must never be completely domesticated; it transforms. Faith must retain its strangeness, its power to question us. Because the gospel is supracultural and supranational, it is the norm by which all cultures are relativized.

Christian faith has the stamp of culture upon it, but it must also speak a prophetic word to culture. God is accessible in our specific cultures, but God must not be captive to our culture. God's interests are greater than our particular cultural interests. Since Christ and culture are in tension, Christ must never be merged with culture. Sometimes the gospel renews culture; other times it uproots it. Christians are often too critical of culture or not critical enough of culture.

Witness to other religions, which takes us beyond our secure walls to encounter other beliefs, involves risks, but risk is preferable to inaction. We should be guided by the early church, which in absorbing powerful intellectual and cultural elements from Greek and Roman cultures, needed to decide whether to resist or to selectively accommodate. Fortunately, the gospel which translates so naturally into culture also has a tradition of prophetic critique.

Contextualization

Contextualization (inculturation) is the process by which God's word is applied to concrete situations in ways relevant to the culture. When the gospel is addressed to human beings who share a common language, customs, or religion, it must communicate truth in the language and symbols meaningful to the culture. But the gospel must be gospel and not merely a product shaped by culture. Some formulations of the gospel portray the culture more than the gospel. Jesus cannot only be tailored to the particular cultural ideal; he is larger than any cultural formulation. Jesus must be permitted to address the total context in which people live.

The Bible itself is a multicultural and contextual document: the events, times, places, and people are shaped by specific cultures. Hebrew culture or Greek culture is not the ideal culture for Christian faith, though Arab culture is regarded as ideal for Islam. Since there is no universal pattern for personal and social behavior as in Islam, each community must express the fruit of the gospel in its own cultural forms. For this task Scripture translation is indispensable, so each culture can discover fresh insights. Some parts of the Bible will be more meaningful in specific cultures. Yet the Bible is a normative account of God's action which is universally valid.

As the gospel encounters each culture and religion afresh, some of the most critical issues in theology emerge. A crucial issue is the relationship between religion and culture, because in some sense religion is an expression of culture. Since culture and religion are so closely intertwined, we need as much as possible to differentiate between what is a cultural or a religious value, and what is a cultural or religious impediment to belief.

Some will reject Christ because he conflicts with their religious values. However, it is regrettable if persons reject Christ because of the church's cultural insensitivity. John Mbiti, an African Christian theologian, criticized those who insisted on "cultural circumcision" as part of accepting Christian faith. On the other hand, Arab Christians describe much of their culture as Islamic and live comfortably with most of it. Repentance and conversion to Christ involves a transfer of religious allegiance but need not result in complete separation from one's sociocultural world.

Cultures should not be destroyed in the process of introducing Christian faith. Christian faith has a *mission to culture*; sometimes it is *against culture*. But in its dependence upon language and custom, it is also a *debtor to culture*. Cultural forms and some religious forms can be reshaped to express the gospel. There will be different cultural incarnations of the faith as Christ takes form in varied cultural expressions. The "Salvation Today" conference at Bangkok in 1973 stated, "Culture shapes the human voice that answers the voice of Christ."[18]

Contextualization and "Inreligionization"

Recently it has been proposed that we should not only work for inculturation (contextualization) but also for "inreligionization,"[19] an engagement of Christian faith with other religions whereby elements in other religions are incorporated into Christian faith. Because Christian concepts can be translated into the language of non-Christian peoples, we assume there is some continuity between Christian faith and other religions. And since the Holy Spirit is working in all cultures preparing people for the gospel, we can expect that in all cultures there are "truth paradigms," signs pointing toward the gospel.

C. S. Song argues that Christian faith in relation to other religions should result in *enfleshment*, not *disembodiment*.[20] Those who become Christian don't leave everything behind. Their being, thinking, and living may contain much that comes from God and can be reoriented toward Christ. For instance, divine transcendence in Islam is not denied but conditioned by the incarnation. Aspects of divine immanence in Hinduism can be affirmed but need correction by the transcendent sovereignty of God.

The New Testament records the encounter of the gospel with religiously plural contexts. In that encounter, the name for God in the New Testament is *theos*, taken from the Greek religious environment and filled with new meaning. Some words and titles for Jesus were taken from Jewish, Greek, and Roman religions. The apostles, attempting to understand the philosophical and religious worldview into which they were communicating, quoted Greek poets, prophets, and philosophers (Acts 17:22-31; Titus 1:12). Paul in his letter to the Colossians adapted his vocabulary to the thought forms of Greco-Roman religious culture, using terms such as *fullness, knowledge, wisdom;* but he introduced new content compatible with the gospel.

Christians must give more attention to how they communicate divine sonship to Jews and Muslims, or monotheism to Chinese who emphasize either impersonal heaven or popular polytheism, but have little understanding of one high God. How does one speak of sin and repentance, or of justification by faith and sanctification, when addressing morally upright Chinese and Japanese who believe in the inherent goodness of nature, humans, and ancestors?

We need to introduce Christ to others in a way that is faithful to Scripture and sensitive to each particular context. Christians should be able to witness to the grace of Jesus Christ in the context of hints of grace in Pure Land Buddhism. In Thailand, where spiritism is very present, I was told that Christian faith must deal more with animistic and spiritualistic concerns. At Varanasi in India, a sacred site on the Ganges River for Hindu pilgrims, a Christian told me that Hindus who read the Bible discover they need no longer search for God because God is searching for them, and in this they find peace. In Hong Kong, I learned that people are attracted to the church because of the sense of family and community. The story of the prodigal son was important for the Chinese because the father accepted the undeserving son.

Christian faith and the church can be enriched by "possessing" religious forms as vehicles for the gospel, or by developing new forms as "functional substitutes" for those religious forms that must be rejected. Inculturation (contextualization) and inreligionization will have an impact on the names used for God (e.g., Allah for Arabs, Kami for Japan). To the question asked during the Gulf War, "Is Allah of the Muslims the same God as the Christian God?" we can respond confidently, "Allah is the same God but understood differently." Forms of Christian community, the nature of religious leadership, patterns of decision making, methods of nurture, and styles of worship—all these will reflect principles of inculturation and inreligionization.

As the universal gospel becomes dynamically present in local frames of meaning, it is more fully localized and less abstract. But local theologies must not be provincial. The transcendent gospel frees from excessive localism; it de-provincializes. Contextuality and universality should be mutually interdependent. Contextualization is not adequate until it links indigenous culture to a new understanding of universality. It is important for churches to be both local and cross-culturally aware—local so they embody God's particular message, and cross-culturally sensitive to keep them from being swallowed by the culture. When the church's vision of the context-transcending elements of the gospel grows dim and the particular culture assumes control, de-contextualization needs to occur. Contextualization and de-contextualization will be in tension with one another if we are truly in the world yet not of the world.

The church often wants to maintain its own security instead of risking contextualization of the gospel. But as Newbigin said, "True contextualization accords to the gospel its rightful primacy, its power to penetrate every culture and to speak within each culture, in its own speech and symbol, the word which is both No and Yes, both judgment and grace."[21] That happens when the word is embodied in a community which lives the story.

10

Forms of Witness: Church, Presence, Service, Evangelism

In the history of Christian mission, most witness has focused on the more responsive populations. Those areas of the globe where major world religions predominate have tended to remain on the periphery of the church's interest. But with increasing globalization has come greater exposure to the plurality of religions. If we believe the gospel should be communicated in the midst of the world religions, witness is not a question of *whether* but *what* and *how*. The forms of witness should not call the content into question. What forms of witness are appropriate in the context of religious pluralism?

Church as Embodiment of the Gospel

Witness emerges from the character of the church. If witness announces the gospel, the church needs to embody it. The church as the people of God images the kingdom; it is a sign of the kingdom. The church, as sign of the kingdom, has a witness *dimension* and a witness *intention*. The witness dimension characterizes the church's community life. The witness intention is the church's conscious attempt to move beyond its walls in sharing the gospel with the world. Witness dimension attracts seekers to the church; witness intention is the centrifugal movement of the church toward the world.

It is important to keep a dynamic and creative tension between dimension and intention so they nourish and stimulate each other. Intention is only possible as it emerges from dimension, for without dimension, the intention quickly dissipates. Witness dimension is integrally linked with a theology of discipleship. The discipling community is part of the gospel, not additional or peripheral.

In Acts 2 the new life of the community attracted the attention of seekers. Without those characteristics, the spoken message would have been deficient, lacking credibility. Believers are concerned with what the church *is* and *does* as well as with what the church *says*. Through evangelistic declaration, the gospel is *taught*, but that cannot be separated from the community through which the faith is *caught*. There must be no conflict between the Spirit-directed word and the Spirit-embodied community.

It is important for the church to give attention to the character of its presence, recognizing that its presence has often been hollow and ineffective. Many churches are present in the wrong way. Some mouth verbalisms or formulas but lack credibility. Some appear aloof, self-righteous, or phony. Sometimes the church's presence speaks loudly of a reality different from what is proclaimed. Churches can no longer rely on institutional power to make their presence felt. The church must be a Christocentric community.

The church is not only an "ark of salvation" or a "safe haven." It is also for "pilgrim people." The church demonstrates to other religions that it is on the way; it is not itself the goal. In the face of religious plurality, we are called to give up parochialism. We are to be salt and light, not simply withdrawn from encounter with people. The church asks what it should do in the world that the world cannot do for itself. Christian communities should be signs of hope. Community can be part of the attractiveness of the gospel, either because of the absence of community in other religions, or because of the uniqueness of Christian community when compared with other forms of religious community.

The church as a body is important; it is more than a collection of Christian individuals. The church is a community where relationships are prior to ideas or program. The church is a community where Christians live out their convictions. Several aspects of this community are particularly important in the context of other religions.

Messianic Community

The community is a new order under Messiah's rule. As a firstfruit of the messianic movement, it is an instrument for messianic purposes. Its identity and role is in relation to the kingdom. While the church is visible evidence of the kingdom, the church and the kingdom are not synonymous. The church is part of the "now" of the kingdom, but there is more—the "not yet" of the kingdom, anticipated when Christ returns.

Because the church is the body of Christ, there is vital unity among believers in Jesus. Believers are dependent upon and in union with Christ the head. Believers are "in Christ," in the body and community of Christ. Christians are saved through their union with Christ, and they follow Christ's model and teaching in faith and ethics.

Jesus as the head of the community differs radically from Buddha, who is an example; the Hindu guru, who guides; the Islamic prophet, who instructs; or Judaism, which has Torah without Messiah.

Community of the Spirit

Pentecost became the connecting link between the historical Jesus and the new community, a link effected by the living presence of the Spirit. The gift of the Spirit at Pentecost should not be understood primarily in individualistic categories. The heart of what happened at Pentecost is the interaction of the individual and the community. The community consisted of Spirit-filled persons who experienced God's presence. It was not merely a contractual arrangement between individuals who shared common commitments or goals; it was the gift of God. It was a dynamic, organic, spiritual community. It was more charismatic than organizational, more movement than institutional.[1]

The community of the Spirit differs from Judaism as the community of Torah or the Islamic community, of law (*sharia*). Christians do not devalue instruction or law, but the formative basis of community is the Spirit. On the basis of biblical revelation and the revelation in Christ, the Spirit serves as moral guide and enabler.

Covenant Community

The church is a peoplehood experiencing *koinonia* (fellowship) together. Covenant is a relational category. Christians are a community gathered around the risen Jesus. He is the head, and believers are members of his body. Believers are brothers and sisters in the household of God, where Christ is the elder brother. Christ is the foundation, and believers are living stones. Jesus did not introduce a new principle, idea, or law so much as a new relationship. The church is a visible community, not just a mystical entity. It is the extension of the incarnation of Jesus in a human community.

This understanding of community is in contrast to the Buddhist *sangha* or the Hindu *ashram*, where each person is on a private search for meaning with little relationship to others even if they search together. For Hindus, enlightenment comes to individuals through gurus; communities lack universality because they function around a variety of gurus and are divided by caste.

In India, I met a Hindu outside his cave, where he lived for seven years, withdrawn from the world in search of spirituality. He sought peace on his own, with no concern for relationship within community. Christian community differs from Islamic community, which has a unity of doctrine, devotion, and ritual regulated by the Quran or Muhammad's teaching and example. But it lacks the organic connectedness of individuals in community. Judaism has a profound sense of covenant community to which Christians are indebted.

Believing, Discipling Community

The church is a fellowship of believers, those personally committed to Jesus Christ. The church is composed of voluntary disciples. Biblically, one is not a member of the church on the basis of citizenship, ethnic identity, or birth into a particular group. The community of Christians is a gathered church, a called-out-of-the-world fellowship. It is a particular group with a universal mission.

Those in covenant with God agree to a covenant of discipleship based upon an experience of Christ. They also covenant with the discipling community, convinced that life in the community is necessary in order to remain faithful. The community is a reconciled community, a community of love, peace, and mutual care. Through personal wholeness and social righteousness, the discipling community resists values of the world's kingdoms. Discipleship places community in tension with the world by demanding a new social orientation and a new view of history. Such tension often leads to suffering, persecution, and the way of the cross.

This community differs from Judaism, where one is technically a Jew if one's mother is Jewish; or from Islam, where one is Muslim if the father is Muslim. Because Judaism with little exception is for a particular people, the covenant with Judaism is not as universal as the new covenant community. The structures of Jewish faith assume Jewish ethnicity. Islamic community (*ummah*) is not confined to one people on the basis of nationality, kinship, or ethnicity. But once one becomes a member, there is no freedom to reject the community. Children are automatically members of the community. The Islamic ideal is that the whole social community become Muslim. The Islamic community is not "called out"; there is no distinction between faith and society, believer and citizen, doctrine and culture, or church and state. Islam accepts a divine pattern for community and is willing to use political power to effect it.

Incarnational Community

The incarnational community seeks to embody the divine presence. Christian faith does not idealize a disembodied spirituality. The incarnational community, believing that the gospel is for all, can be contextualized in any culture. It is a universal community transcending cultural divisions but must also be particularized in each cultural environment. Without contextualization within culture, the community becomes a ghetto, isolated from its cultural setting. It is important that specific forms of community be appropriate to the culture. Christians in Latin America have found the base ecclesial community to be a powerful expression of the gospel. Believers in India have experimented with Christian ashrams as a contextualized witness.

Implications of Community

The church as embodiment of the gospel is an essential form of witness foundational for presence, service, evangelism, and dialogue. We must think more about the visible church than about latent or anonymous Christianity. Christian community is the legacy of Christ that both embodies and announces the presence of the kingdom; it is an instrument of divine communication, an interpreter of the gospel. Committed communities provide creative ferment: salt, leaven, light, mustard seed. They are communities of the resurrection. Community is crucial for those who come to Christ from other faiths because of their need for nurture and understanding, especially when ostracized by family or friends.

Theoretically, the uniqueness of Christian community stands in contrast to other forms of religious community. But what is the church's record? In Jordan, I heard a pastor describe the church in a Muslim environment as "living in a glass house." A glass house is completely vulnerable! But vulnerability is of two kinds: the vulnerability of unfaithfulness, and the vulnerability of the cross. How do other religions perceive the church? Regrettably, the church's failures are obvious. Can the church recover the vulnerability of Christ, the weakness of the cross? Perhaps the church's greatest weakness is its failure to be weak. Is it possible that the suffering love of Christ is so seldom grasped by other religions because the church's preoccupation with power has distorted the essence of redemptive suffering?

Presence

Our understanding of church will affect the quality of Christian presence. Christians should be authentically present in the midst of other religions. But Christian presence is difficult for Westerners to learn because our tradition has taught us to act decisively and formulate carefully. It is easy for us to creedalize or institutionalize the gospel. But we need to learn to communicate relationally before we communicate rationally. In the New Testament, actions were inspired and confessions verbalized after encountering Jesus. We are so action or idea oriented that we fail to ponder the quality of our presence.

Western Christians should learn from Eastern churches in the Middle East and in China. In Egypt, I have been impressed with and blessed by the quality of Christian presence in the Coptic Orthodox Church. The church in China has by its presence been an effective witness, pointing to transcendence beyond the official ideology.

Christians are not free to choose or reject a theology of presence. Presence should not be just one of the options if no other options are available. Though not limited to restrictive situations where action and word are severely limited, presence is particularly important in cultures where major religions dominate.

Presence is the foundation for action and word. It is the most difficult form of witness, for it affects the credibility of action or word. Presence defines the basis on which one begins, not the limits of what can be done as opportunities arise. Presence does not by definition exclude explanation of action or proclamation of word; verbalization can be part of presence. Indeed, one can verbalize with greater credibility as one is authentically present. But a presence theology cautions one against over-verbalization or superficial verbalization. It is not a question of being verbal or nonverbal, but a matter of what one verbalizes and whether the word has integrity.

A theology of presence is not an attempt to diminish the place of evangelism; presence can be a vital part of evangelism. Christian presence anticipates that men and women might discover Christ's presence and receive his presence into their lives. When people discover the presence of Christ, they cannot remain neutral indefinitely. A decision is required.

From one perspective presence is pre-evangelism because it enables people to meet and acknowledge Jesus. But to define presence as only pre-evangelism is too limiting. Presence is witness whether or not it leads to evangelism or obtains a particular result. One should not insist that presence is a first link in a chain and is authentic only if all the other links (service, evangelism, church formation, dialogue) are clearly visible at the beginning. In that scenario, when other links cannot be guaranteed, presence receives a low priority and is practiced as a last resort. The validity of presence must always be granted apart from whether other forms of witness can follow. One cannot separate word from being, or action from being. God's presence must permeate our being, acting, and speaking.

Presence is more than passivity, apathy, or silence. There are times when silence is important. Some situations demand waiting and listening. Sometimes a painful silence is required as one waits with patience for the ripeness of time. Some witnesses are brash, aggressive, or cheaply verbal when silence, restraint, or reserve would be more acceptable. There are times when evangelism is inappropriate or forbidden, as when I taught at Haile Selassie I University in Addis Ababa, where open witness in the classroom was restricted. North American public school teachers live with a similar restriction.

Silence can be an implicit witness so long as Christians are more than the "quiet in the land." If they are apathetic or uninvolved, silence is counter-witness. Christians then succumb to an isolationist ghetto mentality. They are not present with people and for people. Christian presence must always be for others, sharing gladly in life together. A clear Christian identity must be expressed by identification with others if it is to avoid fossilization. On the other hand, total assimilation to a particular culture is equally dangerous, for then Christians lose that clear identity which makes a distinguishing presence so important.

Christians are embodiments of the gospel; they represent something. They are committed to engagement on behalf of people in whatever ways possible. Christ's presence is manifested in such engagements. There is no substitute for life involvement; people understand more readily when they see faith in context. Such a pro-active stance stimulates curiosity and elicits questions. A friend of mine who taught Muslim students reported that students would sometimes seek him out after school to ask faith questions. His presence was an invitation to learning by discovery.

Presence helps us understand the importance of living winsomely as Christians. It demands a theology of relationship, solidarity with others, and intense participation in the lives of people. From the depths of relationship can emerge an invitational theology which calls people either explicitly or implicitly to "come and see." Inquirers can then feel comfortable in their search for answers to real questions rather than receive pre-packaged answers to questions they have not asked. When the United Mission to Nepal was forbidden to do evangelism in the Hindu Kingdom of Nepal, it emphasized development ministries. Yet it was reported that wherever the United Mission was present, a church emerged.

Christian presence cultivates the gift of hospitality, the outstretched hand. Sadly, Gandhi was rejected at a church door in South Africa. The South African church had a coherent theology, a well-verbalized faith, but its door was closed. How might Gandhi's response have been different if Christian hospitality had been extended to him? Christian presence through hospitality is concerned for personal communication rather than mere information. Christian presence is behavioral. The communicator is not just a vehicle for the message but a major component of the message.

Sadly, some people have never had a relationship with anyone for whom the gospel has made a significant difference. Christian presence is a life message; life messages elicit word messages as the taste of good food arouses interest in the recipe. Friendship, compassion, listening, and naturalness in relationships commend the gospel.

Presence demands new understandings of time, goals, and success. Our agenda will need reshaping. By neglecting the significance of presence, we often start with the wrong agenda. Presence does not always have a clear agenda; it does not start with "management by objectives." Presence requires patience because the validity of what we do cannot be immediately measured. Presence is a needed corrective to our service mentality (a Christian motivation) or North American pragmatism, which emphasizes dynamic activism. A theology of presence demands that the church seek creative ways of being present.

Presence must never be a new technique. Regrettably, some are interested in a theology of presence only as a new strategy. Presence is a response to the gospel, a spirituality, not a strategy. When presence is strategy, it is second-best witness. For too long Christians have married witness to a success theology.

Since presence is spirituality rather than strategy, the Holy Spirit enables authentic presence. Christ's presence breaks in and is not produced or manipulated. Spiritual formation is essential. There needs to be a strong sense of call and a clear commitment to Christ. If one witnesses primarily by life, there must be no equivocation in regard to faith, because this will eventually be perceived in how one lives. Presence requires more of one, not less.

Presence is always contextual; it is never prepackaged. Its shape varies from culture to culture as Christ takes on flesh in each new setting. Christ is present in the world even where Christians are not present, but Christian witness is a call to personify that presence. When the Spirit energizes presence, we are surprised and overjoyed at ways in which Christ manifests himself through us.[2]

Service

Christians have opportunity to serve all people, including those of other religions. The church has a long record of service in the name of Christ in Buddhist, Shinto, Hindu, Taoist, Muslim, and primal religious contexts. Many have served in ministries of relief, teaching, health care, development, justice, peacemaking, and economic empowerment. Christians take their model from Jesus, who announced the kingdom of God through preaching and ministries of compassion.

Philippians 2:1-11 encourages us to pattern our lives after Jesus Christ, who modeled downward mobility. As God, Jesus became a human being, as a slave (*doulos*), and was obedient unto death, even death on the cross. In light of Jesus' example, we are to model humility, compassion, empathy, unity, concern for others' interests before our own, downward mobility, and suffering servanthood.

Witness to neighbors of other faiths must be characterized by solidarity, participation, vulnerability, and authentic praxis. As servants of God, we take up the cross as suffering servants of the world, renouncing the privileged status and authority of Western Christianity with its self-confidence, self-assertion, and triumphalism. As recipients of God's grace, we do not claim a privileged status for ourselves, only for Christ. Action in the service of others is an implicit witness to Christ.

Service must have integrity; it is not an inducement to conversion, though caring for others has evangelistic dimensions. We must not capitalize on human problems or wretchedness but listen to the cries of the disadvantaged. Neither should service be merely programmatic; persons must come before programs. Service is not response to guilt or attempts to make amends for past injustices. Service originates from love for people and thanksgiving to God. Service from a guilty conscience creates unhealthy relationships and dishonors Christ. Service is part of the gospel and not an appendage to it.

After Jesus lived as suffering servant, he became the exalted Lord whose name is above every name, the name to which every knee should bow in heaven and on earth and under the earth. Every tongue should declare that Jesus is Lord, to the glory of God the Father. Christ's lordship was accomplished through humility, self-emptying, and servanthood, not through conquering; servanthood preceded kingship (Phil. 2:5-11). If we are willing to be downwardly mobile in service to people of other religions we can thereby recommend the suffering servant who became the exalted Lord. But if we talk about the exalted Lord in an exalted manner, we detract from the meaning of his lordship.

Perhaps the Christian failure to model the suffering servant has kept people of other faiths from seeing the exalted Lord. Driven by the desire for success, we often recommend the exalted Lord without modeling the suffering servant. When we start with the exalted Lord, we are prone to exude power, overconfidence, and abrasiveness.

Conversely, some emphasize the suffering servant and talk about service but neglect or equivocate about the person of Jesus Christ. They fail to acknowledge that all will some day confess that Jesus Christ is Lord. I recall comments of a service volunteer among Muslims who wasn't sure Muslims should consider becoming followers of Jesus Christ. We should avoid both extremes by keeping the suffering servant and exalted Lord together in our consciousness and ministry.

Not only do we serve people of other faith traditions; we can sometimes serve with them for the common good. In the face of injustice, oppression, war, poverty, overpopulation, environmental deterioration, and natural catastrophes, we offer assistance along with people of other faiths in spite of our faith differences. Such cooperation centers on social, economic, or political goals.

Since religious pluralism is a social phenomenon, not just an ideological issue, we can participate in promoting religious freedom and justice for all. Christians are pluralistic in terms of equality and freedom for people of all religions. They insist on tolerance for all but are not indifferent to truth. We share the world and common experiences even if we don't share the same faith. We can celebrate the many things we share in common in spite of varying creeds and lifestyles.

Some North American Christians are reluctant to cooperate with other religions for the common good, fearing they might be unequally yoked together with unbelievers. Yet they work daily with secular nonbelievers in North America. Cooperation with other religions does, however, call for discernment. It is a challenge to discover the meeting point between ourselves and other religions. We cooperate with people of other faiths in projects which are consistent with the Christian's understanding of God's caring: famine relief, education, justice activities, humanitarian concerns. Other religions may not agree with our view of the kingdom of God, but working cooperatively need not compromise either faith.

I was part of a group (including one Muslim) which visited congressional offices in Washington, D.C., to urge that greater consideration be given to justice for Palestinians in the Middle East. I contributed money to an interfaith experiment in reconciliation between Jews and Arabs in Israel. We should support efforts for peace between warring factions in Northern Ireland, Hindu-Muslim-Sikh tension in India, and the Hindu Tamil-Buddhist Singhalese conflict in Sri Lanka.

Serving together may be less problematic than worshiping together. Christians have learned to appreciate joint Christian ecumenical services. But when ecumenical is widened to include interfaith worship services, a central focus is compromised. Historically, the ecumenical movement was centered on Jesus. Does participation in interfaith services show a desire for improved relationships, and does it celebrate cooperation and common concern? Or does it gloss over crucial faith differences, relativize the name of Jesus, and distort Christian witness?

Aspects of joint worship services may be dishonest or compromising. We must be sure that we do not embrace the totality of another religious tradition by certain acts of worship. Shared vocabulary is not necessarily shared meaning. Worship cannot be separated from faith or theology. Even if other religions worship the one God (as in Judaism and Islam), our understanding of God varies widely. I recall the disruption in chapel when a seminary student in Ethiopia read from the Quran.

We should not give the impression through worship that all religions are in essence one. Parts of an interfaith service may be in conflict with our essential beliefs. Prayers that respect everyone's feelings and convictions, lose the essential focus of worship. Joint worship services easily become experiments with God. Shortly before the Gulf War, I attended in an interfaith worship service to express solidarity with those who were concerned about the impending war. We listened to readings from differing faiths, but I felt I was an observer rather than a full participant. Careful thought, prudence, and sensitivity must be balanced with religious integrity when considering interfaith worship services. I prefer to retain ecumenism for the Christian family and see limited value in interfaith worship services that include various religions.

Evangelism

The witness of the church includes presence, service, and dialogue, but also evangelism. Though each form of witness seeks to *actualize* the gospel through life or word, evangelism is particularly concerned with *announcing* the *kerygma* (word of witness). It is equally wrong to exclude evangelism from witness or to reduce witness to evangelism. The church should be involved in all forms of witness with personal and theological integrity.

Sometimes presence, service, or dialogue seem easier because they tend to affirm and enable people in their cultural settings rather than make demands upon them. Evangelism, by inviting people to a new commitment and a new community, can be disruptive. We should see evangelism as enablement rather than imposition. The tension between different forms of witness can be resolved by a vision of the kingdom of God which incorporates multiple dimensions of witness. We should not strengthen one dimension of mission by denying or ignoring other dimensions. All are strengthened when they are part of a common vision.

Word of Witness

Israel and the early church were surrounded by other religions. The prophets proclaimed the lordship of God, and the apostles proclaimed the lordship of God in Christ. Peter called on people to repent and be baptized so that they might be forgiven and receive the gift of the Spirit (Acts 2:38). Paul proclaimed repentance, forgiveness of sins (Acts 13:38-39; 17:30), and salvation through confession of Jesus Christ (Rom. 10:9). He asks, "But how are they to call on one in whom they have not believed? And how are they to believe in one of whom they have not heard? And how are they to hear without someone to proclaim to them?" (Rom. 10:14).

Evangelism is concerned with life's ultimate questions: the nature of humankind and the nature of God. New Testament evangelism calls people to repentance and faith in Jesus Christ. Christians have the privilege of sharing the light and truth which have come in Christ so that people have the opportunity to freely give allegiance to him. If we disown evangelism, we are inconsistent with centuries of Christian witness and infer that Christ is only for Christians. But evangelism in the context of other religions is difficult and often brings limited results. Yet we can be encouraged by Kenneth Cragg's statement: "Mission is not a calculus of success, but an obligation to love. . . . We present Christ for the sole, sufficient reason that he deserves to be presented."[3]

The church witnesses through deeds and words to Christ, who saves. Is it arrogant to believe people need redemption? If people are in need of redemption, can we choose not to share, as though Christ were for a few and not for all? Christ is not just *a* window but *the* window of God. To say "Christ is risen" or "Jesus is Lord" means little if not shared. Tolerance of other religions does not mean silence about one's own faith. Sharing of good news is part of the church's existence; the church by impulse is evangelistic. The gospel provides resources not found elsewhere: forgiveness of sin, regeneration, reconciliation. The church, not another social organization, is entrusted with the gospel.

If the fullest revelation is found in Christ, then this truth must be shared universally. If in Christ we have been shown the way, we do not keep it to ourselves; we invite others to walk with us on the way. Evangelism is generosity. It is the test of our belief in the truth and the test of our love. The ministry of reconciliation is based upon the truth in Jesus, conditioned by the love of the cross.

The gospel we announce is a whole gospel: atonement, forgiveness, and ethics. Conversion cannot be separated from obedience nor obedience from conversion. Radical discipleship and holiness are not elective elements; instead, they are essential to the faith. Instead of prioritizing aspects of the gospel, we should put the gospel in all of its aspects at top priority. However, specific situations may call for some priority of service in response to urgent needs. During the famine in Ethiopia, the immediate task was to feed the starving, but Christians there likewise engaged in evangelism.

Conversion

The Christian gospel is conversionist.[4] If we deny conversion, we deny the hospitality of God in Jesus Christ by assuming that Christ is only for those who grew up in a Christian environment. But the gospel is not only for some; it is for all. The gospel and privacy cannot coexist.[5]

Conversion is the work of the Holy Spirit. But we need to be faithful in following Jesus and telling his story so the Holy Spirit can do the work of conversion. For those converted from other religions, the process is often gradual. Conversion does not bring complete discontinuity with one's past. Rather, one's allegiance is changed and one's past is reoriented.

Presenting a call to conversion may be considered a threatening act. In the minds of some, conversion is associated with insensitivity, manipulation, emotionalism, naïveté, and code words. Others associate conversion with arrogance, triumphalism, and crusading. We acknowledge that conversion has sometimes been prostituted to exploit others. But abuse of conversion does not invalidate conversion. When we see such abuse, we need to seek more clarity in understanding and practice.

Some Christians respond to this dilemma by suggesting that we ourselves need to be converted. This takes numerous forms: conversion to the oppressed, conversion to the poor, conversion to the world. Conversion in this sense implies consciousness-raising which leads to insight, commitment, and transformation. This indeed is necessary.

The example of Peter and Cornelius is instructive. It reminds us to share the Christian faith and not simply our brand of Christianity. It prepares us for judgment and correction as we witness. Peter was "converted" in the process of meeting Cornelius. His understanding of Christian faith and his attitudes were changed. This is an essential correction to overconfidence. Like Peter, some of us are "converted" anew in the act of witness.

However, some overcorrect themselves by going to another extreme. Their regret for abuses in the past, immobilizes them. They are either uncertain about faith or embarrassed to invite persons to convert to Jesus. Lesslie Newbigin argues that what is said "about the conversion of Peter must not be used to overshadow the conversion of Cornelius, without which there would have been no conversion of Peter."[6] This new definition is helpful so long as it does not displace the earlier meaning of conversion; both aspects of conversion must be held together.

Some people suggest that the one who witnesses is acting as though in a superior status. They object to the power connotation of "proclaiming the good news" or even "sharing the good news." They prefer to "exchange good news." While the spirit of this communication can be applauded, one must ask how the good news is defined. In the encounter with other religions, we exchange ideas and experiences. But what is the good news we exchange? Where knowledge of Christ is lacking, is what we exchange really good news as defined by the gospel? Is it unnecessary for the believer to share good news? Witnessing to good news need not be *against* people but *for* people, assuming that the manner of witness is appropriate to the content.

In our efforts to correct the mistakes of witness, it is important to identify whether the problem is the message, our understanding of the message, or the manner of presenting the message. Our fallenness and finitude demand modesty and humility. Our convictions must be expressed with respect. But this need not minimize conversion.

Professor Milan Machavic of former Czechoslovakia, a Marxist participant in Christian dialogue, said, "I don't trust a Christian who isn't interested in converting me."[7] Some Marxists understand the gospel better than Christians! Yet while we anticipate conversion, we are not the ones who exercise the power of conversion. A Jewish rabbi friend told me, "I think you would like me to believe in Jesus."

I responded, "Did you ever believe in something so much that you wished others would also believe?"

We do not do the converting. But if something good happens to us, we like to share it. We encourage others to see the truth in Jesus, but they are converted as they turn to the one who beckons them. I believe more and more in conversion through knowing friends who have turned from Islam to Christ.

Conversion is being changed from within (Matt. 18:3), an experience described as "new birth" or being "born from above" (John 3:3, 7). Openness to that change must be voluntarily chosen. Jesus did not force people into choice but freely invited them.

Integrity in Evangelism

Adherents of other religions frequently use the term "proselytization" in a pejorative sense when referring to Christian evangelism. Proselytization is associated with coercion, manipulation, or exploitation of weakness. Though Christians object to equating evangelism with proselytization, we must divest ourselves of questionable evangelistic behavior. Unethical methods and abuse of authority deny the gospel. Explanation of the gospel must be clear. Words and actions must be sensitive, not aggressive. Warfare vocabulary like strategies, crusades, campaigns, targeting people, fighting or waging warfare for souls—these must be excluded from our thinking and conversation. Ephesians 6 attests to "spiritual warfare," but the warfare is between Christ and the cosmic forces of evil. God in Christ wars against spiritual enemies, but that battle was won in the suffering of the cross. Our words and style must reflect the cross, not soldiers going off to war.

I was at a Sunday morning worship service in Jerusalem, to which an observant Jew came with a friend. The sermon was based upon the Sermon on the Mount, but the closing song included phrases such as

"You soldiers of the cross, . . . marching off to war." Though I know the intended meaning of this song, I was troubled because of the triumphalism and aggression that has often characterized Jewish-Christian relationships. While Christians have tried to change these negative relationships, the message of this song can inadvertently communicate the reverse of what is intended.

How we think and speak impacts our attitude and style. Can we move away from the language of conflict and conquest in witness? Bethlehem and Calvary are not images of conquest. Faith is not a weapon. Proclamation is not propaganda. Evangelism is not an imposition; it is a gentle witness. Faith claims are made on the basis of truth and love.

Witness is not passive. We witness with hope that there will be a response, but we respect the limits of evangelism and accept people even if they reject our witness. It is not unethical to witness if we model ethical behavior. We should be vulnerable; we should not exploit another's vulnerability. Evangelism should grow out of meaningful relationships with living subjects, not be directed to objects.

I recall taking students to the mosque in Washington, D.C., to interact with Muslims about faith issues. I later learned that one student left a tract behind. It was not given personally to a Muslim but placed in the building. I respected the urge to witness, but I felt uncomfortable with the method, because we were guests of Islam. This attempt to witness appeared underhanded. I prefer a more open discussion of faith issues in a trusting relationship.

Jesus spoke with authority but was not domineering. His life manifested weakness and suffering. When Christians who are in a position of power or privilege invite people to follow Christ, their invitation may appear corrupted by a spiritual imperialism. Sometimes Western claims to superiority and the uniqueness of Jesus are entangled. We must frankly acknowledge the often-scandalous failure of Western Christians to submit to the authority of Christ. How tragic when we have argued for the truth and failed to embody it.

We acknowledge with regret that Western Christians have wrongfully used the triumph of Christ by triumphalistically calling people to faith. Christ has been associated with imperialism, with ruling ideologies and elites, and with race and class. Syncretistic accommodations of Western dominance and evangelism must be rejected. But Christian faith is not merely Western, either historically or currently. We must recover a biblical view of witness and evangelism.

Fear of being labeled arrogant can make us timid, but arrogance and timidity both compromise the gospel. Can we regain confidence in the universality of the gospel that calls people from all cultures? As we see the gospel take shape in multicultural forms, our faith is renewed. Regret for past mistakes is not regret for the gospel.

Lesslie Newbigin believes that embarrassment for the gospel is frequently evidence of shifting belief:

> The contemporary embarrassment about the missionary movement of the previous century is not, as we like to think, evidence that we have become more humble. It is, I fear, much more clearly evidence of a shift in belief. It is evidence that we are less ready to affirm the uniqueness, the centrality, the decisiveness of Jesus Christ as the universal Lord and Savior.[8]

Can we combine confidence in evangelism with a winsome manner? James Scherer reminds us, "The Christian witnesses to Christ not out of conviction of sinless perfection, but as *redeemed sinner*; not boasting of new-found moral superiority, but wanting to share the gift of life with other human beings."[9] Humility and Christlike identification with people is essential. We need to be "soul friends," hospitable and openhearted. Evangelism is a process, a journeying together with people.

Christian faith needs to continue its witness to Jesus Christ as the fulfillment of the religious quest in other religions by discovering those forms and expressions that are compatible with the gospel. Tom Finger recognizes that there is interplay between Christian uniqueness and the impulses of other religions, though it is impossible to construct an overall theory to fit each situation. Instead, constant reflection on the Christian message within each cultural context is necessary to see how God is relating the gospel and impulses of other religions.[10] Dialogue with other religions, the subject for the next chapter, is one way we can relate the gospel to the impulses of other religions.

11

Forms of Witness: Dialogue

Witness assumes that conversations must occur between Christians and adherents of other religions, that there should be dialogue between the Christian story and other stories. We can be committed to Christ and to the gospel and still be open to and accepting of the other. Holding to our confession can make us more sensitive to others rather than less sensitive. Roelf Kuitse notes, "Without a true concern for the Gospel, dialogue becomes a pleasant conversation and exchange of ideas. Without a concern for the other person, it becomes irrelevant, unconvincing, and arrogant."[1] Because Christian faith has a dialogical nature, dialogue should not preclude witness but enhance witness.

Biblical Basis for Dialogue

Dialogue follows the pattern of God and Jesus in dialogue with humans. Jesus' incarnation made possible an ongoing dialogue with humans. Jesus was in the temple listening and asking questions (Luke 2:46). He entered into serious conversation with Nicodemus (John 3) and the Samaritan woman (John 4) rather than giving neatly-packaged presentations in replying to their questions. He called for responses by asking people questions about his teachings so that their minds and consciences would be engaged (Matt. 21:40; Luke 10:36).

The apostle Paul argued in the synagogue at Thessalonica, explaining, proving, and persuading people about Jesus Christ (Acts 17:1-4). In Athens, he argued in the synagogue and in the marketplace (17:17). At Corinth, he was in the synagogue, trying to convince Jews and Greeks (18:4). In Ephesus, he discussed faith in the synagogue and in the hall of Tyrannus (18:19; 19:8-10). Paul later had a dialogue with Festus (24:25).

Such dialogue included argument, reason, and debate. For Paul, dialogue was part of witness; the subject of his dialogue was Christ, and he hoped that his hearers would trust Christ. Dialogue was not the primary or only witness of the early church, but it was significant. The New Testament does not support a sharp distinction between proclamation and dialogue.

Types of Dialogue

Dialogue takes many forms. Formal, intellectual dialogue is only one and often not the most important level of exchange. A *first* form of dialogue is "living dialogue." Such informal dialogue is important. It occurs when Christians living in the same vicinity with non-Christians, through normal daily contacts in homes, at school, at work, or at market. Such dialogue is not official and professional, but a living in relationship, a sharing of life, an attitude, a style of approach, a dialogical manner.

Dialogue is as much living together as talking together. It is interpersonal involvement and communication. In a new culture it is not enough to meet people in books; we must meet them in the street. Personal encounter is important since we share a common humanity and are all in God's image. Dialogical living inspires inquiries about faith. Those who teach English in China or in Muslim societies, report that students inquire about issues of faith.

A *second* form of dialogue (informal and formal) occurs through cooperation in practical areas of living or communal concerns: justice, peace, crime prevention, drug rehabilitation, better education, health, or development. Though our rootage and methods sometimes differ, we cooperate with people of other faiths in projects that are consistent with God's concern in the world. Christians and Muslims consult together for human rights in Palestine; Jews, Christians, and Muslims work together for peace between Israel and Palestine. I participated in an International Jewish-Christian Conference on Modern Social and Scientific Challenges in Jerusalem, dealing with common concerns faced by both communities. I joined an interfaith study tour to Galilee, visiting projects in which Jews, Christians, and Muslims cooperate to promote peaceful coexistence and reconciliation.

A *third* more-formal type of dialogue is concerned with interreligious conversation about issues of history and theology: belief, ethics, community, tradition, experience. Usually this kind of dialogue is a planned engagement between Christians and other religions. It is mutual inquiry, often scholarly or institutional, and is usually intended to promote greater understanding between religions. Christians affirm the importance of all these aspects of dialogue but are particularly concerned for dialogue about theological issues and understandings of truth. Such dialogue should go beyond mere exchange of information and opinions. It should include reflection on real faith issues, even if this involves risk or discomfort.

To Meet and to Greet

Dialogue is needed to overcome *isolation*. Recently I heard a Jewish person say that Jews and Christians have lived beside each other for hundreds of years without knowing each other. Christians must resist the temptation to withdraw into safe places. Isolation may be a result of geographical factors, but many believers have been isolated from those who live in close proximity. We tend to think of religion as a private matter, not to be discussed even if we live in the same community, work together, or have children who go to the same school. Sometimes power relationships are a factor in social isolation.

Dialogue is also needed to overcome *hostility* when people feel threatened by another regarded as the enemy. Interfaith relationships are sometimes thwarted by *competition* between religions. Some feel reluctant to develop a *partnership* with another religion for fear it will avoid real religious questions, leading to compromise or indifference. David Lochhead notes that theologies of isolation, hostility, competition, or partnership each hold a particular perspective on other religions.[2]

In *To Meet and to Greet*, Kenneth Cragg encourages people of different religions to meet one another.[3] Faiths are strangers to each other unless there is meeting, questions, and inquiry. We need to move beyond our parochialism, beyond our religious walls and hedges, beyond our shores. We need to give up our isolation and security in order to explore the meaning of faith. Though we prefer to live in our religious fortresses, faith is not always kept pure by isolation. Refusal to dialogue results in isolation of the Christian community and in compartmentalization of religion, as though faith had no impact upon society.

Dialogue begins when people meet and cultivate relationships, relationships based upon life involvements and conversation. In dialogue we seek to be present to the other, to let our eyes meet, to extend to the other the invitation to speak even if we think the other is mistaken. We combine confidence in our identity with the desire to know the other.

Dialogue involves two things, *content* and *relationship*. Often relationships will determine how the content is heard. In our fear of compromising the content of the gospel, we sometimes view others with suspicion and withdraw into religious ghettos to give our witness. Instead, we must build bridges, look for places of meeting, be involved with people, and engage the minds of non-Christians. Meeting can happen in homes, consultations, or assemblies. Meetings might be regular or occasional, person-to-person, or group-to-group. We need living contact with theologians and philosophers, but also with less-reflective loyal adherents of the faith. Religious meanings are not in words but within people and, like electricity, flow best where there is good contact.

Dialogue can help to cultivate new attitudes by breaking down barriers of distrust, prejudice, caricature, and hatred. But this can only happen if dialogue is honest, with no hidden agendas, and if participants renounce intellectual and cultural superiority. A dialogical manner is more important than formal times of dialogue; dialogue requires living together more than talking together. We need to share our lives, have common activities, and develop relationships with neighbors. "Suspicion is lived away, not talked away."

The more we know each other, the more careful we will be in our pronouncements. Resisting the temptation to disfigure another, we look for the best in their point of view rather than trying to win arguments and score points. Personal attack or hurtful and misleading statements produce resentment. Arguments lose persons when things are said that irritate and injure them. Arguments encourage a spirit of rivalry which is not conducive to spiritual understanding. Dialogue must be open and sensitive to others, a token of Christian love and respect. Trust overcomes animosity; patronizing words make enemies.

Dialogue, in its concern for the identity of the other, "passes over" to the other religion and then "comes back."[4] When we shift our standpoint in order to understand another's religious standpoint, we come back with new insights. When we enter sympathetically into the feelings and insights of the other, we return a different person. We do not just learn new things; we learn to look with new eyes on what we already knew. Such encounter with other religions both enlarges our understanding and helps us to see them more critically. We are forced to create a common language in order to translate what the other has said into our language. We are obliged to uncover assumptions and presuppositions which govern our thinking and theirs.

Dialogue for Understanding

Personal Understanding

Dialogue contributes to mutual understanding and growing friendship. Our common humanity is an important basis for inter-religious relationships. We meet not only academically but as persons struggling with real-life issues.

We may discover that people in other religions are reluctant to enter into dialogue with us. The term seems to them to be a change of words but not really a change of Christian attitudes about witness. Given the centuries of strained relationships, much mistrust and suspicion has to be overcome. Sometimes proximity between the religions has led to defensiveness and hostility in relationships.

In other cases religions are self-confident and feel no need for conversation with other religions. In the 1994 Jewish-Christian conference in Jerusalem, the chief rabbi of Israel boycotted the conversation because, in his words, "Jews have the Torah. Why do we need to talk with Christians?" The impetus for dialogue has usually come from Christians, who are often more eager to talk with other religions than other religions are to discuss Christian faith.

Christians must demonstrate willingness to take the other person seriously, as one created in the image of God, and only secondarily Hindu, Buddhist, or Muslim. If God loves all people, we need to love all without discrimination. We dialogue because of love for our neighbor, not from duty to salve our guilty consciences. We cannot claim to love our neighbor without getting to know our neighbor. People are more important than their religious labels.

Since people on both sides have apprehensions concerning religious dialogue, it is important that we refrain from heated and destructive arguments, scoring points, and blaming or denouncing others. Polemical dialogue usually produces alienation and enmity. Our stance should not be adversarial. We must divest ourselves of mistrust, stereotypes, prejudices, caricatures, and misconceptions. We must not misrepresent or injure the adherent of another faith by comparing their worst with our best. Christians can too quickly isolate other religions through a fortress mentality, an insider-outsider paradigm or an us-them syndrome, which leads to aloofness or inaccurate assumptions. Dialogue begins by accepting and respecting the neighbor. In dialogue we encounter people, not just concepts; ideas must not displace personal relationships. And as we develop relationships with one another, we grow in understanding.

Understanding is helped by courtesy, winsomeness, reverence, tactfulness, and trust. People of deep religious experience should, of all people, be sensitive to another's experience of religion. There needs to be a meeting of hearts, not just minds. Dialogue can symbolize humility and love, a sign we are willing to give up our prejudices. Love implies that we are taking the other seriously, that we are interested and open. Love forges friendships without preconditions. Love respects the other's dignity; love goes beyond tolerance. Encounter, interaction, exploration, and *informal* dialogue are preparation for *formal* dialogue. Love does not mean that we totally agree with the person or approve all conduct; love is both sympathetic and critical.

Dialogue is other-centered rather than self-centered. Dialogue refuses to force another to a particular point of view. Understanding and acceptance happen best when there is no pressure. We should not be obsessed with contemplating results but relax and let the outcome of the dialogue rest in God's hands.

Dialogue, not Monologue

Dialogue implies that communication should be more than a remote monologue. It may be more comfortable to communicate with people from a distance, but this is often characteristic of a coward who feels insecure about faith and is unprepared to meet objections. Or one may assume a position of power so one's own imperfections are less apparent. But we must be willing to be seen and known for what we are—human, needy, dependent on grace.

Dialogue is bidirectional, a two-way relationship. Talking is important but so is listening. Dialogue is not a one-way street. Dialogue is concerned about speaking *with*, not speaking *at*. It guards against a "teacher" demeanor that cuts off listening. It insists on reciprocity. There must be opportunity to ask questions, state objections, and clarify what is heard. Personal relationships, personal conversation, and group discussion provide an atmosphere for listening.

Listening to Another's Self-Definition

Dialogue demands that we listen with sympathetic appreciation to other religions. Sensitive hearing counteracts hearsay, which breeds prejudices. Why should another listen if we have no willingness to listen? Why should another learn if we have no desire to learn? It is so easy to listen to ourselves speaking instead of listening to another. Without authentic listening, we are deaf to what other religions are saying. In dialogue we take time to hear those who practice their religion interpret their religion, rather than interpreting it for them.

It is important to understand the difference between the meaning we project onto other religions, and what other religions understand as their own meaning. Even if we know well the religious system, we must listen to the person's perspectives of faith and truth, and be open to the faith as the faithful hold it. It is misleading to interpret what others are saying in terms of our concepts and worldview. We must come to terms with another's self-understanding and have the courage to change our misconceptions. I have personally benefited from Muslim and Jewish teachers, and from listening to Hindus and Buddhists explain their faiths. Listening can help us correct errors and caricatures and learn to appreciate new images of the religion or person. We need to move beyond an understanding of theoretical ideas or the worldview, and begin to see the questions and problems which other religious believers encounter.

Other people have the right to define themselves. How do Muslims understand *jihad* (struggle)? Self-definition of religion is a needed corrective to our proneness to see only the dark side of religion. Probing the mystery of other faiths must be done with great sensitivity. Do Hindus worship idols? Attempting to be sensitive, I used the term *image* in India (instead of idol), but some Hindus used the word *idol*. Are we willing to re-envision the other? Meeting people keeps us from merely surmising what they think and from perpetuating untruth about them. Such encounter is crucial since it is so hard to understand words and concepts that are not part of our experience.

The more secure we are in faith, the more open we can be to learn from others. Muslim observance of Ramadan can remind us of our need to fast. Two hours of prayer and study before breakfast in the Hindu temple, rebukes our lack of devotion. Eastern religions remind us of contemplation; Africa recalls for us the wholeness of life and divine power. Can we feel the tug of the other in challenging our faith?

Mutual Questioning

Christians must open themselves to the questions of others. A Jewish person once asked me how Christians understand the Holy Spirit. During a Jewish-Christian conversation in Jerusalem about the Christian understanding of the eucharist (holy communion), a Jewish rabbi asked, "To understand the Eucharist, must I understand psychology or chemistry?"

Mutual questioning leads to self-interrogation. We should not be indifferent to the problems others have with our faith. Critical questions can lead us to more mature understandings of faith. Indeed, we must take some responsibility for people's misconceptions of our faith. Dialogue should not avoid all critical questions for the sake of a friendly relationship.

Sometimes we should risk inquiring about how our religion gives the person pain, even if hearing another's criticism of our faith is painful to us. When we try to walk in the sandals of another, we begin to glimpse our faith and theological tradition through different glasses. Then we may discover what prevents the person from hearing the gospel. As we listen with empathy and discernment, we discover felt needs which call for modification of Christian clichés.

By listening to others, we can sometimes anticipate their questions. We should also invite them to address questions to us, even if questions are difficult. It is important to hear another's perceptions of our teachings and practice. By thus exposing ourselves, we gain a deeper understanding of ourselves. We should welcome the probings and questionings of others for the way in which they identify crucial issues and for the clarity they demand from us (Col. 4:6). In dialogue we have a chance to hear people's questions and not merely imagine them. Many of the presentations in Acts were responses to queries.

We need to model vulnerability as we attempt to give reasons for the hope in us (1 Pet. 3:15). We must be aware that our difficulties and weaknesses are already known, and that there is a great gap between our ideals and our practices.

Dialogue insists that we discuss the meaning and interpretation of the gospel. This helps our own understanding of the gospel and gives us insights for discussing it with a partner. We especially need to think about and discuss faith in the presence of other religions. Of what value is our belief in a unique salvation if we are unaware of how it is good news to the one who hears? Dialogue helps us to see how the gospel corresponds with the deepest human longings.

Mutual questioning is essential because theology is rooted in biography. Sharing one's pilgrimage is important for understanding. To answer the question, "Who am I?" it is important to ask the question, "Who are you?" To answer the question, "Who is my God?" it is important to inquire, "Who is your God?"

Christians may wish to address questions to Muslims concerning the generosity of God. Does God only command, or does God also reach out in mercy to sinners? Is prophecy enough, or do we also need salvation? If works determine human destiny, how are we to understand God's mercy? If God is merciful, how is mercy expressed? Is God only powerful, or does God suffer?

Christians also have puzzling questions for Hindus. Does monism take the individual seriously enough? Is evil part of ultimate reality? If the world is illusion, is not human life devalued? What resources do Hindus have for social transformation? How does karma relate to the equality of people and to social justice? To the Buddhist, who has not been taught about a loving, personal God, the Christian asks, Why did a religion that was antimetaphysical begin to develop god-belief? Does nirvana satisfy the longing for transcendence?

There is nothing to fear from mutual questioning; those who care about truth must not suppress questions. Questions which seek to clarify another's faith can clear away wrong perceptions, create mutual accountability and rapport, sharpen differences between religions, and show the uniqueness of Christian revelation.

Christian Self-Understanding

Dialogue can help Christians come to terms with their own cultural and theological presuppositions. We are forced to ask how much our faith is based on the gospel or whether our beliefs and practices are simply inherited. Christian terms often lose their value because they have not been portrayed faithfully. We must be prepared to receive judgment and correction so that we recover the integrity of Christian faith and action.

Encounters with persons of other faiths can purge us of dross by helping us to see our imperfections, failures, and sinfulness. When we see ourselves from the other's perspective, that forces us to self-criticism. We need to admit our mistakes, accept responsibility for them, and correct them. Criticism might cause our "Christianity" to be at risk, but not our faith in Christ. In encountering other religions, we become aware of dimensions of divine reality that we have neglected, and we are forced to encounter Christ afresh.

It is not that biblical revelation is inadequate, but that our understanding of and commitment to God's revelation is inadequate. Dialogue helps us to reread and sharpen our understanding of Scripture. As we listen to the questions and difficulties of non-Christians, we are forced to examine our faith affirmations in the context of Scripture. As we discover another's points of reference, we reinterpret theological abstractions and clichés. We communicate faith afresh in response to new questions, cultures, and religions.

Seeing ourselves as others see us and responding to their perceptions and questions, can spur us to new depths of faith. That which was obscure or forgotten can be recovered. Gandhi helped many

Christians gain a new perspective on the Sermon on the Mount. We need to give a fresh account of our faith in the context of other religions. Contrary to some Muslim perception, Christians do not understand Trinity as God, Mary, and Jesus. We are forced to look seriously at *what* we know about God and *how* we claim it. How do we explain our theology so that it is understood?

In conversation between Jews and Christians in Jerusalem, Christians were asked, "What is meant by presenting your body as a living sacrifice? How can you believe that Jesus was Messiah when peace has not yet come? What does it mean to you Gentile Christians that Jesus was a Jew?" I believe dialogue can help us work more carefully at theological self-definition.

Dialogue can help us distinguish between the Christian message and its cultural framework. We often absolutize our understanding of Christian faith instead of celebrating the varied cultural "editions" of faith. How can we tell the "old, old story" in fresh ways? Interaction with other religions pushes us to examine theological formulations which were developed in a particular culture, and to reformulate the faith for new religious environments. New questions and new issues drive us back to the source of our faith.

Commonalities and Differences

There are commonalities in religions, but there are also differences and conflicts. If we only emphasize what is common and minimize differences, what is there to discuss? We should never surrender the *essence of Christian faith* in the name of *common essence*. Real encounter begins at the point of disagreement. Occasionally we fear discussing underlying theological assumptions because of their potential for divisiveness, but we must not ignore key theological issues. We are not indifferent to conflicting truth claims. Dialogue is not the search for agreement or uniformity, but for clarity of understanding.

We need intentionally to explore commonalities and differences. Denny Weaver describes religious commonalities against the background of religious trajectories. He writes, "Trajectories may intersect. That intersection indicates some kind of commonality, and it is at these points of intersection that dialogue can properly begin."[5] For example, we can speak of Christian nonviolence and Native American nonviolence because their trajectories intersect. Yet Weaver notes that there are also differences: "The image of intersecting trajectories provides a way of understanding possibilities of cooperation and dialogue at points of common purpose or interest, but without necessarily implying that the points of intersection indicate a common foundation."[6] Such concern for commonalities is the entry point for dialogue.

Dialogue should not deal in generalities; it is important both to examine commonalities and to honestly recognize differences. Some religious concepts reflect or affirm Christian faith; other ideas oppose Christian faith. Dialogue should not degenerate into a mutual affirmation of differing religious beliefs, where all the critical questions are excluded. It is important to discuss, debate, and question, but in a congenial way. There should be no limitation on subjects for dialogue, so long as dialogue does not bargain with the other or threaten the other.

Processing Dialogue

Christians need time to converse among ourselves about issues that are raised in dialogue. Visits to religious centers can be helpful when there is adequate processing by the Christian community. The methods we adopt should not put at risk our commitment to Christ or assurance of faith. When I have invited persons from other religions to make presentations in class and participate in discussion, we have taken time in a subsequent class period to evaluate what we heard. Similarly, when I have gone with students to visit religious centers, I have asked them to respond in writing to ideas presented and to their personal observations. This feedback then forms the basis for further class processing. As we explore other traditions, we should not lose touch with our roots. It is important for us to keep in touch with the faith community so we can remain grounded in faith. If we are not grounded in faith, we have no faith to share.

Dialogue and Witness

Dialogue and witness are not identical, nor are they necessarily opposed to each other. Dialogue need not diminish or eliminate witness, nor should it be a substitute for communicating the gospel. Each is valid in the context of the other. Instead of precluding witness, dialogue can invite, extend, and deepen witness. Dialogue can be a prelude to witness, have witness dimensions, and be a witness in itself.

Though dialogue is compatible with witness, dialogue is not explicitly evangelistic or only pre-evangelism. But when we are committed to Christ, a dialogical relationship provides opportunities for authentic witness, a witness that recommends the freshness of the gospel and illuminates grace. Dialogue is not simply to make the Buddhist a better Buddhist, the Hindu a better Hindu, or the Muslim a better Muslim. Christian faith has a dialogical nature, but not at the expense of its witness nature. Since Christian faith is missionary, is it improper to invite adherents of other faiths to consider Jesus Christ? Christian faith cannot surrender the conviction that God sent Jesus, who provides forgiveness, justification, and a new life. It is not that Christians have a better chance of being saved; it is that Christ saves.[7]

Conviction and Discernment

Some hesitate to dialogue because they fear losing their identity or betraying their basic faith commitment. Others are afraid that encounter with another religion will weaken their faith or that they lack adequate answers for probing questions. While dialogue can be risky or threatening, it can also be a faith-strengthening experience. Dialogue that is always safe is neither serious nor interesting.

However, dialogue calls us to critical discernment. We do not enter dialogue with empty hearts and vacant minds; it is important to be clear about our identity. It is not necessary to suspend our faith to respect another, or to denigrate ourselves to be more accepted by the other. We should not relativize our convictions to have an equal footing in dialogue, as though harmony, mutual understanding, and enrichment were the primary goals of dialogue. When anchored in Christ, we need not fear dialogue. We can be loyal to ourselves and committed to our convictions.

Faith and belief are important in dialogue; without particular faith, dialogue dissipates. Dialogue cannot function without conviction. Kenneth Cragg insists that there must be inner faith for interfaith. He writes, "Inter-faith necessarily tugs at inner faith."[8] But conviction must never be an excuse for imposing beliefs on others; profound conviction must be matched with reverence for the other. Faith held with honesty and tolerance for the other is the foundation for authentic dialogue.

Truth and Dialogue

Some Christians ask, If Christian faith has the fullest truth, what is there to discuss? If all truth is found in Christ, why dialogue? Christian attitudes toward dialogue depend on the presuppositions and purpose of dialogue. Some question dialogue because of its association with universalism, God's revelation in all religions, or a relative understanding of truth in all religions. They are understandably critical of a roundtable kind of approach where all religions are assumed to be equal and where there is a mutual search for a coming higher synthesis of religion.

They raise important questions: Does dialogue demand that one accept the other's religion as an equally genuine expression of the divine? Is it bigoted to deny the legitimacy of another's religion? Is every defense of Christian faith ethnocentric or triumphalistic? For them, dialogue does not distinguish enough between belief and unbelief, or between Christian faith and other faiths.

Dialogue should not be seen as the road to an uncritical syncretism. Instead, dialogue can be a safeguard against syncretism by discerning the essential differences between Christian faith and other faiths. We should not reject dialogue but clarify our understanding of it. What are theological implications of dialogue? How does one value other faiths? Must dialogue be neutral, minimizing faith commitments? Is dialogue restricted to generalities? Will dialogue blunt the edge of witness? Must the commitment to witness be abandoned to engage in fruitful dialogue?

Dialogue can symbolize both solidarity with non-Christians and a commitment to witness. If we are not concerned with the gospel, dialogue is just pleasant conversation. If we do not respect the person, dialogue is irrelevant or unconvincing. We do not come to dialogue with detachment, indecisiveness, or surrender of what we consider to be true. Dialogue is not so much to discover new religious truth as to understand it. We enter dialogue so truth might become more evident.

In dialogue we learn new dimensions of truth that we have not comprehended before. Though we understand the truth in Jesus, this does not mean that we cannot learn from people of other faiths. Dialogue is more than an exchange of truths, as if some truths were possessed by Muslims, some by Christians, and some by Hindus. Each of these traditions has insights from which we can benefit. Yet we do not discover different truths so much as different perspectives on the truth.

Instead of deciding in advance how much truth others possess, we need to discover truth perspectives in conversation with people. Wisdom of other religious communities should not threaten us; if all truth coheres in Christ, truth from other sources need not undercut faith. We learn from the wisdom of other religions and also share the saving wisdom of Christ. Instead of sacralizing the diversity of truth claims, we use diversity as an opportunity for conversation.

Dialogue must not exclude issues of truth. Jürgen Moltmann says, "A dialogue that does not revolve around the question of truth remains irrelevant."[9] Dialogue need not corrupt the truth; it can illuminate truth. Truth should not be defended *against* dialogue but *in* dialogue. We are not custodians of the truth; we are communicators of truth. Though we have found truth, we do not fully comprehend it. Our interpretations of truth are sometimes mistaken or distorted. Yet in penitence we attempt to speak the truth in love (Eph. 4:15).

Dialogue is not consensus by compromise. In an effort to find a common ground for dialogue, we should not reduce religion to the least common denominator. For Christians, the gospel is true and not negotiable. Christ is the foundation from which we begin. Dialogue presupposes honesty about our faith commitment. We don't sacrifice our position.

Clark Pinnock says, "Truth that is trivialized or sacrificed on the altar of religious unity is not in anyone's best interests."[10] David Bosch is convinced that "an 'unprejudiced approach' is not merely impossible but would actually subvert dialogue."[11] The basis for dialogue is the equality of persons, rather than the equality of religions. Our openness to others is in the context of a prior commitment. Real dialogue is only possible if we are sure of our identity in Christ. We can feel the heart of another religion without being disloyal to our own faith, just as one who is married can identify with another's marriage.

We can take a confessional position in dialogue: we listen to others, and we witness to our deepest convictions. But our confession of the ultimate authority of Jesus Christ should not sound omniscient because Christ is infinitely greater than our understanding of him. A confessional stance implies that truth is to be found in a life of obedient discipleship to Jesus Christ. Yet those who take a confessional stance can also be seekers. Pinnock notes, "Paul was able to expose himself to truth-seeking encounters without being intimidated and without being anxious about the outcome."[12]

We believe in revealed truth (confession-making) and seek to understand it (truth-seeking). But our confession, spoken with passion and conviction, must not be self-righteous or defensive. Dialogue is a process of confession and exploration. Dialogue can lead us beyond ourselves and back again with new understandings.[13] The Christian confession motivates us to dialogue but also becomes the center from which we dialogue. We need not be embarrassed about a strong Christocentric focus in our confession—if we allow space for another's confession we must allow space for our own confession.

In dialogue we seek to grasp new truth according to those ways of thinking and valuing which we have already learned from the gospel. We don't regard revelation given in Jesus Christ as merely one of many options; we regard Jesus as the criterion by which other ways are tested. Interfaith dialogue only has integrity as we take seriously the reality of our faith for understanding other religions. Yet we are not possessors of salvation. We do not control the truth and holiness of God; we witness to truth and holiness by which we are all judged. We are stewards of the gospel, not its owners.

Conversion and Dialogue

The question is often asked whether it is possible to believe in dialogue with other religions and still believe in conversion. Many people suggest that the nature and spirit of dialogue are destroyed if either of the parties wants to convert the other. They accept dialogue as simply a matter of sharing, getting to know one another, and gaining a new understanding of the respective faiths.

These important goals for dialogue should not be discounted. However, dialogue in Acts was part of a fuller witness. If we delete the possibility of conversion in dialogue, that is not consistent with apostolic dialogue. Whenever Jesus Christ is part of the dialogue, conversion is part of it as well. If we exclude the possibility of conversion, we stand in the way of Christ drawing people to himself. We do not argue people into conversion, but we cannot rule out the power of the gospel to transform.

Dialogue is not a secret weapon in the witness arsenal. Clandestine efforts to convert others must be renounced. We enter dialogue not as manipulators but as fellow pilgrims on life's journey. We do not apply ready-made formulations of the gospel. Instead, we seek to relate the gospel to the needs and questions which arise. In the process the gospel is affirmed, not undermined. The message becomes more intelligible, applicable, and relevant.

Openness and Dialogue

To what extent is Christian faith an open or a closed system? For the Christian, there is ongoing tension between commitment and openness. We don't come to dialogue with a blank mind or suppress our convictions. Gayle Gerber Koontz believes Christians are open but not empty. There is openness with conviction.[14] We are open to take seriously those who differ from us, but this does not mean that we hold less firmly to belief. Koontz believes a confessional orientation can be more committed to truth-seeking than positions which want to eliminate norms and absolutes. She believes we should maintain the integrity of a particular tradition and foster openness to growth and change.[15]

There is more danger in being totally closed to other religions than in being courageously open. As Christians, we seek transparent openness, though we are not totally open. There is a difference between openness and open-endedness. Total openness can lead to meaninglessness, indifference, and disconnectedness. It is impossible to approach any question with a completely open mind. Along with other religions, we have a frame of reference. We should encourage the dialogue of open heart to open heart, honest conviction to honest conviction. We hold openness and conviction in balance; we are open to others and confident in faith. Because we are confident about the gospel of truth, we can be humble about our formulations, open to learn, and discerning about another's understandings and claims. Confident Christians can be gracious Christians.

Trusting God in Dialogue

Possible tension between witness and dialogue can be resolved if two affirmations are kept together. First, God has left a witness in the world. Second, God is revealed uniquely in Christ.

We believe God is at work in ways that surpass human understanding and in places that are least expected. In dialogue we may discover that God has gone before us in preparing people in the context of their own culture and convictions. God accompanies us and comes toward us; we don't just take God to others. Perhaps we cannot resolve the potential tension between dialogue and witness. But we need to live with the adventure of both—an adventure that involves risk and surprises as the Spirit leads us.

The Christian's task is to be present with others and leave the rest to God. We believe the Holy Spirit can lead our conversations. He can use dialogue to convict our partner and ourselves. Trusting ourselves and others to the Holy Spirit keeps us from manipulating others, talking more loudly, or using more sophisticated arguments.

Witness and dialogue are not primarily a conversation between human beings but a conversation in which God speaks to both partners. D. T. Niles says, "In missionary communication the Christian is not first of all concerned to bring Jesus into the life of one of another faith; his chief concern is that Christ brings him (the Christian) into the life of the other."[16] Verkuyl believes that with the benediction of the Spirit, dialogue becomes a "trilogue."[17]

The Holy Spirit is ahead of our witness. Since the Spirit goes before and prepares the hearts of people to respond to the gospel, we need to be aware of the Spirit's action and sensitive to the work of the

Spirit. The Spirit creates expectancy but also restrains us from aggressiveness or from over-zealous and self-generated activity. In dialogue the Spirit enables us to listen, to speak, and to discern what God is doing in the lives of our dialogue partners. Those who are in God's image have an insatiable longing for God and spiritual reality. This spiritual search creates an atmosphere of openness that enables dialogue empowered by the Holy Spirit.[18]

Our willingness to learn from other faiths should not undermine Christ's supremacy or finality. Indeed, it is possible that the Spirit uses experiences with other faiths to draw us closer to Christ. Vinay Samuel claims, "The Spirit of God will enable us to discern the signs of God's presence in the religious experience of others."[19] Christians who take Christ as their criterion will be able to find new illuminations of Christ from the experiences of other faiths. Can the church both discover and bring to light and fullness all the riches God has hidden in creation and history? We trust God, who is renewing creation and history in ways that amaze us. We admit that our knowledge is finite and fragile, partial and provisional.

Dialogue About Christ

Dialogue is frequently a mere exchange of ideas and opinions based on a religious tradition: history, belief, ritual, ethics, and community. Real theological conversation is often neglected. If human beings are subjects, not objects, it is important to engage living persons at a deeper level. Dialogue should be a personal encounter, not just intellectual gymnastics or social convention.

If dialogue is person-centered, going beyond comparative doctrinal ideas, people take precedence over impersonal religious systems. Dialogue is more than talking about religion. The subject of dialogue is the essence of faith, not tradition. We need to talk about the depth of our experience of faith. How do we understand God? Who is God to us? A Christian friend of mine teaches English to Muslim students. His students ask him about his experience in prayer.

If faith is poetry of the heart, dialogue needs to be on the wavelength of the heart rather than just on the intellectual level. It is precisely in the area of personal experience that hunger expresses itself. We violate the integrity of the gospel if we regard the gospel only as a system, rather than as a relationship with Christ. It is the relational dimension of the gospel that corresponds to the deepest longing of the human person.

The essence of Christian faith is not its teaching but Jesus himself.

Many religions would like to separate Jesus' message from his person, but his teaching derives from the authority of his person. That is why the center of Christian faith is not the book (Bible) but the person of Jesus. This is in contrast with Judaism, which stresses the *Torah,* and with Islam, which emphasizes the *Quran.* The name of Jesus is often downplayed for the sake of religious generalities. But for Christians, dialogue which talks about everything but Jesus is inadequate. We do not have to speak of Christ first, but neither can we exclude him. Dialogue should not merely compliment Jesus but explore the meaning of commitment to Jesus.

Jesus is not a background figure. He is central. If we make Christian faith into a general idea or redefine Christian faith to get the broadest human agreement, we rob Jesus of his uniqueness. We should not talk less of Jesus and more of religion. Jesus is not just one negotiable variable.[20] The distinctiveness of Christ should not be softened or abandoned. Dialogue is richer if we are candid about the center of our faith—Jesus Christ.

If we believe Jesus Christ is unique, we should engage in dialogue. Is this why Christians have led the way in dialogue? We should represent in word and action how Jesus is unique. The gospel of Jesus Christ is not a formula of words but the story of redemption in one's life.

In dialogue we are concerned that the people we converse with see Jesus. Dialogue also gives us the opportunity to tell the story of Jesus. When we speak of Jesus Christ, we speak of one who wants to meet the needs of all of us. But speaking is only part of witness; our faith needs to be open for others to explore its richness. In dialogue we discover how great is the gap between the gospel and our expression of faith.

Jesus Christ can be a barrier to dialogue, but he is also a bridge. We are often surprised that people know so little about Christ. Yet there is also renewed interest in Christ. Ideas in dialogue can be quite arid, but the subject of Jesus brings life to dialogue. Participants in dialogue may want to hear more about Jesus, just as I inquire more about Buddha or Muhammad. Many people are finding Jesus attractive. Jews and Muslims are more willing than before to talk about Jesus; some give more place to Jesus than their religious systems do. It is a mistake to downplay Jesus. Nevertheless, how Jesus is introduced is crucial. We need a balance between too quickly imposing Jesus and unduly postponing any mention of him for fear of causing offense.

Yet no serious discussion with people of other religions can go far without serious consideration of Jesus Christ. Sometimes we sense that persons are on their way to discovering God in Christ as they seek for something that is absent from their tradition. Their present location may not be their final destination. Can we dialogue in such a way that the uniqueness of Christ can be understood in their context, confident that the Holy Spirit can glorify Jesus, who is the subject of the dialogue? Our primary concern is not to commend ourselves but to commend Christ (2 Cor. 4:5).

Ted Peters notes that in many religious dialogues, Christians suddenly begin boycotting the name of Jesus Christ. Christ is removed from prayers and benedictions lest his name create offense if spoken. Peters wonders why the name of Jesus is taboo. He asks whether Christians should stop giving witness to their faith as they understand it. Then Peters concludes that it is not other religions who want to suspend the name of Jesus, but Christians themselves. Martin Marty comments that it would be eerie to dialogue with Jews without mentioning the God of Israel, with Muslims without mentioning Allah or Muhammad, or with Buddhists without mentioning the name of Buddha.[21]

Is it possible to talk about Christian faith without speaking of Christ? If Buddhists speak of "Lord Buddha," can we not speak of the "Lord Jesus Christ"? Temple Gardiner sought to exhibit a true portrait of Jesus to Muslim friends. Kenneth Cragg wants to show Muslims the Christ they have missed.[22] Cragg and Gardiner understood the essence of Christian faith. If Jesus Christ is the heart of our faith, he must not be marginalized. Christian dialogue invites people to accept not merely better ideas, a dogmatic system, a sociocultural code, or one's personal views. Christians invite all to consider Christ.

Christians are not threatened by what dialogue includes but by what dialogue excludes. Dialogue with the right presuppositions is integral to witness because it insists that hearing must occur. And hearing is only possible when the message touches the point of need.

12

Those Who Have
Not Heard

Traveling through Cairo in a bus with students, weaving our way through masses of people, one student asked, "What is God going to do with all of these Muslims?" Many African believers ask, "What will happen to our forebears who died before Christian faith was brought to us?" Once a North American student asked, "Was I just fortunate to have been born where I heard the gospel? What if I had been born in India?" These are perplexing and provocative questions that won't go away.

If the way to God is through Jesus Christ, and the way of forgiveness and acceptance is through atonement effected on the cross, how shall we regard those who have lived and died without hearing of Christ? What happens to those who through no fault of their own have had no opportunity to respond to the gospel? Are they denied salvation because of accidents of history? Will God condemn a whole group of people because they have not heard? Since the majority of human beings have lived and died without hearing of Jesus, does God have another way of saving them? If God does, why is the church called to witness?

There are no simple answers to the question of the unevangelized. Though we know that God desires all men and women to be saved, we also know that many people have not had a chance to respond to God's offer of salvation in Christ. How do we balance the two poles of God's revelation—God's universal saving will and salvation through Christ? Must we surrender particularity, uniqueness, and the finality of Christ to accommodate our questions?

Sensitive Christians are understandably troubled by questions. Are only those who know Christ saved? Must non-Christians explicitly call on the name of Jesus to benefit from his work? Can people benefit from grace even if they have not heard of it? Does God have two standards, one for those who have never heard, and one for those who have heard? Will God judge those who have heard by their response to Christ, and those who have not heard by their deeds or by the light they have? What about those who have not heard of Christ but repent of their sins and turn to God? Is there hope for the eventual salvation of all?

These questions are difficult because they relate to our understanding of God's character. If people who have not heard are lost, then is God all-good, all-knowing, or all-powerful? Should people be judged for things they do not know to be right and true, or are those excused who are innocently ignorant? Have people rejected Jesus if they have not heard? How do we balance the justice of God and the love of God? Is God only just? Or is God also fair and merciful? Does God really love the world if redemption is limited to those who have an opportunity to respond to Christ? How could a God of love create men and women and then reject the majority of them? From a human perspective, it seems unjust to condemn people to an eternal hell for failing to receive a medicine about which they have not heard.[1]

Those who have not heard include several categories of people. Some lived in the centuries before Christ came (B.C.). Others lived after the incarnation of Christ, but since they have not heard of Christ, they are informationally B.C. Some have heard facts of the gospel but have not really understood the gospel. Others have been alienated from the gospel because of inconsistent Christians, or because of negative experiences with institutional forms of Christianity. Examples of the latter are Christians who mistreated Jews and Muslims, collaborated with gunboat diplomacy in China, and projected superficiality and deception on radio and television.

Through contacts with other religions, we have discovered that many people love God and hold some beliefs which parallel Christian beliefs. We have friends who are pleasant, sincere, and ethical. Adherents of other religions are no longer strangers; it is much easier to judge a stranger. Acknowledging that witness to other religions has not been very effective, we ask whether an explicit response to the gospel of Jesus Christ is necessary for those who have not heard.

Wider Hope

Rationale for Wider Hope

In earlier chapters we considered inclusivists and pluralists with their more positive perspectives concerning the salvation of people in other religions. Other groups have also struggled with this question, seeking to hold the *particular* (Jesus as Savior) and the *universal* (of the world) together in responding to the question of the unevangelized. Some evangelists in past generations theorized that people in other religions might be saved without *explicit knowledge* or *explicit confession* of Christ. John Wesley characterized those saved outside the Christian community as *servants*, not *sons*. If they continue in their faith, they will become sons.[2] C. S. Lewis thought that those who commit themselves in trust to the one who lies behind all truth and goodness will be saved though ignorant of the Savior.[3]

More recently John Sanders and Clark Pinnock opt for a "wider-hope" position. They believe that Jesus provides atonement and reconciliation, but that many do not know about this salvation. So they explore the possibility of a more universally accessible salvation through Jesus apart from evangelization.

Pinnock believes that harshness about the destiny of those who haven't heard, elicits the reaction of radical pluralism. For him, the church is the "instrument of salvation" more than an "ark of salvation." He argues, "All who achieve holiness, whether in the church or outside it, achieve it not as a result of their own efforts but by the grace of God, which they have received by faith."[4] Pinnock is exclusivist in affirming a decisive redemption in Christ, but he does not deny the possible salvation of non-Christian people. He is inclusivist in refusing to limit the grace of God to the confines of the church, but hesitates to regard other religions as vehicles of salvation in their own right.[5]

Old Testament and Wider Hope

The Old Testament provides perspectives on those who have not heard. There were *two kinds of believers* in the Old Testament. The *first group* were pre-Abrahamic people (Abel, Enoch, Noah) and God-seekers (Melchizedek, Jethro, Abimelech, Naaman, Job). The God-seekers saw the fallacy of their "pagan" religion and were saved by trusting in God. The *second group* consisted of those in the covenantal tradition.

From the New Testament perspective, we believe Old Testament saints in the covenantal tradition looked forward in faith to Messiah. Their salvation was at God's initiative and based on Christ's sacrifice, yet to come in history (Heb. 9:15; 11:39-40). Chris Wright asks,

> If it was possible, then, for people at that time to be saved by Christ without actually knowing Christ because it was historically impossible, is it not likewise possible for people today to be saved by Christ even if they don't know him because of geographical obstacles?[6]

It is assumed that those who are theologically pre-Christian are similar to Old Testament believers. If God has through Christ redeemed those who had not heard *then,* can God not also redeem those who have not heard *now?* Do those who abandon themselves to the mercy of God find mercy, saved by God's grace in Christ even if they have not heard?

New Testament and Wider Hope

General revelation is also used as a possible basis for wider hope (Rom. 1:19-20; 2:5-16; 10:18). General revelation is thought to mediate saving grace because the source of general revelation is the saving God. Revelation does not save; God saves. Since truth, morality, and values find their source in God, the sense that one should do right and follow the truth is from God. People are then saved or lost depending on their response to general revelation. Those who develop a trusting relationship with God are saved, but those who reject God are without excuse (Rom. 1:19-20).[7] In Romans 10:18, Paul uses Psalm 19 to confirm the universal extent of grace as God speaks through general revelation. Even if one affirms the possibility of salvation through general revelation, that does not deny the sinfulness of humanity (Rom. 3:9, 11, 23); none are saved by their good efforts (Rom. 1:21; 2:23). The issue is not salvation by moral perfection, but whether God grants opportunity for salvation.

Those who base wider hope on general revelation argue that if general revelation is enough to produce guilt and condemnation, it can also lead one to salvation. The light provided in general revelation is sufficient to open the way to salvation for those who have not heard the gospel. When humans respond with a sense of need and abandon themselves to God's mercy, salvation is possible. However, if seekers do find God through the light of general revelation, it is because of God's provision of grace; religions do not save. When seekers hear about Christ, they sometimes respond, "This is the one I have been following all along." Those who embrace the light of general revelation sometimes turn from their former religion in anticipation of something new. General revelation does not devalue special revelation; it is a framework within which the Christian message can be understood, pointing the way to salvation for those who have not heard.

Some believe the Logos and the Spirit enable us to be more optimistic about the salvation of those who have not heard. The Logos is said to produce light, thereby making salvation available to all. Salvation is then possible through the Word (Logos) even if one doesn't know the earthy Jesus. Likewise, the Spirit, who broods over creation and history, uses general revelation and opens the door for humans to respond. The Spirit works before and after the incarnation, convicting people of sin in all ages and cultures.

The story of Cornelius is used as a basis for wider hope. Sanders argues, "The story of Cornelius is to inform us of God's desire to include all races in the fellowship of the church, not to teach that until someone is a member of a church and is baptized, he or she is eternally damned."[8]

Explicit Faith and Implicit Faith

Does God want all to be saved or only those who have conscious faith? A wider hope is often linked with how one defines faith. Can we assume that God will take into account the faith of one who has never heard, even if it occurs in the context of general revelation? Is *explicit faith* in Christ necessary, or is *implicit faith* sufficient?

The issue is whether the benefits of the atonement are made available, in some way, to every human being, even if there is no knowledge of Christ's death. Pinnock says, "The problem is that God cannot save those he would like to save if indeed it is true that there is salvation only where the gospel is preached and accepted."[9]

Implicit faith acknowledges that information for salvation can be found outside of special revelation. According to this view, those who have no contact with the Bible or Christ, knowing of God's existence through nature and conscience, and being aware of their alienation from God, are drawn to God for care and protection. They are then saved by God's grace expressed in Christ's atonement even though they have no conceptual knowledge of Christ, as one may be healed by medicine without knowing the name of the medicine. Thus their faith in Christ is implicit.

Pinnock understands the "principle of faith" by the people of faith in Hebrews 11, on the basis of three ways in which people relate to God: (1) cosmic covenant established with Noah, (2) covenant made with Abraham, (3) new covenant in Jesus. It is important to note that each of these covenants had validity and that many were commended for their faith, but they "did not receive what was promised, since God had provided something better" (Heb. 11:39-40).[10]

The principle of faith allows for the possibility that the unevangelized can be saved because one doesn't need to be conscious of the work of Christ to benefit from it. Christ's grace applies to people whether or not they understand it. For Pinnock, "What God really cares about is faith and not theology, trust and not orthodoxy."[11] God's grace saves, not a perfectly developed theology. According to Pinnock, it is not so much a question of whether the unevangelized know Jesus as whether Jesus knows them (Matt. 7:23).

People who advocate a wider hope criticize those who use Acts 4:12 to assume that God's grace is not at work, and the hope of eternal life is not a possibility, apart from explicit faith in the name of Jesus. They are convinced that salvation is available only by the authority of Jesus because God in the person of Jesus provided it. But they understand this text to speak to the power of Jesus for those who hear and respond to the good news; it does not address the question of the unevangelized. They insist that Peter was affirming more than limiting. They want to avoid the idea that Acts 4:12 intends to exclude most people, thereby magnifying the severity of God. They argue that it was not Peter's intention to deny that God has been at work saving people before, but to affirm that God is now saving people in a unique, new, and messianic way through Jesus. "No other name" means that salvation for any human being comes only through Jesus.

Sometimes a distinction is made between *believers* and *Christians*. Believers in Hebrews 11 all trusted in God, though not knowing Christ. Believers are defined as those saved through faith in God; Christians are those who understand God by participation in Christ. All Christians are believers, but not all believers are Christians. According to this view, ignorance does not disqualify from grace; intellectual errors need not keep one from trusting God. Attitude is more important than knowledge; acts of faith and a positive response to God are necessary for salvation. The focus is on the direction one is moving more than on one's position. Some are going toward Christ, and some are moving away. People with little knowledge can be accepted by God as believers moving in the right direction.[12]

We recognize God's concern for the salvation of all (1 Tim. 2:3-4; Tit. 2:11) and God's response to seekers (Ethiopian, Acts 8; Cornelius,

Acts 10). Therefore, some suggest that God will in some way grant to all those who seek, an opportunity to hear the gospel of Christ and to make a decision.[13] God then may save seekers on the basis of their humble repentance and faith, not on the basis of their piety and good works, because salvation in the Bible is never by sincerity or merit.

Wider hope is also based on God's response to unknowing children or the mentally impaired, who are incapable of understanding the gospel. We believe God accepts them because they have not deliberately rebelled against God. If one accepts this premise, it is difficult to say that God loves the unevangelized adult less than infants or the mentally impaired, unless one assumes that infants and the mentally impaired don't have the ability to respond and adults do.

Wider Hope and Judgment

Those looking for wider hope, probe the meaning of judgment. They argue that people will be judged on the basis of what they know rather than on what they do not know. How can people who have not heard of Christ be condemned for denying Christ? Would it not be unjust to condemn those who have never heard for their lack of response to an unknown offer of grace? God is said to accept all people prior to human response. God includes all in grace and excludes in judgment only those who resist that grace. Only those who know the good news and reject it, are guilty of spurning the divine offer of grace. God has no pleasure in the death of the wicked. God wants no one to perish.

Judgment is on "those who do not know God and on those who do not obey the gospel of our Lord Jesus" (2 Thess. 1:8). Condemnation is for explicit disbelief in Christ; Jesus is ashamed of those who are ashamed of him (Mark 8:38). If Jesus denies those who deny him (Matt. 10:32-33), we assume there is knowledge of him. Punishment is for obstinacy (Heb. 6:4-6). Those who refuse to believe are judged (John 3:18, 36). Only people aware of Jesus have no excuse (15:22).

Some believe judgment is on the basis of people's response to the revelation they have, or how they would have responded to Christ if they would have had an opportunity. Persons are responsible for light that they have, not for the full light of grace not revealed to them. Those holding this view call attention to the fact that in the judgment there will be surprises. Some will be saved by Christ even if they are unaware of him (Matt. 25:31-46); those who do deeds of mercy to "the least of these" do them to Christ, and they are saved apart from recognizing him.

However, since good deeds are not in themselves the basis for salvation, it is not action that justifies. But behavior manifests one's basic attitude toward God, and such response is counted as faith. It is further suggested that the unevangelized will not be punished as severely as those who have explicitly rejected Christ, since Scripture seems to hint at degrees of punishment (Luke 10:12-14; 12:47-48), and Christians are warned that judgment begins with the household of God (1 Pet. 4:17).

Some want to be more optimistic concerning salvation. They believe God encounters people at the moment they are dying, giving them a chance to believe (this is not the same as an after-death opportunity). For others, a wider hope is based on the possibility of "eschatological evangelization" or "postmortem encounter" with Christ for those who did not encounter Christ and the gospel in their lifetime (cf. 1 Pet. 3:18-20; 4:6; Eph. 4:8-9; 1 Cor. 15:29). God perseveres and will not abandon to eternal punishment those who did not know of Christ and did not, therefore, decline grace. Thus these people are said to have an opportunity after death to make a decision about Christ. Anyone who will receive Christ is given opportunity to do so. This view seeks to preserve God's love and power as well as the conscious choice to trust in Christ.[14] (Cf. 2 Macc. 12:39-45; Matt. 12:32; and the Roman Catholic doctrine of purgatory, after-death expiatory purification for those who die in God's grace.)

Critics ask whether one should build a doctrine of after-death opportunity on such little evidence. Many Scriptures seem to regard death as the end of opportunity. Furthermore, texts used to support this view are unclear and controversial.

Witness and Universality

Those who recommend wider hope do not intend to diminish the importance of Christian witness. But they believe God's wrath or "hell insurance" should not be the primary motivation for mission. The love of God should motivate Christians to share the love of Christ. They insist that seekers who find God through general revelation need to be exposed to the brightness of the light in Jesus. Persons of implicit faith (believers) need to know more about Christ. If people see God in nature and hear God in the conscience, should this not increase our responsibility to build connections to Christ? Those who are not believers also need to hear the gospel. All need to hear, those who have responded to light, and those who have not responded. Those who have responded to light will learn the source of the light and can be led to a fuller experience of life.

Pinnock declares, "God's word has gone out in all the world in general revelation—but it is not the same high wattage as the light which shines in the face of Jesus Christ. No one at all, whatever his or her spiritual condition, should be denied access to that light."[15]

It should be noted that wider hope is not the same as universalism (that all will eventually be saved). Wider hope is concerned for more universality, that all will have an *opportunity* to be saved through Christ. Pinnock rejects universalism because it denies human freedom and warnings of judgment. He believes there is a difference between a universalist outcome and a universal opportunity.[16] Universalists usually do not distinguish between objective and subjective reconciliation. Pinnock insists that salvation must be subjectively (personally) appropriated; salvation is only universal if it is universally accessible. He affirms God's universal will to save through Christ, not through religious systems or meritorious actions.

Assessment of Wider Hope

Though we are free to ask questions about a wider hope for those who have never heard, it is difficult to make statements with certainty. No attempt is made here to answer all the questions posed. The Scriptures should be our guide, but the fate of the unevangelized is not directly, systematically, or conclusively addressed in the Bible. Since the issue is at best addressed indirectly, there are biblical perspectives that must inform our speculations, but we have insufficient information to adequately resolve the issue. The debate will continue, but so also must love and respect for the subjects and participants in the discussion. Crucial to the discussion is how we interpret and use the Scriptures. We must immerse ourselves in the main thrust of the Bible and look at the variety of texts rather than merely proof-texting.

Two Themes in Scripture

Some texts suggest a universal salvation. Other texts speak of a particular or limited salvation. Do we subordinate the universal to the particular, or the particular to the universal? Paul claimed the universal and the particular. Can we let both kinds of texts be answers to different questions? Paul is certain that salvation is particular because it is *only* in Christ; Christ's salvation is universal because Christ defeated the powers of sin and death. John Toews says, "The universal does not deny the particular, but affirms it, and the particular needs the universal to be authentically and divinely transformative.["17]

Two themes in Scripture must be held together. Jesus is *exclusive* and *inclusive*. Jesus is *Lord* (exclusive) of *all* (inclusive). Exclusivity and inclusivity are polarities that must engage each other. God loves the world and desires the salvation of *all* people. God is making all things new and reconciling the nations through Christ. The Lord wants no one to perish but *all* to come to repentance (2 Pet. 3:9). Christ draws *all* people to himself (John 12:32). God our Savior desires *everyone* to be saved (1 Tim. 2:3-4). Jesus tasted death for *everyone* (Heb. 2:9) through his sacrifice for the sins of the *whole world* (1 John 2:2).

Do these texts imply that all without exception will ultimately be saved, or that all are invited to salvation? The universal promise of salvation implies that all have need of it, and that God wishes the salvation of all through Christ. But is the universally intended salvation universally accessible?

If Christ's death is for all people, some argue that it is not universal unless it is accessible to all. If God wills everyone to be saved, does God give everyone a chance? Is the language of *all* or *whole world* all inclusive or representative?

Interpreting General Revelation

The presence of God in general revelation and the fullness of God in Jesus are complementary, not contradictory. But crucial to our understanding is the amount of continuity we see between God's revelation in Christ and God's activity among all people everywhere.

General revelation is God's attempt to establish communication with humans and develop a relationship with humankind; the Creator is pursuing humankind. But awareness of God through such revelation needs to be followed with human response to God. It is important, therefore, to distinguish between revelation and salvation. Divine self-disclosure in creation may have a saving intent but is not itself saving without the human cry for help. General revelation is not the means of salvation, but it can point toward salvation as people become aware of their sinfulness and powerlessness and abandon themselves to the mercy of God. Some people who hear the gospel instinctively recognize it as truth because they were searching for mercy. J. N. D. Anderson observes, "I have heard of more than one Muslim whose study of the Quran made him seek after Christ."[18]

Scripture indicates that human beings are accountable for the general revelation they have. Those who have knowledge through general revelation are not necessarily innocent (Rom. 1:19-21). Humans may know something about God but refuse to acknowledge the truth they know. They often compound their guilt by creating false religions (Rom. 1:22-25). Religion can be both an honest attempt to search for God and a rejection of what God is revealing. A crucial issue is to what extent religious people are prepared for the fuller revelation of God in Christ, or to what extent they resist the revelation of Christ.

Sin and Judgment

General revelation must be held in tension with the power of sin. People bear responsibility for their sin; having distorted general revelation, they are without excuse (Rom. 1:20). Those who know the law and those who do not know the law are both in need. Gentiles who don't have the law have no excuse for their sin (Rom. 2:14-16). All are given light, but none lives up to the light. All people fall short of God's holiness (Rom. 3:23). Sin can blind one's eyes to the light. The issue is not just knowledge in contrast to ignorance, but the presence of evil. Sin condemns; not all will be saved. In the spirit of Romans 1:21-23, many people refuse God's self-revelation in creation and worship the created rather than the Creator. Hence, they incur the wrath of God.

The Bible speaks of God's love and wrath. Sin and judgment cannot be removed from Scripture. There are consequences of sin—darkness and lostness. The New Testament wants people to believe Christ and thereby to be released from already-present condemnation and judgment (John 3:16-18). God's wrath is revealed against ungodliness and wickedness (Rom. 1:18); no one is righteous (Rom. 3:10, 23). There are saved and lost, those condemned and those free from condemnation.

There is eternal life and eternal death, heaven and hell. Hell is designed to show God's judgment on the consequences of sin, not to portray a cruel God who delights in torturing sinners. The counterpart of human freedom and responsibility is the fact of God's judgment. The possibility of judgment is a call to consider salvation. God's holiness and judgment must be held in tension with God's love and mercy. God hates sin but loves the sinner. Sin separates from God, yet God wills all to be saved. ,

We sometimes think people are lost only if they have knowingly rejected Christ. But are humans who have not heard of Christ innocent? Or have they perhaps repudiated and perverted the light they have through general revelation? Goodness in other religions must not blind us to depravity. We are judged by the light, the light of the cross. The cross brings judgment on all, including religious people, and on Christians. God, wishing to save us, calls us to repentance. Those who have never heard are also called to repentance. Repentance cannot be removed from the faith equation. Faith does not simply evolve from general revelation to Christ.

Sin and Grace

In our discussion about those who have never heard, the universality of sin and the universality of God's grace must both be stressed. Does one emphasize sin, or God's power to save? How do we balance God's holiness with God's grace? If sin and death are universal, grace and life are universal (Rom. 5:12-21). We believe God's grace is present in all of God's universe. No one seeks God apart from the influence of grace. Everyone seems to have some awareness of God's grace; the light of general revelation reflects the brightness of Christ.

However, awareness of God's grace or good behavior do not in themselves constitute salvation. Goodness does not justify. Those who cry for mercy are justified. The effect of grace is conditioned by human response (1 Cor. 15:10-11; 2 Cor. 6:1; Phil. 2:12-13). Those moved by grace or toward grace must be open to grace. Grace is only saving if accepted. The self-righteous stand condemned; those looking for mercy find it.

If God saves some who have not heard of Christ, it is not because of their religious sincerity or good works but only because of the grace of Christ. It is not the pious and those who are obedient to law who are guaranteed a place in heaven. General revelation does not make Christ's sacrifice unnecessary; his passion, death, resurrection, and ascension provide sufficient covering for all sins, for all people, and for all nations throughout history. God's universal will to save is expressed through the particular Christ (1 Tim. 2:4-5). Salvation from beginning to end is the work of Christ. Christians should not seek to control or restrict God's grace; it is God's grace. Yet humans are the ones who limit God's free grace by their rebellion against God.

Surprising Grace

Sometimes God's redemptive activity is wider than the boundaries of our preconceived notions of revelation. People have awareness of God through the Logos and through the Spirit, but that awareness is not automatically saving unless they act on the awareness. The Holy Spirit who works through general revelation and special revelation is the bridge between general revelation and special revelation.

The Holy Spirit seeks to create faith in us regardless of the kind of revelation we know. The Spirit prepares people for the gospel, and the Spirit testifies to Scripture and to Christ. God draws people by the Spirit.

The Holy Spirit may use dreams, visions, mystic contemplation, or miracles to bring people to repentance. Norman Anderson says, "One cannot deny that some of the great Muslim mystics have sought the face of God with a whole-heartedness that cannot be questioned; and I do not doubt that in some cases it was God himself whom they were seeking, not self-justification."[19] He conjectures that they may be responding to the grace operative in the cross and resurrection, the grace of the One whose story they had never really heard.[20]

There are numerous stories of persons who humbly sought eternal life and had a vision or dream in which they have seen the figure of Jesus or learned the name of Jesus. Sometimes we hear people say, "This is what I have been looking for all these years. Why didn't you tell me before?" A Burmese woman abandoned Buddhism because she knew in her heart that there is one God and sought God's mercy. When she heard the gospel for the first time, she was convinced that this was the answer to her quest.

As God works through the Spirit, it is indeed possible that in exceptional circumstances God is revealed independent of gospel witness. Through a special revelatory initiative, God is disclosed to persons, so that those who have had no contact with the explicit message of the gospel can respond to God in faith and trust. We should expect to encounter people who are drawn toward God's fuller revelation.

These wider redemptive activities are clearly consistent with the Old Testament when people came to know God *outside* the covenant with Israel (Melchizedek, Job, Jethro, Balaam). However, when those who have never heard are compared to Old Testament believers *in* the covenant of Israel prior to the coming of Christ, the analogy is less helpful. Such a comparison provides important insights, but the situations are not parallel. Old Testament believers had a covenant relationship with God grounded in special revelation. They had symbols which anticipated and pointed to the Messiah. Those who have not heard are informed more by general revelation.

When considering the significance of general revelation to those who have not heard, we should focus more on the attitudes of adherents of other religions than on religions as systems. Seekers who move toward Christ do so not because of their religion but in spite of their religion. A Sufi Muslim said, "When you see Jesus, you see

God."[21] There are no alternative ways to be saved because there are no alternative gospels; there is no alternative gospel because there is no other Christ. The central theme of the gospel is that Christ reconciles.

Trusting God's Sovereignty

What is the eternal destiny of those who have never heard? Someone asked Jesus, "Lord, will only a few be saved" (Luke 13:23)? Jesus was not very explicit but gave a *yes* and *no* response. He told them to enter the narrow door, suggesting that only a few will be saved. But after discussing the agony of the lost, he said people would come from the east and west and north and south and take their places in the kingdom. He concluded, "Indeed, some are last who will be first, and some are first who will be last" (Luke 13:23-30). His teaching indicates that not all will be saved (Matt. 7:13-14). If all will be saved, the New Testament would not speak of the final "day of judgment" (Matt. 12:36; Rom. 2:16; 2 Pet. 2:9; 1 John 4:17). But Jesus is warning us not to look for simplistic answers to the mystery of God's sovereignty concerning the saved and the lost.

Lesslie Newbigin, in noting the surprises concerning human destiny which are found in the New Testament,[22] writes, "It is the sinners who will be welcomed, and those who are confident that their place was secure will find themselves outside."[23] Those least expected will be welcome (Matt. 22:1-14). There will be astonishment among the saved and among the lost (Matt. 25:31-46). Parables teach that some who are confident will find themselves excluded and some will be welcomed who do not anticipate it (Luke 15). The righteous will be shocked by the generosity of the Lord (Matt. 20:1-16) and by his severity (Matt. 7:21-23).

Are we being asked to leave the judgment to God? Yes, if the final judgment is in the hands of God, we refrain from definitive judgment. If the Lord refused to answer conclusively, perhaps the answer to the question will need to remain ambiguous.

Salvation is a free gift, but we are not the ones who dispense it. We do not have the authority to determine who is going to be saved or lost on the last day. If we are always trying to decide who is saved and who is lost, we so easily place people in categories and erect relational barriers. Belief in lostness understandably makes us uptight. In Ethiopia one of our children asked whether our Muslim gardener would go to hell. We replied that we don't decide who goes to hell; that's God's decision. Our task is to witness to Christ, who saves from judgment, not to assign people their places. We must refrain from definitive judgment, whether positive or negative. We do not acquit or condemn. God alone has the right to answer our questions about those who have never heard. Since we cannot see from God's perspective, we must not play God, but trust God and let God be God. We are perplexed because our knowledge is finite and fallible.

Revelation calls for obedience; it does not satisfy all our curiosity. Speculation may be a useful exercise, but we need to be more cautious about drawing conclusions from our speculations. We too quickly conclude that what *might* be possible *is* possible. It is unwise to build elaborate theological systems on speculation which goes beyond what God has revealed to us.

We cannot point to any other way of salvation except Jesus Christ, but we are not authorized to limit grace or give a "final examination" for salvation. Perhaps a "reverent agnosticism" (we don't know for sure) or modesty is preferable to negative or positive judgments, since our hopeful speculations cannot be definitive. There is much mystery concerning those who have never heard. The presence of mystery and paradox means that we can explore but cannot fully explain. We need space in our theology for the unknown.

This is especially hard for Westerners, who want to arrive at answers on the basis of human logic. But some things are best left to God's knowledge and wisdom. Our questions about what God will do need to be footnotes, not our major thesis. How much energy should we spend on issues about which God reveals so little? If our questions are really God's, can we be content to let them in God's hands? God's prerogatives are beyond human interrogation.

Our response to wider hope is largely theoretical. Our arguments are based on assumptions or inferences from biblical examples and principles more than from explicit statements from the Bible. It is not our task to declare that people who have not had an opportunity to hear of Christ are automatically lost. Similarly, it is not our task to declare that they are automatically saved. All of us would like to have a wider hope, but our knowledge remains uncertain; we have to remain open to unresolved issues and surprises. We should focus more on the gospel consensus that can be known.

I have no desire to keep the doors of hell ajar. I will not be sad if God finds a way to redeem those who have not heard of Christ. I will be delighted if God saves more people than I expect. But I want to be faithful to my calling and not spend my life speculating about God's intentions or pronouncing either condemnation or false assurance.

These issues have an impact on our moral sensibilities. Our probings are so intense because they are related to the justice of God (Gen. 18:25; Matt. 11:20-24). We ask, "Is it just for God to condemn those who have never heard?" The central issue becomes the justice of God rather than the adequacy of salvation in Christ. Will a loving God provide everyone with an opportunity to be saved? Will God judge people on the basis of the light they have or the light they don't have? How will God express love impartially? Our struggle is sometimes related to our Western sense of justice and tolerance, which leads us to sentimentalize the love of God.

Do we think God will be unfair? Was Jesus ever unfair? We have limited knowledge and misperceptions of justice and fairness, but God revealed in Scripture is loving, gracious, merciful, patient, just, holy, and righteous. We need to balance God's justice and God's love, God's justice and human responsibility, knowing that divine love and divine power never override human freedom. We don't know all of God's thoughts, but we know that God's love reaches as far as love can reach. We don't know for certain the fate of those who have never heard, but like Abraham we ask, "Shall not the Judge of all the earth do what is just?" (Gen. 18:25). Yes, we know God will do what is just and right, and we trust God. If we can trust God *for* salvation we can trust God *with* salvation. There is wideness in God's mercy, but God alone determines it.

Witness More Than Speculation

If God loves the world and wishes all to be saved, does this suggest everyone has access to salvation? Or should such an understanding encourage witness? If God desires the salvation of all, sharing the gospel witnesses to the wideness of God's mercy. Many have not heard or have misheard. Others have not heard because they have been blinded to the truth. Witness does not require complete clarity about all theological questions. We are called to witness to what we do know. Whatever wider hope we grasp for, let us not forget that our task is to witness. When we ask about those who have not heard, the situation calls for urgency in witness, not equivocation. Too often this question is raised as an excuse for inactivity. Posing the question in a particular way can dull the edge of witness. When we wonder, "What will happen to those who have not heard?" we must ask an additional question. "How does God want us to respond to these people?"

If God is drawing people toward the kingdom and they are open to grace, we have incentive to witness. No speculations about what might be should keep us from sharing the message. Redemption is objectively provided. We witness so that the story of redemption is made accessible and can be subjectively appropriated. I believe there are Cornelius-type people to whom God would lead us so that they can respond to God's provision in Christ. Those who have responded to the light that they have, need to know the source and nature of that light. They need access to the fullness of light in Christ. They need teaching and assurance.

We need not apologize for wanting all to know and follow Jesus. We witness to grace precisely because it is such good news in contrast to all the bad news of alienation from God. This is our "operational principle," taught in Scripture and modeled in the New Testament.

13

Style of Witness

Keshab Chandra Sen, leader of Reform Hinduism, said he loved Jesus more than any other and wanted his life patterned after Jesus. But he was turned off by Western forms of Christian life. Gandhi admired Christ but rejected Christianity because of the style of inconsistent Christians. Some people say, "The problem with Christians is that they are not Christian."

The first task in witness is reconversion of Christians to Christ. Christian witness can point the way to Christ by declaring, "I decided to know nothing . . . except Jesus Christ and him crucified" (1 Cor. 2:2). The crucial issue is not Christianity and religions, but Christ and the religions; yet people are often attracted to Christ or repelled from Christ because of the Christian's manner or attitude of witness.

There is reason to criticize the history of Christian witness. It is important to examine whether such criticism focuses on the content of witness, the forms of witness, or the style of witness. Yet the content of witness is often judged by the forms and the style of witness; likewise, legitimate forms of witness are conditioned by the style of witness. We have already noted the importance of witness and have looked at appropriate forms of witness. But these need to be understood as part of one whole witness, a whole which includes content, forms, and style of witness.

Christian religion is a human response to revelation in Christ. Because it is a human response, it is not free from flaw and must, therefore, be critiqued by the Scripture and the life of Christ. Christian witnesses are fallible, as seen in their misuse of power, divisiveness, aloofness, religious pride; their reduction of the gospel to doctrine, ritual, or morality; and their identification of the gospel with Western culture. Encounter with other religions increases awareness of Christianity's weakness and lukewarmness. Many people from other religions have what one Muslim author called "tattooed memories" of the encounter with Christendom.[1]

Today many Christians are embarrassed about past insensitivity to culture and the entanglement of witness with remnants of colonialism. Or they feel uneasy about the style of current involvements. Others feel guilty about their noninvolvement in witness. Some are critical and negative about witness. Others are critical and positive about witness. Christians should intend to transcend their negative feelings about witness. If we only react against our past, we become immobile and apathetic; we withdraw and become complacent.

We must sincerely repent for failure to accept the authority of Christ for the content and manner of witness, and not be captive to what was done in the past. If there is danger in denying those failures, there is equal danger in agonizing over our unfaithfulness. Repentance should lead to more appropriate action, not inaction. New learnings and increased sensitivity should foster more credibility in witness. Perversion of witness brings shame because it is bad news; good news must again emerge. How can we be rooted in Christian faith and not be stuck in old styles of witness? Can we be creatively faithful to our faith?

Western theological interpretation must not be the normative standard for witnessing to Christ in varied cultural contexts. The church in every nation needs to have the freedom to develop its own theological vocabulary and style of witness appropriate to its specific culture. Christians in other cultures can help us distinguish between Western culture and the essence of the gospel. No theological or missiological reflection can be complete without their voice.

Western Christians must listen to brothers and sisters in the international church who live in the context of other religions. At a 1991 meeting in Cyprus cosponsored by the Middle East Council of Churches and Evangelicals for Middle East Understanding, I listened to Christians from the East and West converse about the meaning of Christian witness. It was especially important for Western Christians to hear Arab Christians who live in a Muslim cultural environment. For them, the relationship of Christian faith and other religions is a daily issue. They wrestle constantly with how to live as neighbors and be faithful witnesses to the gospel. Listening to these churches forces us to reflect more realistically about a theology of witness in the context of other religions.

Sometimes Western Christians, because of past tendencies to denigrate other religions, idealize other religions. Many Western Christians who speak positively of religious pluralism have never lived under another religious system. On visits to Hindu centers in India and in conversations with Christians from Hindu background, I observed that Hinduism is not the "pure spirituality" some in the West have come to believe.

While it is important to listen to people who have lived all of their lives in the context of other religions, we also need to hear from people who have turned to Jesus Christ from other religious backgrounds, to see how they experience the uniqueness of Christ.

Priority of Relationships

Witness often commences with a rush of activity instead of cultivating moments of opportunity through relationships. Friendship, a meeting of hearts, is possible even if our religious reflections are not similar. Personal conversation is often more important than a formal agenda or detailed theories of dialogue. People like to speak about themselves and inquire about others; through conversation about daily life, trust and confidence is established.

In conversation we discover the deep feelings and sometimes the wounds of people; these need to be heard and healed. Christian causes, even if just, can ignore or injure real people. Christians need to love people for who they are and for the sake of Christ. But love must have integrity; if love is manipulated, it is no longer love. We cannot always define these relationships as presence, evangelism, service, or dialogue. But we relax and let the Spirit direct our relationship.

If God is primarily revealed in the human life of Jesus, who could be seen and touched, human relationships must have higher priority. We in the West are inclined to explain the gospel rationally, but many people are more likely to receive it intuitively through personal relationships. If living faith is more important than rationalizing faith, the gospel must be modeled through life-transforming relationships.

David Bosch proposes relationships that are not like water pipes, which have no connection with the water they carry, nor like sterile surgical instruments, untouched by human hands; we are not diplomatic mailbags; we are diplomats.[2] Our *being* must be in harmony with our *doing* and *saying*. Visualization must be integrated with verbalization. Witness needs to flow from our person as fresh water flows from a spring. The medium or form of witness is effective to the degree that it creates a relationship. When a relationship is created, witness is inductive; it has some knowledge of the person being addressed. It is not enough to say that the gospel is relevant. The gospel must be seen to relate to particular need.

In the history of the Christian church, faith has often been reduced to ideas. But Christian witness is not merely an intellectual defense of an idea; it is good news, an invitation to enter into a relationship. When the gospel is prepackaged, it becomes a salvation formula, and salvation is dispensed as pills without diagnosis of the patient. Sometimes Christian witness creates information overload, with many words but little communication of truth. Doctrinal truths seldom penetrate the heart and lead people to repentance. Doctrinal overload can inoculate people against the gospel. Faith needs to be demonstrated, not merely defined.

Belief by itself is insufficient without models of Christian behavior consistent with the message. Authentic Christian discipleship is an invitation to acknowledge the lordship of Jesus. We must become good news before we share good news. We must love the neighbor before we win the neighbor. Deeds and words must interpret each other; behavioral language and spoken language complement each other.

In one project, I interviewed first-generation Indian Christians from Hindu background to discover why they had become Christian. I discovered not only why they were drawn to the gospel but also the important role of specific Christians in their pilgrimage of faith. A Hindu lawyer was impressed with how Christians seemed close to God when they prayed. A student gave up his plan to commit suicide because a Christian befriended him, suffered with him, and shared his life. Another student was attracted by Christian modeling of nonviolence, good family life, and disciplined ethical life.

Theology must be translated into relationships. Winsome relationships are prior to theological issues. Kosuke Koyama encourages us to practice an "invitational theology" rather than an "answer theology."[3] The gospel should be seen as invitation, not imposition. Do we hear the questions before responding with answers, and inviting people to faith? Sometimes we have right answers, but they don't match the questions. We need a theology that responds invitationally to real human quests.

Since the gospel flows from people to people, we can only recommend a relationship with Christ if we model relationships with people. Perhaps people have never experienced a relationship with anyone for whom the gospel made an attractive difference.

Christians who believe in witness should take initiative in bridging the gap to other religions. As a whole, Christians have little significant contact with other religions. If this is to be corrected, there will need to be a move away from provincialism to engagement with other religions. Some Christians are reluctant to encounter other religions because they feel inferior or fear rejection.

I recall an experience on the ship from North America to Ethiopia in 1961. A rather sophisticated retired gentleman, observing how uninformed I was on many issues, with some condescension asked, "Where have you been all your life, in a cave?" Some of us may feel like we've been in a cave or ghetto. We have a quarantine mentality toward other religions. We emphasize the "pure message" but are anxious, timid, sometimes even defiant toward the world and its religions. Total isolation for the sake of purity is not possible, nor is it an adequate Christian stance, because it resists religions instead of encountering them.

Rather than restricting our contacts, we look for ways to enter other people's frame of reference on their turf. Such engagement is neither pietistic retreat nor total accommodation; it is an attempt to express solidarity and caring love. A relationship which says, "I love you if you respond to Christ," is not invitational but patronizing and calculated.

Christians should be outward-looking, not defensively erecting barriers of self-protection. Apathy, uncertainty about faith, or defensiveness confuse one's identity and close the door to meaningful relationship. The Christian calling is to open one's heart, one's mind, and one's house, offering Christ because we have nothing of greater value to offer. In that offering, we discover the gospel's meaning afresh.

If Jesus ministered freely, risking rejection, we can respect people's freedom of choice. Rejection of our witness should not elicit harshness or cool a relationship. Christian witness to the truth must be gentle, conditioned by love.

To some extent our understanding of truth makes us theologically exclusive, but this should not translate into sociological exclusivism. We can maintain clear theological perspectives and still be inclusive in our relationships. Though Christian communities are concerned for their identity and for the boundaries between Christian faith and other faiths, Christian communities need not be a barrier to witness. They can be a source of strength as they hold to Christian distinctives, rather than homogenize belief by looking for a common core of belief.[4]

H. D. Beeby suggests that the church, the new Israel, is only the church when it wrestles with the nations; he contends that " 'pietistic retreat' or 'liberal accommodation' to the nations are equally ways of ceasing to be the church."[5] The nations will receive blessing only if the church is truly the church; in wrestling with the world, the church is blessed. But this can only occur when the church, as the people of God, develops meaningful relationships with the world's people.

Critique and Judgment in Witness

Witness should be a positive statement about the gospel rather than a negative statement about religions. Christians should be reluctant to make judgments about religion in general. If religions combine truth and falsehood, Christian witnesses will need to discern and critique them, affirming some aspects of religion and rejecting others. But discernment and critique are not to accuse or to scorn. The Christian's manner should be reconciling and redemptive. Since Jesus is the norm, some elements of religion will be excluded. But Christ is the one who excludes, and Christian witnesses must defer to Christ's prerogative. We have no authority to be more inclusive or exclusive than Christ. Our witness should point to the claims of Christ. Lesslie Newbigin has taught us that we are not on the judgment seat but on the witness stand.

Since redemption is defined by its center more than by its boundaries, it is not our task to set limits on God's grace by pronouncing judgment. Christian witnesses must exercise caution. Verkuyl notes that "no theologian of religions has a right to make an ultimate value judgment on a person's faith. There is within everyone a deep secret which none but God knows."[6]

Several years ago I heard a visiting North American preacher speak in the chapel of Union Biblical Seminary in India. In his address he unequivocally declared, "I can tell you, Gandhi won't be in heaven." The Indian students were upset, not because they wanted to assign Gandhi a place in heaven, but because the preacher had stepped beyond the bounds of his responsibility.

I dislike hearing anyone being condemned to hell. I also dislike seeing people made "honorary Christians" against their will. We know the Bible speaks about hell, and that Jesus warned people to repent so that they might not perish. But for us to pronounce another's destiny goes far beyond our authority. Though we believe that salvation is made available through the grace of God as manifested in Jesus

Christ, we can only entrust persons who have not received Jesus Christ to the judgment of a wise and merciful God.

However, there is another kind of judgment. If there are some who declare, "You are not okay," there are others who declare, "You are okay." Some confidently assert that people of other faiths or no faith will be saved through their sincere following of the light they have; they are also making a judgment. If it is not our prerogative to condemn, and it is also not our prerogative to acquit.

I listened to a dialogue between a Christian and a Jew. The Jewish person said, "I don't believe in hell. God is love, and hell doesn't sound like a loving place to me." It is sad that hell has been exploited by making God into a cruel God who delights in punishing sinners.

Sometimes Christians also assume that a religion of love eliminates hell from the Scriptures, but the Bible clearly teaches lostness, condemnation, and judgment. Jesus in conversation with Nicodemus said, "Those who believe in him are not condemned; but those who do not believe are condemned already, because they have not believed in the name of the only Son of God" (John 3:18). Jesus also said that he will be ashamed of those who are ashamed of him (Mark 8:38), and he will deny those who deny him (Matt. 10:33). Those who are not with Christ are said to be against Christ (Matt. 12:30). Jesus taught the principle of judgment in his stories of the faithful and the unfaithful slave (Matt. 24:45-51), the parable of the ten bridesmaids (Matt. 25:1-13), the parable of the talents (Matt. 25:14-30), and the story of the division of sheep and goats in the judgment of the nations (Matt. 25:31-46).

Lesslie Newbigin says there are

those who seem anxious to keep the doors of hell wide open so that there may not be any lack of funds and recruits for mission work. There are, on the other hand, those who seem to think that God governs the universe on some referendum principle, and that it is intrinsically impossible that the majority should be wrong.[7]

It is tragic that the threat of hell has so often been misused. Yet judgment cannot be removed from Scripture.

The cross of Jesus Christ cannot be understood apart from sin and judgment. The cross judges self-salvation, human conceit, legalism. Jesus was crucified not only for sinners but also for religious people. In the New Testament there is mercy and judgment, salvation and destruction, life and death. Christian witnesses are not faithful if they ignore sin and judgment; they function as prophets warning of coming judgment.

Judgment and salvation are not separated in the Bible because God's nature is both holy and gracious. Yet Jesus' mission was to seek the lost, like a father runs toward his prodigal son, or like a mother hen gathers her chicks. God is merciful and "patient with you, not wanting any to perish, but all to come to repentance" (2 Pet. 3:9).

Jesus judges people on the basis of their relationship with him. Jesus gave and gives people freedom to choose, with the condition that they would bear the consequences of their choice. The possibility of hell reinforces both the reality and consequences of human freedom. Heim says, "Judgment . . . is something like having your passport checked. Where is your citizenship? Where do you belong?"[8] Humans are involved in judging themselves by the choices they make.

The main thrust of witness should not be to threaten punishment. Jesus didn't threaten the Samaritan woman; he invited her to drink. Witness is too often a negative statement about religion rather than sharing faith; assault must give way to invitation. We call attention to human sin and need, but we share good news more than bad. If we try to convince men and women of their lostness before they come to know the Savior, we become judges of our fellow human beings. But we are not God's accountant; our judgments are premature. We are cautious about expressing the wrath and judgment of God precisely because we cannot do it justly. Rather, we witness with the realization that some day "every knee should bend, in heaven and on earth and under the earth, and every tongue should confess that Jesus Christ is Lord, to the glory of God the Father" (Phil. 2:10-11). All will meet Christ into whose hands judgment has been given.

We believe the finality of Christ is a judgment upon other religions, but it is also a judgment upon ourselves. The Scripture says judgment begins with the household of God (1 Pet. 4:17). This awareness keeps us from using the finality of Christ as a club and helps us to avoid confusing the lordship of Christ with our particular interpretation of his lordship. Judgment must arise from the gospel, not from cultural Christianity. Jesus pronounced "woes" on those within the covenant (Matt. 23). In fact, judgment was most severe on those who confessed Christ but didn't live accordingly. Not everyone who says "Lord, Lord" will be saved (Matt. 7:21-23). Those who know the will of God and don't do it will be treated more harshly than those who didn't know the will of God (Luke 12:47-48).

Jesus was more generous than his disciples. Some people who

were not part of the disciple group, cast out demons in the name of Jesus. When the disciples complained, Jesus said, "Whoever is not against us is for us" (Mark 9:38-40). When James and John wanted to command fire to come down from heaven to punish the Samaritans, Jesus rebuked them (Luke 9:54-55).

I invited a Bahai person to speak about his faith to my class on new religious movements. At the end of the class he turned to me and asked, "What do you think of what I said?"

After my response, which included the claims of Jesus Christ, he replied, "What does that do to me?"

I knelt on the floor, suggesting, "We all need to kneel under the authority of Christ." When we acknowledge that all are under the judgment of Christ, we share the message of Christ with humility, realizing how inadequate is our response to Christ.

When Karl Barth lectured at Fuller Theological Seminary in 1963, he was asked, "Do you believe in hell?" He replied, "No, I don't believe in hell; I believe in Jesus Christ." Hell exists, but this is not the focus of our witness; we are not hell's gatekeepers. We do not publish the list of the doomed. Jesus wants to give life, light, and freedom to people; salvation is more than escape from hell. The apostles did not deny lostness, but their witness was motivated by the possibility of salvation through the death and resurrection of Jesus the Messiah.

Attitudes in Witness

Christians concerned about belief in Jesus must also be concerned about the beliefs of others. Theological convictions must be presented with sensitivity to other religions. A Christian's attitude and approach to another should recommend the truth which is being communicated. Some of these attitudes have been implicit or explicit in earlier chapters, especially in chapters 10 and 11, but they are stressed here because one's attitude toward others is so crucial in witness. Attitudes which commend the gospel include understanding, respect, humility, tolerance, and vulnerability.

Understanding

If Christians want to be understood, they must understand. Zeal for witness is no substitute for knowledge of the religious background of persons to whom one witnesses. Knowledge of religion is of two kinds: religion as systems, and religion as experience. A thorough knowledge of contemporary religious systems is helpful. Whenever possible, Christians should know as much or more about other religions than many of their adherents.

This demands careful thought and empathetic understanding. It is important to understand the function of religion in society and in the personal lives of committed people. As much as possible, we should try to vicariously participate in the religious history of others, learning from their writings and from writings about them. Such understanding helps us to correct misconceptions and avoid false accusations or unfounded pronouncements.

We soon discover, however, that people's experience of religion is as important as history and theology. Since much experience and practice deviates from the philosophical and theological ideals, "expert knowledge" of the tradition can blind us to important dimensions of religious experience and practice. Many have a religion by birth but have not made it their own. Others make it their own, but it is not very consistent with the official version of the religion. No Christian is a perfect Christian, and no Muslim is a perfect Muslim. It is important, therefore, to distinguish between religions and the followers of religions. There is value in seeing religious systems as a whole so long as we do not forget that the Muslim and the Buddhist may differ from Islam and Buddhism.

On the other hand, we cannot relate to individual Muslims without taking Islam and Islamic culture seriously. If we ignore the religious culture, we ignore part of the person. When we take time to converse with people about their religion and culture, we affirm their personhood, even if we cannot accept their religious faith.

Religions should be seen as a basic faith response rather than systems, programs, traditions, and institutions. We should avoid assigning people to institutional boxes. Objective religion may or may not lead to faith. Since the meaning of religion does not reside in systems but in people, we must converse with people, asking how they express piety, faith, and fear of God. It is important to observe the direction which people are moving. Some have faith which goes beyond the institutional religion to which they are committed.

The Samaritan woman was part of a system, but she was restless and moving. Some Buddhists fear God even if Buddhism is considered agnostic. An Ethiopian friend reported to me that in his adolescence he was not well behaved. So his mother took him to a Muslim witch doctor, who told her not to be anxious because her son would soon become a believer in Jesus and change his behavior. If God's light shines everywhere, religious experiences sometimes anticipate the gospel, and persons are drawn toward Christ.

As we cultivate inner understanding, not just intellectual understanding, we are better able to deal with bitterness, aloofness, and fear between the religions. When understanding results in empathetic love, our own commitment makes us more sensitive to the commitment of another, not less sensitive. In our Western "self-confidence" and because of our Christian concern for witness, we are conditioned to speak. But how much do we know about listening? If we are not actively listening and learning, we engage in irrelevant arguments and ineffective communication, which produces bigotry, hostility, and defensiveness on both sides.

We need patience, openness, and transparent honesty. We probe, we observe, we question. Although we believe in the uniqueness of the gospel, that gives us no excuse for ignorance or for condescending, derogatory statements born of ignorance. For too long Christians have been unwilling to learn from other cultures and religions.

Understanding develops as we recognize differences, not by ignoring or denying them. We share a common humanity with other religions. We are human beings before we are Jews, Christians, Muslims, Hindus, or Buddhists. When we speak of Islam as a system, misunderstandings quickly emerge. But when we befriend Muslims, we respond to real persons with their hopes and anxieties. When a basis for friendship is established, people may be more willing to discuss personal faith issues—health, guidance, family, spirituality, prayer—rather than only theoretical issues. In this context witness can be both person-centered and truth-centered because truth is always tied to personal relationships. As we witness, new questions emerge, but the new questions are an opportunity to refine witness, not abandon it.

As we begin to understand another faith, we grasp new dimensions of our own faith. There is always tension between understanding another religion and understanding one's own faith. This risk should not frighten nor make us complacent. It highlights the importance of being secure in our own understanding of faith if we are to relate meaningfully with other religions.

Respect

In addition to understanding, we need genuine respect and appreciation for other religions. Increased understanding of other faiths affects our attitude toward other religions. My experience of living among other religions and teaching religions has given me a new appreciation for other faiths as well as a greater appreciation for the significance of Jesus Christ. We can affirm the finality of Christ and still respect other religions. We can only present Jesus with integrity if we fairly represent others. Witness to Christ that belittles or denigrates people of other faiths is counter witness. Conviction should be spoken with confidence but also with respect and graciousness.

Metaphorically and sometimes literally, we take off our shoes lest we tread irreverently on another's sacred ground. I met a Christian who refuses to take off his shoes to enter a mosque, choosing thereby to remain outside. Though I want to respect him for his conviction, I'm disturbed by some of his attitudes, which seem disrespectful and stifle meaningful communication with Islam.

Respect goes beyond coexistence to appreciation. We can appreciate another's religion by focusing upon the truth and richness of the religion. We do not deny error, but error should force us to sympathetic understanding rather than denunciation. Religious encounter should focus on the positive rather than on the negative and be characterized by tact and gentleness. Respect for the other person demands that we reject dishonest handling of religious issues or deliberate misinterpretation. We should not needlessly offend people. It is unchristian for us to violate the dignity of the other by verbal abuse, insult, or embarrassment.

Christian conviction must always be matched with reverence. People deserve hospitality and courtesy, especially since some have been the objects of suspicion. It is unfortunate when disagreements have led to a breach of trust or resentment; truth must be explored in a trusting way. In Jerusalem, Krister Stendahl once asked Christians, "How safe are other religions in our orthodoxy?" Christian witness must always be with sensitivity. In 1 Peter 3:15-16 we are encouraged, "Be ready to make your defense to anyone who demands from you an accounting for the hope that is in you; yet do it with gentleness and reverence."

Love for God should not keep us from respecting human beings. If we respect the other, our thoughts and actions build relationships. Respect does not demean the other; we see the other as a subject and not as an object. Respect is enhanced when witnesses are generous and congenial. What is the quality of our interaction with people? Can we develop natural relationships as we do with the salesman and carpenter we meet, people who may be only nominally Christian?

Care must be given to both words and actions because some aspects of religion elicit disdain rather than respect. In Nepal, I remember how unsettling it was for me to observe many goats being sacrificed to Hindu deities. Sometimes we are insensitive in the language we use for customs that we find objectionable—"pagan rites," "stupid ceremonies." But we must always respect people and guard against feelings of hostility or ridicule toward those who seem misguided.

Rabbi Irving Greenberg, in a speech to Jews and Christians in Jerusalem, said we should "love God more, not religions less."[9] David Lochhead writes, "To love one's neighbor as oneself is to be in a dialogical relationship with one's neighbor."[10] If our manner of relationship is dialogical rather than polemical or defensive, we will be respectful in social interaction and theological discussions. Our attitudes are often more objectionable than our theological stance.

Witness demands rapport, and there can be no rapport without mutual respect. Respect does not imply less concern for the truth; it is not indifference to the truth. We witness to Christ with both confidence and sensitivity. But when we witness to the Christian story, we listen to other stories, we respect their integrity, and we grant others the freedom to receive or reject Christ. If they reject our witness, we do not cease to love. As a Christian leader said to a Jewish-Christian conference in Jerusalem, "Jesus' blood did not call for retaliation but for reconciliation."[11]

Humility

Humility is necessary in our relations with other religions. In the history of Christian witness, the triumph of Christ has caused people to become triumphalistic in manner. John H. Yoder notes, "The error of triumphalism was not that it was tied to Jesus, but that it denied him, precisely in its disrespect for the neighbor. . . . Its error was not that it propagated Christianity around the world, but that what it propagated was not Christian enough."[12]

For many Jews, Christianity is linked with memory of the Holocaust. For many Muslims in the Middle East, Christ is still associated with memory of the Crusades. E. Stanley Jones said that when the Crusaders conquered Jerusalem, they found that Christ was not there because they lost him through the spirit and methods with which they sought to serve him.[13]

Perhaps we feel no responsibility for past mistakes, which we regard as accidents of history before our time. But this does not erase them from the minds of the injured persons. Christian faith is not alone responsible for all the sins of the West. Yet we should repent and denounce obvious Christian entanglements with triumphalism.

Even today Christian witness can easily be associated with power, privilege, position, authority of money, cultural origin, political position, knowledge, or technology. In Cyprus, I heard Elias Chacour, an Israeli Arab Christian leader, criticize Western ethnocentrism by declaring, "Jesus wasn't born in Washington, D.C.!"[14] In Syria, I listened to the Greek Orthodox Patriarch of Antioch and all the East. He said to a group of us from America, "Sometimes we think you believe that Christ was incarnated in America or that the gospel is an American book."[15]

Unfortunately the church sometimes displays a competitive mentality in witnessing to other religions. How do we divest ourselves of a superiority complex? Frequently the claims of Christ have been seriously misrepresented as claims to superiority and power. Even if other religions express aggression and violence (such as is true of some religious fundamentalism), we should not respond in kind. Christian attitudes should not be conditioned by the stance of other religions toward us but should be motivated and directed by the Spirit.

A conviction for the uniqueness of the gospel doesn't give us the right to be smug. Far too many Christians have unconfessed sin in relation to other religions. Sometimes we have denigrated other religions by scapegoating them or considering them enemies. It is so easy to have patronizing attitudes toward other religious people. Such attitudes may be rooted in our unconscious mind and find nonverbal expression. A Hindu said concerning Christians, "They went out to give and not to receive, to talk and not to listen."[16] Often in interreligious relationships, other people are more aware of our hearts than we ourselves are.

Those who are humble are self-critical. We dare not claim personal superiority over followers of other religions; we are saved by grace. Interactions with other people can help us correct our misunderstandings concerning Christ and make sure that our deeds do not betray our confession. Authentic discipleship is more important than cheap advertisement.

We must acknowledge that we have sometimes misinterpreted the gospel by presenting it with the accretions of our own thought and culture. Our practice has fallen short of our theological position. We do not apologize for confessing Christ. We apologize for triumphalism, because Christ's triumph was a triumph of the cross. We apologize for our mistakes, not for the gospel. We aren't embarrassed for the truth, but for our misrepresentation of the truth.

Some have claimed the name of Christ but have perverted its

content. Others affirm the content without the name. For example, Gandhi liked the ethical-communal message of Jesus but refused to call himself a Christian. His refusal was in a context where "Christian" meant empire or racism. Which Jesus was Gandhi following?[17] The issue is crucial: Which Jesus do we follow? To which Jesus do we witness?

In witness we must find our way between arrogance and neutrality, between triumphalism and timidity. When we declare that Christ is the way, that is not triumphalism if it is said in humility and love. However, it is not a sign of humility to relativize the message of the cross as a corrective to imperialism and triumphalism. If we are embarrassed about ethnic or cultural exclusivism and our move toward greater acceptance of the larger culture, that should not make us reluctant to uphold the unique character of the gospel. Those who criticize us for being Christocentric can also be self-righteous.

Many are afraid they will be seen as arrogant or imperialistic if they hold distinctive beliefs. But arrogance has more to do with how beliefs are held; not all styles of witness are appropriate. We should not forsake the center of our faith in the interest of humility. Humility does not call for deprecation of our values or lessening of our convictions. Humility is not indecision about Christ; what Christ has done on our behalf must not be negotiated away.

Arrogance, contempt, and conquest are a violation of the cross. If people object to the gospel, let it be because of the cross, not our lack of love. Authentic witness is not rude, intimidating, or manipulative. Witness is not dominance and control but suffering (*marturia*). I recall listening to an Egyptian clergyman who had spent time in prison for his faith. He spoke of suffering as a "divine gift."[18] Koyama urges us to have a "crucified mind."[19] If the cross is the center of our message, it must be the center of our life and attitude.

Witness is not an imposition. We do not trample on another. Embracing truth with confidence should not lead to conceit or dogmatism; the gospel cannot be communicated with condescension. We entreat people on behalf of Christ to be reconciled to God (2 Cor. 5:20), and we commend the gospel (2 Cor. 4:2). Truth is not merely asserted but must be recognized. Truth stands at the door and knocks. There must be consent from within; too much pressure keeps one from opening the door.

In a Jewish-Christian conversation in Jerusalem concerning Jewish understandings of Messiah, a Christian student, shaking his finger, insisted that he could prove from Hebrew Scriptures that Jesus was

Messiah. But conviction stated forcefully is not always convincing. When one enters the Church of the Nativity in Bethlehem, one has to bend low because the door is so small. This is a fitting symbol for the mystery of the incarnation and a model for Christian witness.

Zeal sometimes causes people to go beyond the bounds of propriety in their manner; such zeal can destroy bridges rather than build them. Once I listened to a zealous sermon in which the tone seemed quite abrasive. After the sermon a young believer challenged the speaker for his use of fear as a primary motivation, citing his own experience in which he had come to faith because of positive aspects of the gospel. But the speaker responded by quoting Paul: "Therefore, knowing the fear of the Lord, we try to persuade others" (2 Cor. 5:11). I empathized with the young believer. Fear can be misused. We must make sure that the tone of witness is invitational. Meekness and gentleness recommend the truth of the gospel.

Humility and courtesy provide the right context for religious truth. Confidence in the truth is not bolstered by arrogance; one who is confident can afford to be gentle. Witness and civility belong together. Insulting people's religion is like misbehaving in their house or expressing hostility at their table.[20] There is an intimate relationship between people and their religious convictions. It is irresponsible for anyone to respond to other religions with unkind remarks or derisive humor. We must stand alongside others, not in opposition to them. The most profound religious convictions require an empathetic atmosphere.

Witness to what God has done in Christ need not be arrogant. We have not invented the gospel; we are messengers and stewards of it. Karl Barth reminds us that we never "have" the gospel; we perpetually receive it. The privilege of witnessing to Jesus Christ should not make us feel superior in status or character; it is Christ who is superior. But fear of a superiority complex should not drive us to an inferiority complex or a persecution complex. With confidence we witness to faith, hope, and love in a gentle spirit.

The gospel is leaven, not a hammer. People are not argued into faith; witness is an invitation to consider Jesus. Since we are concerned that people voluntarily make decisions for Christ, witness is characterized by patience rather than by pressure.

Tolerance

It is important for us to define tolerance in our attitudes toward other religions. While we seek to cultivate appropriate attitudes toward non-Christian religions, we are not faithful to the truth if we neglect the content of the gospel. Are we self-righteous or intolerant if we believe in the uniqueness of Christian faith? Is it intolerant to believe that the gospel should be shared with others, so that they might have an opportunity to follow Christ?

From one perspective the Christian confession is intolerant, for if the gospel is true and does not accept all ways as equally valid, it is intolerant. The gospel wouldn't be the gospel if we removed its claim to universal validity. If something is true, its antithesis is untrue. There are limits to tolerance in belief and morality. Error should not be permitted to thrive in the name of tolerance. We cannot be tolerant of all intellectual ideas or religious practices. If tolerance is the highest virtue, we need not be concerned for truth, but if truth is the highest virtue, tolerance needs a more careful definition.

Tolerance should not demand that personal conviction be relativized. We cannot concede the essence of our faith. This is precisely what we bring to our relationship with others. If truth matters, we cannot accept a "lazy tolerance" which makes room for any expression of religion. Cragg says, "For some, tolerance becomes almost a faith in itself, with little awareness of things that divide." He continues, "Entire tolerance is bogus. . . . Truth demands more of us than mutual politeness."[21] Truth must not be pushed aside but held with modesty. Tolerance is not indifference, timidity, or fear.

Does one make choices on the basis of preference or on the basis of enduring norms? Is the cross pointing in every direction, or is it the place where people are meant to kneel? The study of comparative religion should not make us comparatively religious. Christians should be intolerant of religious relativism, theological compromise, and syncretism. When truth is relative, indifference replaces commitment and uncertainty replaces confidence. We are not obliged to give up our belief in normative truth. Though a religion of tolerance is said to be the religion of the future, this challenges our basic understanding of the nature of truth, for truth by its nature is intolerant.

On the other hand, though the gospel is not tolerant of all religious ideas, the spirit of the gospel is forbearance, with no limit on tolerance for people as people. We argue for the truth but honor all persons, keenly aware that we can sometimes mar the truth by the spirit in which we contend for it. A tolerant attitude is itself a witness to the gospel. We are tolerant of others because of God's grace in Christ. We must not hate one another for the love of God or for the love of truth. Love for God makes possible a loving, tolerant disposition toward all of God's children. We don't just tolerate people with a stiff upper lip; we can be genuinely accepting of them. Social tolerance, respect, and coexistence are basic human rights.

Tolerance does not mean we are prevented from saying anything negative about religion. But disagreement does not have to be with a spirit of intolerance. We need to critically evaluate the beliefs and practices of religion, accepting the person holding conflicting beliefs or practices without accepting the validity of those beliefs and practices. Courtesy does not avoid contradictions. But unless our convictions for truth are matched with courtesy, the spirit of our witness invalidates the truth we commend. This understanding of tolerance suggests that tolerance has more to do with attitude than belief, more with open-handedness and open-mindedness than open-endedness. Faithfulness to Christ should make us open to others but not to all ideas.

Vulnerability

It is important to be aware of our cultural identity as Western Christians, because there is often a power factor in our relationships. A Buddhist said, "The strain between the Christian communities of the world and the non-Christian communities is not only due to the theological distance between them but [is] also in considerable measure due to their power relationship."[22]

Christians need to divest themselves of the burden of power in their witness. Spiritual violence is never justified in the name of witness. If witness is done from power or prestige, it is corrupting rather than liberating. We so easily succumb to condescension, spiritual pride, and elitism. Sometimes our self-assurance, aggression, or insensitivity wounds others. Jesus' conquest of death gives us no authorization to conquer other religions. From Christ's death we learn surrender and sacrifice. Without vulnerability in relationships, the lordship of Christ becomes harsh.

Some Jews say that after Auschwitz Christians can no longer maintain that in Jesus Christ salvation has come. Many Jews have no desire to accept Jesus as one of their own because of the pain he symbolizes to their people. It is tragic when our failure to live as Christ taught, has denied or perverted our confession of Jesus Christ. A Jewish friend of mine said, "Jews have nothing good to say about Jesus because of the church's mistreatment of the Jews." Another Jew said, "Christians believe in the cross; Jews carry it."

Religious people find it difficult to admit guilt, preferring to vindicate or exonerate themselves. But repentance and self-criticism must be part of witness. Our position should be one of vulnerability for the times when we or "our" people have had feelings of superiority or have invaded another's religion with dominance and aggression. Sometimes we need to carry the sins of those who have gone before us. Penitence, rather than pleading innocence, seeks forgiveness even if we are not the primary perpetrators. Is this going the second mile? Penitence is more than regret; penitence seeks to correct, and by so doing, it opens the door for new and more hopeful relationships. Repentance must be honest; it is not a new strategy.

Kenneth Cragg says, "Christianity needs self-accusation as much as any. Yet guilt does not always prove a wise counselor. A true repentance is not served by a false penance."[23] If the cross is to be believed, we must take our position at the foot of the cross. Repentance is not disengagement from witness but another kind of engagement.

Vulnerability and repentance are concerned for reconciliation that overcomes enmity. Christians who are sometimes the cause of others' wounds need to help heal those wounds. Our task is to incarnate the good news of reconciliation, acknowledging and rectifying our insensitivity to others and confessing our prejudices, such as shown in anti-Semitism and caricatures of Islam.

Misunderstandings and misinterpretations must be corrected. Many prejudices are partly false or partly true. In Israel, I heard a Jewish person speak who still carried an impression of Christians based on past actions, and on statements which blamed Jews for the death of Jesus. He had not erased those impressions even though there have been Christian attempts to correct such pronouncements.

Even when others mistrust us, we are called to love them. Love promotes nonretaliation. The church not only witnesses to personal reconciliation through Christ. The church also needs to model reconciliation through commitment to peace and peacemaking. As individuals we are called to model the peace teaching and example of Jesus in our personal lifestyle, seeking to mediate Christ's reconciling love in all our relationships.

Vulnerability is not always chosen voluntarily. Today the institutional church in the West is losing much of its power and influence. This could help it to recover its primary task. Nevertheless, the church must consciously choose a new vision. Can the church in the West learn from other churches which have been forced to be vulnerable? During the Marxist revolution, the Ethiopian church was stripped of its power and security. Egyptian Christians have learned to live a precarious existence as a minority in an Islamic society. In their times of vulnerability, renewal made the signs of the kingdom more apparent. Can Western Christians learn from these examples and voluntarily choose vulnerability?

Our vulnerability must be patterned after the vulnerability of God, yet many of us never see God in failure, only in success. We make a mistake if we think we can have the power of the resurrection without the mark of the cross. On Easter evening 1995, in a vesper meditation in Jerusalem, Thomas Stransky noted that when Jesus accomplished that most important part of his mission on earth, he was in a position (on the cross) of being unable to *do* anything: he couldn't walk, minister with his hands, or even speak.

Christians are often preoccupied with success, but the gospel of weakness is not shared by powerful means, as measured by the world. God uses our strengths and gifts but also our weakness and brokenness. We do not have a perfect understanding of the gospel. We know personal failure. But the power of the gospel does not depend on the flawlessness of the messenger. When we are strong, we are dangerous and least effective.

When Jesus sent out his disciples on their mission, he showed them his hands and his side (John 20:20-21). They would share his mission as they shared his passion.

Epilogue

In Jerusalem, I heard a story of a man lost in the expanse of the Judean desert. In his distress he found a Bedouin who said, "I'll show you the way back to Jerusalem."

Christ wishes to show us the way to God because he *is* the way. Sometimes we doubt, question, or become confused about Jesus being the way because his claim seems so exclusive. Can we affirm again that Christ is the way? We don't need to shout louder. Sometimes we whisper in love. Our confidence is not in the superior claim of our religion but in Christ and the cross.

Jesus Christ keeps confronting us with the question, "Who do you say that I am?"

Many of us have answered, "You are the Christ, the Son of the living God."

As Christian witnesses, we are not doing the questioning. Jesus poses the question. The uniqueness of Christ is not something we have invented; it is the truth entrusted to us as stewards of witness. We bear witness to Jesus so that people hear the impact of his question.

We are not disinterested witnesses. The love of Christ inspires our witness. But as Jesus gave the disciples time to answer, so our hearers must be given space to ponder the significance of the question. Some people will confess, "You are the Christ." Others who hear his question may reply, like the disciples, that he is one of the greatest prophets. We entrust such persons to Jesus with the hope that they will discover him to be the Christ.

We witness with *patience*. Witness in the context of other religions is a difficult task. People need time to ponder the significance of Jesus

Christ. I had a student, formerly Muslim, who took many years before he could confidently confess to Jesus, "You are the Christ."

We witness with *hope*; hope that others will be drawn, though ever so slowly, to the one who moves toward them with arms outstretched.

We witness with *trust*, with a long-range view. Perhaps our witness will contribute to an awakened understanding of Christ within religious movements or will reach persons beyond our lifetime. It is difficult when we do not see the harvest. We feel like we are only gathering the stones from the field, plowing the field, or planting the seed.

We witness with *prayer*, prayer that we will not, as Peter, stumble over the meaning of Christ; prayer that we will not confuse our claims with the claims of Christ; prayer that the manner of our witness will commend the vulnerable, compassionate Christ.

Notes

1. Introduction to Religious Plurality

1. Harvey Cox in a public lecture on "Many Mansions—Christians in a Religiously Plural World." Bridgewater College, Bridgewater, Va., March 20, 1989.

2. Harvey Cox, *The Secular City* (New York, N.Y.: Macmillan, 1966).

3. Harvey Cox, *Religion in the Secular City* (New York, N.Y.: Simon & Schuster, 1984).

4. Peter Berger, *The Sacred Canopy* (Garden City, N.Y.: Doubleday, 1967).

5. Peter Berger, *A Rumor of Angels* (Garden City, N.Y.: Doubleday, 1969).

6 Allan Bloom, *The Closing of the American Mind* (New York, N.Y.: Simon & Schuster, 1987).

2. Response to Religious Plurality—Exclusivism and Inclusivism

1. Carl E. Braaten, *No Other Gospel! Christianity Among the World's Religions* (Minneapolis: Fortress, 1992), 13.

2. Ibid., 13.

3. Harold A. Netland, *Dissonant Voices: Religious Pluralism and the Question of Truth* (Grand Rapids: Eerdmans, 1991), 34.

4. Wilfred Cantwell Smith, "An Attempt at Summation," in Gerald H. Anderson and Thomas F. Stransky, eds., *Christ's Lordship and Religious Pluralism* (Maryknoll, N.Y.: Orbis Books, 1981), 202.

5. Peter Cotterell, *Mission and Meaninglessness: The Good News in a World of Suffering and Disorder* (London: SPCK, 1990), 59.

6. Krister Stendahl, in a lecture at Union Theological Seminary in Richmond, Va., at a conference on "Christ's Lordship and Religious Pluralism," October 1979.

7. Wesley Ariarajah, *The Bible and People of Other Faiths* (Geneva: World Council of Churches, 1985), 25-27.

8. Donald G. Dawe, "Christian Faith in a Religiously Plural World," in Donald G. Dawe and John B. Carman, eds., *Christian Faith in a Religiously Plural*

World (Maryknoll, N.Y.: Orbis Press, 1978), 13-32.
    9. Braaten, 89.
    10. John Sanders, *No Other Name: An Investigation into the Destiny of the Unevangelized* (Grand Rapids: Eerdmans, 1992), 226.
    11. S. Mark Heim, *Is Christ the Only Way? Christian Faith in a Pluralistic World* (Valley Forge, Pa.: Judson, 1985), 120-122.
    12. Summarized by Cotterell, 44-50.
    13. See interpretation of Martin Goldsmith, *What About Other Faiths?* (London: Hodder & Stoughton, 1989), 122-124.
    14. Interpreted by Cotterell, 51-52.
    15. David Wright, "The Watershed of Vatican II: Catholic Approaches to Religious Pluralism," in Andrew D. Clarke and Bruce W. Winter, eds., *One God, One Lord: Christianity in a World of Religious Pluralism,* (Grand Rapids: Baker Book House, 1992), 208, 216.
    16. Basil Meeking and John Stott, *The Evangelical-Roman Catholic Dialogue in Mission, 1977-1984* (Grand Rapids: Eerdmans, 1986), 45.
    17. David Bosch, *Transforming Mission* (Maryknoll, N.Y.: Orbis Press, 1991), 480-481.
    18. Chris Wright, *What's So Unique About Jesus?* (Sussex, Great Britain: Monarch Publication, 1990), 62.
    19. Sanders, 215, 223-224.
    20. Chris Wright, 45.
    21. Goldsmith, 124.
    22. Clark H. Pinnock, *A Wideness in God's Mercy: The Finality of Jesus Christ in a World of Religions* (Grand Rapids: Zondervan, 1992), 76.

3. Response to Religious Plurality—Pluralism
    1. Netland, 196.
    2. Ibid., 196.
    3. Heim, 112-114.
    4. Ibid., 115-117.
    5. Ibid., 117-119.
    6. Paul F. Knitter, *No Other Name? A Critical Survey of Christian Attitudes Toward the World's Religions* (Maryknoll, N.Y.: Orbis Books, 1985), 7-20.
    7. John Hick and Paul F. Knitter, eds., *The Myth of Christian Uniqueness: Toward a Pluralistic Theology of Religions* (Maryknoll, N.Y.: Orbis Press, 1987), viii. See also Gerald Anderson's interpretation, "Theology of Religions and Missiology," in *The Good News of the Kingdom,* ed. Charles van Engen, Dean S. Gilliland, Paul Pierson (Maryknoll, N.Y.: Orbis Press, 1993), 201.
    8. Lesslie Newbigin, *The Open Secret: Sketches of Missionary Theology* (Grand Rapids: Eerdmans, 1978), 184-185.
    9. Netland, 117.
    10. E. David Cook, "Truth, Mystery and Justice: Hick and Christianity's Uniqueness," in Clarke and Winter, 240-241.
    11. J. Andrew Kirk, *Loosing the Chains. Religion as Opium and Liberation* (London: Hodder & Stoughton, 1992), 11.
    12. Knitter, *No Other Name?* 152.
    13. Interpreted by Goldsmith, 25.
    14. Knitter, *No Other Name?* 172.

15. Chris Wright, 51-52. For a survey of Panikkar's views, see Knitter, *No Other Name?* ch. 8.

16. Kirk, 92.

17. Knitter, *No Other Name?* 185. Cf. Timothy D. Westergren, "Do All Roads Lead to Heaven? An Examination of Unitive Pluralism," in William V. Crockett and James G. Sigountos, eds., *Through No Fault of Their Own? The Fate of Those Who Have Never Heard* (Grand Rapids: Baker Book House, 1991), 173.

18. Paul R. Eddy, "John Hick's Theological Pilgrimage," in *Proceedings of the Wheaton Theology Conference, The Challenge of Religious Pluralism: An Evangelical Analysis and Response*, March 26-27, 1992, Wheaton College, Wheaton, Ill., 35. See also Westergreen, 172.

19. Kirk, 93.

20. Alister E. McGrath, "The Challenge of Pluralism for the Contemporary Christian Church," *Proceedings of the Wheaton Theology Conference*, 230.

21. Cook, 239-240.

22. Stanley J. Samartha, "The Lordship of Jesus Christ and Religious Pluralism," in Gerald H. Anderson and Thomas F. Stransky, eds., *Christ's Lordship and Religious Pluralism* (Maryknoll, N.Y.: Orbis Books, 1981), 31-32.

23. Tom F. Driver, "Toward a Liberation Theology of Religions," in Hick and Knitter, 212.

24. Westergren, 175.

25. Bosch, 486.

26. Pinnock, 46.

27. Newbigin, 185.

28. Kirk, 169-170.

29. S. Jacques Dupuis, *Jesus Christ at the Encounter of World Religions* (Maryknoll, N.Y.: Orbis Books, 1991), 10-11.

30. Pinnock, 45.

31. Heim, 143.

32. Chris Wright, 50.

33. Norman Kraus, "The New Pluralism and Missions," *Mission Focus* 17, no. 3 (Sept. 1989): 52.

34. Chris Wright, 45, 58.

35. Pinnock, 70-71.

36. Kirk, 167.

37. Pinnock, 72.

38. James R. Edwards, "A Confessional Church in a Pluralistic World," *Proceedings of the Wheaton Theology Conference*, 89.

39. Editorial, "The Truth of Christian Uniqueness," *International Bulletin of Missionary Research* 13, no. 2 (Apr. 1989): 49.

4. A Biblical Perspective on the Religions—Old Testament

1. H. D. Beeby, *From Moses and All the Prophets: A Biblical Approach to Interfaith Dialogue, Mission-Focus* pamphlet (Elkhart, Ind.: Mennonite Board of Missions, 1990), 4.

2. Ibid., 10.

3. John E. Goldingay and Christopher J. H. Wright, " 'Yahweh Our God Yahweh One': The Oneness of God in the Old Testament," in Clarke and Winter, 46.

4. Ibid., 46-47.

5. J. H. Bavinck, *Introduction to the Science of Missions*, trans. David Hugh Freeman (Philadelphia: The Presbyterian and Reformed Publishing Co., 1960), 13.

6. Bernhard Anderson, *Understanding the Old Testament* (Englewood Cliffs, N.J.: Prentice-Hall, Inc., 1957), 175.

7. J. Verkuyl, *Contemporary Missiology: An Introduction*, ed. and trans. Dale Cooper (Grand Rapids: Eerdmans, 1978), 92.

8. Chris Wright, "The Uniqueness of Christ: An Old Testament Perspective," in Vinay Samuel and Chris Sugden, eds., *A.D. 2000 and Beyond: A Mission Agenda* (Oxford, U.K.: Regnum Books, 1991), 117.

9. Sanders, 133.

10. Goldingay and Wright, 49.

11. Chris Wright, *What's So Unique About Jesus?* 89.

12. Ibid., 90-92.

13. Goldingay and Wright, 49.

14. Ibid., 51.

15. Pinnock, 53-54.

16. Chris Wright, *What's So Unique About Jesus?* 95.

17. Ibid., 101; Verkuyl, 95.

18. Goldingay and Wright, 60.

19. Ibid., 60-61.

20. Chris Wright, *What's So Unique About Jesus?* 103-105.

21. John N. Oswalt, "The Mission of Israel to the Nations," in Crockett and Sigountos, 94-95.

22. Beeby, 19-23.

5. A Biblical Perspective on the Religions—New Testament

1. Chris Wright, "The Uniqueness of Christ: An Old Testament Perspective," in Samuel and Sugden, 123.

2. George A. F. Knight, *I AM, This Is My Name: The God of the Bible and the Religions of Man* (Grand Rapids: Eerdmans, 1983), 49.

3. David M. Ball, "The 'I Am' Sayings of Jesus and Religious Pluralism," in Clarke and Winter, 76.

4. Vinay K. Samuel, "Mission in the Context of World Religions," in Samuel and Sugden, 159.

5. Goldsmith, *What About Other Faiths?* 99.

6. Chris Wright, *Unique About Jesus?* 115.

7. Goldsmith, 99.

8. Wright, *What's So Unique About Jesus?* 117-118.

9. Kirk, 149.

10. J. H. Bavinck, *The Church Between Temple and Mosque: A Study of the Relationship Between the Christian Faith and Other Religions* (Grand Rapids: Eerdmans, 1981), 120.

11. John Sanders, "Mercy to All: Romans 1-3 and the Destiny of the Unevangelized," in *Proceedings of the Wheaton Theology Conference*, 221-224.

12. Cotterell, 55.

13. Brian Rosner, " 'No Other Gods': The Jealousy of God and Religious Pluralism," in Clarke and Winter, 159.

6. Theological Issues Concerning Religious Plurality

1. Bruce Demarest, *General Revelation: Historical Views and Contemporary Issues* (Grand Rapids: Zondervan, 1982), 243.
2. Don Richardson, *Eternity in Their Hearts* (Ventura, Calif.: Regal Books, 1981), 10.
3. Goldsmith, 5-11.
4. David Bosch, *Witness to the World: The Christian Mission in Theological Perspective* (Atlanta: John Knox, 1980), 188.
5. Beeby, 9.
6. Braaten, 72.
7. Paul Clasper, *Eastern Paths and the Christian Way* (Maryknoll, N.Y.: Orbis Books, 1980), 92-93.
8. Interpreted by Gerald H. Anderson, "Religion as a Problem for the Christian Mission," in Dawe and Carman, 112.
9. Dawe, 13-33.
10. Sanders, *No Other Name*, 83-89.
11. Goldsmith, 86.
12. Kirk, 54.
13. Netland, 117.
14. Samuel, 153.
15. Quoted by Kirk, 63.
16. Kirk, 103-104.
17. Cook, 245-246.
18. Goldsmith, 27.
19. Netland, 194.
20. Kirk, 102.
21. Pinnock, 11.

7. Assessment of the Religions

1. Roelf Kuitse, "Christian Faith and Other Religions," study document presented to the Mennonite Board of Missions, Elkhart, Indiana, October 1989, 4-5.
2. Bavinck, *Introduction to the Science of Missions*, 263.
3. Kuitse, 9.
4. Braaten, 72.
5. Gerald H. Anderson, "Theology of Religions and Missiology: A Time of Testing," in van Engen, Gilliland, and Pierson, 205-206.
6. Thomas Finger, *Christian Theology: An Eschatological Approach*, vol. 2 (Scottdale, Pa.: Herald Press, 1989), 309-313.
7. Heim, 30.
8. Kuitse, 5.
9. Heim, 31.
10. The issues raised here are somewhat superficial and with no attempt to be exhaustive. The topics are selected to illustrate divergences, omissions, and denials. Convergences will be addressed later.
11. Verkuyl, 344-347.
12. Goldsmith, 128.
13. Bosch, *Transforming Mission*, 486.
14. Goldingay and Wright, 54.

15. Finger, 316.
16. E. S. Jones, *Christ at the Round Table* (London: Hodder & Stoughton, 1928), 139.
17. Newbigin, 200.

8. Who Is Christ?

1. Braaten, 88.
2. Ibid., 112.
3. Heim, 64.
4. Ibid., 133.
5. Chris Wright, "The Uniqueness of Christ," 115.
6. Heim, 80.
7. John Seamands, *Tell It Well: Communicating the Gospel Across Cultures* (Kansas City, Mo.: Beacon Hill Press, 1981), 69.
8. Stephen Neill, *The Supremacy of Jesus* (Downers Grove, Ill.: Inter-Varsity Press, 1984), 16-17.
9. See John Driver, *Understanding the Atonement for the Mission of the Church* (Scottdale, Pa.: Herald Press, 1986).
10. See Raimundo Panikkar, *The Unknown Christ of Hinduism: Towards an Ecumenical Christophany* (Maryknoll, N.Y.: Orbis Books, 1981).
11. Braaten, 98.
12. Ibid., 39.
13. Knitter, *No Other Name?* 190-192.
14. Kraus, 53.
15. Heim, 51-52.
16. Knitter, *No Other Name?* 180-184.
17. Chris Wright, *What's So Unique About Jesus?* 27.
18. Braaten, 116.

9. Witness to Christ

1. Newbigin, 214.
2. Kenneth Cragg, *Troubled by Truth* (Durham, U.K.: Pentland Press, 1992), 2-3.
3. Neill, 156.
4. Kenneth Cragg, *The Christian and Other Religion* (Oxford: Alden Press, 1977), 34-35.
5. Edwards, 93.
6. Verkuyl, 360.
7. Edwards, 96.
8. Braaten, 89.
9. Newbigin, 193-194.
10. Newbigin, *The Gospel in a Pluralist Society* (Grand Rapids: Eerdmans, 1989), 163, 166.
11. Heim, 133.
12. Finger, 315.
13. Verkuyl, 358-359.
14. Pinnock, 120-121.
15. John D. Ellenberger, "Is Hell a Proper Motivation for Missions?" in Crockett and Sigountos, 223.

16. Newbigin, *The Open Secret*, 197-198.
17. Lamin Sanneh, *Translating the Message: The Missionary Impact on Culture* (Maryknoll, N.Y.: Orbis Books, 1989). I am indebted to Sanneh for several of the ideas in this section on contextualization.
18. Quoted by James E. Scherer, *Gospel, Church, and the Kingdom: Comparative Studies in World Mission Theology* (Minneapolis: Augsburg, 1987), 123.
19. Ralph Covell, "Jesus Christ and World Religions," in van Engen, Gilland, and Pierson, 162.
20. Cited in Bosch, *Transforming Mission*, 478.
21. Newbigin, *The Gospel in a Pluralist Society*, 152.

10. Forms of Witness: Church, Presence, Service, Evangelism
1. I am indebted to C. Norman Kraus, *The Community of the Spirit*, rev. ed. (Scottdale, Pa: Herald Press, 1993), for some of the ideas expressed here.
2. Some of this material appeared previously in Calvin E. Shenk, *A Relevant Theology of Presence, Mission-Focus* pamphlet (Elkhart, Ind.: Mennonite Board of Missions, 1982); and in Calvin E. Shenk, "A Theology of Presence: Implications for Mission," *Mission-Focus* 14, no. 3 (Sept. 1986): 36-39.
3. Kenneth Cragg, quoted in Roger Hooker and Christopher Lamb, *Love the Stranger: Christian Ministry in Multi-Faith Areas* (London: SPCK, 1986), 11.
4. I have drawn from previous material in Calvin E. Shenk, "Conversion in Acts: Implications for Witness to Religions," *Mission-Focus* 14, no. 1 (Mar. 1986): 1-5.
5. Cragg, *Troubled by Truth*, 50.
6. Newbigin, *The Open Secret*, 211.
7. Quoted in Edwards, 93.
8. Lesslie Newbigin, "The Enduring Validity of Cross-Cultural Mission," *International Bulletin of Missionary Research* 12, no. 2 (Apr. 1988): 50-51.
9. Scherer, 88.
10. Finger, 318.

11. Forms of Witness: Dialogue
1. Kuitse, p. 6.
2. David Lochhead, *The Dialogical Imperative: A Christian Reflection on Interfaith Encounter* (Maryknoll, N.Y.: Orbis Books, 1988), 5-23.
3. Kenneth Cragg, *To Meet and to Greet: Faith with Faith* (London: Epworth Press, 1992).
4. Clasper, 122. Clasper interprets and applies this term from John Dunne, the Notre Dame theologian. See John Dunne, *The Way of All the Earth: Experiments in Truth and Religion* (New York: Macmillan, 1977), ix-x.
5. J. Denny Weaver, "Christus Victor and Other Religions," paper presented to Peace Theology Colloquium, Messiah College, Grantham, Pa., June 17-19, 1994, 21.
6. Ibid., 22.
7. Bosch, *Transforming Mission*, 484-488.
8. Cragg, *Troubled by Truth*, 268.
9. Jürgen Moltmann, "Is 'Pluralistic Theology' Useful for the Dialogue of World Relgions?" in Gavin D'Costa, ed., *Christian Uniqueness Reconsidered:*

The Myth of a Pluralistic Theology of Religions (Maryknoll, N.Y.: Orbis Books, 1990), 154.

10. Pinnock, 137.

11. Bosch, *Transforming Mission*, 484.

12. Pinnock, 137.

13. Gayle Gerber Koontz, "Evangelical Peace Theology and Religious Pluralism: Particularity in Perspective," paper presented to Peace Theology Colloquium, Messiah College, Grantham, Pa., June 17-19, 1994, 29.

14. Koontz, 27, who elaborates on John Howard Yoder.

15. Ibid., 29.

16. Quoted in Verkuyl, 367.

17. Verkuyl, 366.

18. Bruce J. Nicholls, "The Witnessing Church in Dialogue," *Evangelical Review of Theology* 16, no. 1 (Jan. 1992): 62.

19. Samuel, 163-164.

20. John H. Yoder, "The Disavowal of Constantine: An Alternate Perspective on Interfaith Dialogue," in *Annals 1975/76* (Tantur: Ecumenical Institute for Advanced Theological Studies, 1979), 59.

21. Martin E. Marty, *Context*, June 15, 1993, 5, quoting from *Dialogue*, spring 1993.

22. David Kerr, "Christian-Muslim Relations," in James M. Phillips and Robert T. Coote, eds., *Toward the 21st Century in Christian Mission* (Grand Rapids: Eerdmans, 1993), 351.

12. Those Who Have Not Heard

1. Cotterell, 75.

2. Sanders, *No Other Name*, 251.

3. Ibid., 252.

4. Pinnock, 92.

5. Ibid., 15.

6. Chris Wright, *What's So Unique About Jesus?* 36-37.

7. Sanders, *No Other Name*, 233-236.

8. Ibid., 67.

9. Clark Pinnock, "The Finality of Jesus Christ in a World of Religions," in Mark Noll and David Wells, eds., *Christian Faith and Practice in the Modern World: Theology from an Evangelical Point of View* (Grand Rapids: Eerdmans, 1988), 63.

10. Pinnock, *A Wideness in God's Mercy*, 105.

11. Ibid., 112.

12. Sanders, *No Other Name*, 225, 231.

13. Ibid., 152.

14. Gabriel Fackre, "Divine Perseverence," in John Sanders, ed., *What About Those Who Have Never Heard?* (Downers Grove, Ill: InterVarsity Press, 1995), 71-95.

15. Pinnock, *A Wideness in God's Mercy*, 179-180.

16. Ibid., 156.

17. John E. Toews, "Toward a Biblical Perspective on People of Other Faiths," paper presented to Peace Theology Colloquium, Messiah College, Grantham, Pa., June 17-19, 1994, 19.

18. J. N. D. Anderson, *Christianity and Comparative Religion* (London: Tyndale Press, 1972), 110.

19. Norman Anderson, *Christianity and World Religions: The Challenge of Pluralism* (Downers Grove, Ill.: InterVarsity Press, 1984), 152.

20. Ibid., 153.

21. Goldsmith, 136.

22. Newbigin, *The Open Secret*, 88.

23. Ibid., 196.

13. Style of Witness

1. Kuitse, 10-11.

2. David Bosch, *A Spirituality of the Road* (Scottdale, Pa.: Herald Press, 1979), 41-43.

3. Kosuke Koyama, *No Handle on the Cross* (Maryknoll, N.Y.: Orbis Books, 1977), 71.

4. Koontz, 20, 23.

5. Beeby, 29.

6. Verkuyl, 355.

7. Lesslie Newbigin, *The Finality of Christ* (London: SCM Press, 1969), 61-62.

8. Heim, 101.

9. Rabbi Irving Greenberg, in a speech at the International Jewish-Christian Conference on Modern Social and Scientific Challenges, Jerusalem, Israel, Feb. 1-4, 1994.

10. Lochhead, 80.

11. Cardinal Ratzinger from Rome, in a speech to the International Jewish-Christian Conference on Modern Social and Scientific Challenges, Jerusalem, Israel, Feb. 1-4, 1994.

12. Yoder, 63.

13. Jones, 10-11.

14. Elias Chacour, at a conference sponsored by the Middle East Council of Churches and Evangelicals for Middle East Understanding in Cyprus, October 1991.

15. His Beatitude Ignatius IV, Greek Orthodox Patriarch of Antioch and all the East, Damascus, Syria, March 1996.

16. K. L. Seskagiri Rao, "A Hindu Response: The Value of Religious Pluralism," in Dawe and Carman, 50.

17. Yoder, 66-67.

18. In a speech at a conference sponsored by the Middle East Council of Churches and Evangelicals for Middle East Understanding in Cyprus, October 1991.

19. Koyama, 8

20. Cragg, *The Christian and Other Religions*, 18.

21. Cragg, *To Meet and to Greet*, 7, 27.

22. Mahinda Palihawadana, "A Buddhist Response: Religion Beyond Ideology and Power," in Dawe and Carman, 40.

23. Cragg, *Troubled by Truth*, 95.

Bibliography

Anderson, Bernhard. *Understanding the Old Testament.* Englewood Cliffs: Prentice Hall, Inc., 1975.

Anderson, Gerald H. and Stransky, Thomas F., eds. *Christ's Lordship and Religious Pluralism.* Maryknoll: Orbis Books, 1981.

Anderson, Gerald H. "The Truth of Christian Uniqueness." *International Bulletin of Missionary Research* 13, no. 2 (Apr. 1989): 49.

Anderson, J. N. D. *Christianity and Comparative Religion.* London: Tyndale Press, 1972.

Anderson, Norman. *Christianity and World Religions: The Challenge of Pluralism.* Downers Grove: InterVarsity Press, 1984.

Ariarajah, Wesley. *The Bible and People of Other Faiths.* Geneva: World Council of Churches, 1985.

Bavinck, J. H. *The Church Between Temple and Mosque: A Study of the Relationship Between the Christian Faith and Other Religions.* Grand Rapids: Eerdmans, 1981.

_____. *Introduction to the Science of Missions.* Trans. David Hugh Freeman. Philadelphia: The Presbyterian and Reformed Publishing Co., 1960.

Beeby, H. D. *From Moses and All the Prophets: A Biblical Approach to Interfaith Dialogue.* Mission-Focus pamphlet. Elkhart, Ind.: Mennonite Board of Missions, 1990.

Berger, Peter. *A Rumor of Angels.* Garden City: Doubleday, 1969.

_____. *The Sacred Canopy.* Garden City: Doubleday, 1967.

Bloom, Allan. *The Closing of the American Mind.* New York: Simon & Schuster, 1987.

Bosch, David. *A Spirituality of the Road.* Scottdale, Pa.: Herald Press, 1979.

_____. *Transforming Mission.* Maryknoll: Orbis Press, 1991.

_____. *Witness to the World: The Christian Mission in Theological Per-*

spective. Atlanta: John Knox, 1980.

Braaten, Carl E. *No Other Gospel! Christianity Among the World's Religions*. Minneapolis: Augsburg Fortress, 1992.

Clark, David K., David L. Melvin, Dennis L. Okholm, James R. Peck, and Timothy R. Phillips, eds. *Proceedings of the Wheaton Theology Conference, The Challenge of Religious Pluralism: An Evangelical Analysis and Response*. Wheaton, Ill.: Wheaton College, 1992.

Clarke, Andrew, and Bruce W. Winter, eds. *One God, One Lord: Christianity in a World of Religious Pluralism*. Grand Rapids: Baker Book House, 1992.

Clasper, Paul. *Eastern Paths and the Christian Way*. Maryknoll: Orbis Books, 1980.

Cotterell, Peter. *Mission and Meaninglessness: The Good News in a World of Suffering and Disorder*. London: SPCK, 1990.

Cox, Harvey. *Religion in the Secular City*. New York: Simon & Schuster, 1984.

————. *The Secular City*. New York: Macmillan, 1966.

Cragg, Kenneth. *The Christian and Other Religions*. Oxford: Alden Press, 1977.

————. *To Meet and to Greet: Faith with Faith*. London: Epworth Press, 1992.

————. *Troubled by Truth*. Durham: Pentland Press, 1992.

Crockett, William V., and James G. Sigountos, eds. *Through No Fault of Their Own? The Fate of Those Who Have Never Heard*. Grand Rapids: Baker Book House, 1991.

Dawe, Donald G., and John B. Carman, eds. *Christian Faith in a Religiously Plural World*. Maryknoll: Orbis Press, 1978.

D'Costa, Gavin. *Christian Uniqueness Reconsidered: The Myth of a Pluralistic Theology of Religions*. Maryknoll: Orbis Books, 1990.

Demarest, Bruce. *General Revelation, Historical Views and Contemporary Issues*. Grand Rapids: Zondervan, 1982.

Driver, John. *Understanding the Atonement for the Mission of the Church*. Scottdale: Herald Press, 1986.

Dupuis, S. Jacques. *Jesus Christ at the Encounter of World Religions*. Maryknoll: Orbis Books, 1991.

Finger, Thomas. *Christian Theology: An Eschatalogical Approach*. Vol. 2. Scottdale: Herald Press, 1989.

Goldsmith, Martin. *What About Other Faiths?* London: Hodder & Stoughton, 1989.

Heim, Mark S. *Is Christ the Only Way? Christian Faith in a Pluralistic World*. Valley Forge, Pa.: Judson, 1985.

Hick, John, and Paul Knitter, eds. *The Myth of Christian Uniqueness: Toward a Pluralistic Theology of Religions*. Maryknoll: Orbis Press, 1987.

Hooker, Roger, and Christopher Lamb. *Love the Stranger: Christian Ministry in Multi-Faith Areas.* London: SPCK, 1986.

Jones, E. S. *Christ at the Round Table.* London: Hodder & Stoughton, 1928.

Kirk, J. Andrew. *Loosing the Chains: Religion as Opium and Liberation.* London: Hodder & Stoughton, 1992.

Knight, George H. F. *I AM, This Is My Name: The God of the Bible and the Religions of Man.* Grand Rapids: Eerdmans, 1983.

Knitter, Paul F. *No Other Name? A Critical Survey of Christian Attitudes Toward the World's Religions.* Maryknoll: Orbis Books, 1985.

Koontz, Gayle Gerber. "Evangelical Peace Theology and Religious Pluralism: Particularity in Perspective." Paper presented to Peace Theology Colloquium, Messiah College, Grantham, Pa., June 17-19, 1994.

Koyama, Kosuke. *No Handle on the Cross.* Maryknoll: Orbis Books, 1977.

Kraus, C. Norman. *The Community of the Spirit,* rev. ed. Scottdale: Herald Press, 1993.

_____. "The New Pluralism and Missions." *Mission-Focus* 17, no. 3 (Sept. 1989): 50-55.

Kuitse, Roelf. "Christian Faith and Other Religions." Study document presented to the Mennonite Board of Missions, Oct. 1989.

Lochhead, David. *The Dialogical Imperative: A Christian Reflection on Interfaith Encounter.* Maryknoll: Orbis Books, 1988.

Marty, Martin E. *Context,* June 15, 1993, 5.

Meeking, Basil, and John Stott. *The Evangelical—Roman Catholic Dialogue in Mission, 1977-1984.* Grand Rapids: Eerdmans, 1986.

Netland, Harold A. *Dissonant Voices, Religious Pluralism and the Question of Truth.* Grand Rapids: Eerdmans, 1991.

Neill, Stephen. *The Supremacy of Jesus.* Downers Grove, Ill.: InterVarsity Press, 1984.

Newbigin, Lesslie. "The Enduring Validity of Cross-Cultural Mission." *International Bulletin of Missionary Research* 12, no. 2 (Apr. 1988): 50-53.

_____. *The Finality of Christ.* London: SCM Press, 1969.

_____. *The Gospel in a Pluralist Society.* Grand Rapids: William B. Eerdmans Publishing Co., 1989.

_____. *The Open Secret: Sketches of a Missionary Theology.* Grand Rapids: Eerdmans, 1978.

Nicholls, Bruce J. "The Witnessing Church in Dialogue." *Evangelical Review of Theology* 6, no. 1 (Jan. 1992): 49-65.

Noll, Mark, and David Wells, eds. *Christian Faith and Practice in the Modern World: Theology from an Evangelical Point of View.* Grand Rapids: Eerdmans, 1988.

Panikkar, Raimundo. *The Unknown Christ of Hinduism: Towards an Ecumenical Christophany.* Maryknoll: Orbis Books, 1981.

Phillips, James M., and Robert T. Coote, eds. *Toward the 21st Century in Christian Mission.* Grand Rapids: Eerdmans, 1993.

Pinnock, Clark H. *A Wideness in God's Mercy: The Finality of Jesus Christ in a World of Religions.* Grand Rapids: Zondervan, 1992.

Richardson, Don. *Eternity in Their Hearts.* Ventura: Regal Books, 1981.

Sanders, John. *No Other Name: An Investigation into the Destiny of the Unevangelized.* Grand Rapids: Eerdmans, 1992.

Sanders, John, ed. *What About Those Who Have Never Heard?* Downers Grove: InterVarsity Press, 1995.

Samuel, Vinay, and Chris Sugden, eds. *A.D. 2000 and Beyond: A Mission Agenda.* Oxford: Regnum Books, 1991.

Sanneh, Lamin. *Translating the Message: The Missionary Impact on Culture.* Maryknoll: Orbis Books, 1989.

Scherer, James. *Gospel, Church, and the Kingdom: Comparative Studies in World Mission Theology.* Minneapolis: Augsburg, 1987.

Seamands, John. *Tell It Well: Communicating the Gospel Across Cultures.* Kansas City: Beacon Hill Press, 1981.

Shenk, Calvin E. *A Relevant Theology of Presence.* Mission-Focus pamphlet. Elkhart, Ind.: Mennonite Board of Missions, 1982.

_____. "A Theology of Presence: Implications for Mission." *Mission-Focus* 14, no. 3 (Sept. 1986): 36-39.

_____. "Conversion in Acts: Implications for Witness to Religions." *Mission-Focus* 14, no. 1 (Mar. 1986): 1-5.

Toews, John E. "Toward a Biblical Perspective on People of Other Faiths." Paper presented to Peace Theology Colloquium, Messiah College, Grantham, Pa., June 17-19, 1994.

Van Engen, Charles, Dean S. Gillilan, and Paul Pierson, eds. *The Good News of the Kingdom.* Maryknoll: Orbis Press, 1993.

Verkuyl, J. *Contemporary Missiology: An Introduction.* Trans. and ed. Dale Cooper. Grand Rapids: Eerdmans, 1978.

Weaver, J. Denny. "Christus Victor and Other Religions." Paper presented to Peace Theology Colloquium, Messiah College, Grantham, Pa., June 17-19, 1994.

Wright, Chris. *What's So Unique About Jesus?* Sussex, Great Britain: Monarch Publications, 1990.

Yoder, John H. "The Disavowal of Constantine: An Alternative Perspective on Interfaith Dialogue." In *Annals 1975/76.* Tantur, Jerusalem: Ecumenical Institute for Theological Studies, 1979, 47-68.

Index

The Author

Calvin E. Shenk was born and grew up in Lancaster County, Pennsylvania. He was educated at Lancaster Mennonite High School and graduated from Eastern Mennonite College with a B.R.E. in biblical and religious studies. He completed an M.S. in education at Temple University and a Ph.D. in religion and culture at New York University.

Calvin's professional life has included pastoring as well as school administration and teaching at the secondary, college, and seminary levels. Sponsored by Eastern Mennonite Missions, he served as an educator in Ethiopia 1961-1975. Since 1976 he has taught religion and mission in the Eastern Mennonite University (EMU) Bible and Religion department, where he served for ten years as department chair.

Calvin has specialized in the interaction of religion, ideology, and culture in cross-cultural and international contexts. This interest resulted in his earlier book on ideologies, *When Kingdoms Clash* (Herald Press, 1988). He also helped inaugurate a required cross-cultural component for every undergraduate at EMU, and with his wife, Marie, has led four Middle East Semesters. In recent years Calvin spent each spring semester in Jerusalem as research scholar at Tantur Ecumenical Institute.

Concerned with integrating theory and practice, the academic and the pastoral, Calvin has traveled widely in Africa, Asia, and the Middle East exploring issues related to religion and Christian faith. He returns frequently to Ethiopia for leadership training. He serves as resource person in consultations dealing with religions and mission and participates in conversations with adherents of other religions in North America and the Middle East.

He and his wife, Marie Leaman Shenk, are parents of three adult children, Douglas, Duane, and Donna. He is an ordained minister in the Mennonite Church and a member of Park View Mennonite Church, Harrisonburg, Virginia.